Metaphor and Emotion

Are human emotions best characterized as biological, psychological, or cultural entities? Many researchers claim that emotions arise either from human biology (i.e., biological reductionism) or as products of culture (i.e., social constructionism). This book challenges this simplistic division between the body and culture by showing how human emotions are to a large extent "constructed" from individuals' embodied experiences in different cultural settings. Zoltán Kövecses illustrates through detailed cross-linguistic analyses how many emotion concepts reflect widespread metaphorical patterns of thought. These emotion metaphors arise from recurring embodied experiences, one reason why human emotions across many cultures conform to certain basic biological-physiological processes in the human body and of the body interacting with the external world. Moreover, there are different cultural models for emotions that arise from unique patterns of both metaphorical and metonymic thinking in varying cultural contexts. The view proposed here demonstrates how cultural aspects of emotions, metaphorical language about the emotions, and human physiology in emotion are all part of an integrated system. Kövecses convincingly shows how this integrated system points to the reconciliation of the seemingly contradictory views of biological reductionism and social constructionism in contemporary debates about human emotion.

Zoltán Kövecses is Professor of Linguistics in the Department of American Studies at Eötvös Loránd University.

STUDIES IN EMOTION AND SOCIAL INTERACTION
Second Series

Series Editors

Keith Oatley
University of Toronto

Antony Manstead
University of Amsterdam

This series is jointly published by the Cambridge University Press and the Editions de la Maison des Sciences de l'Homme, as part of the joint publishing agreement established in 1977 between the Fondation de la Maison des Sciences de l'Homme and the Syndics of the Cambridge University Press.

Cete collection est publiée co-édition par Cambridge University Press et les Editions de la Maison des Sciences de l'Homme. Elle s'intègre dans le programme de co-édition établi en 1977 par la Fondation de la Maison des Sciences de l'Homme et les Syndics de Cambridge University Press.

Titles published in the Second Series:

The Psychology of Facial Expression
Edited by James A. Russell and José Miguel Fernández-Dols

Emotions, the Social Bond, and Human Reality: Part/Whole Analysis
Thomas J. Scheff

Intersubjective Communication and Emotion in Early Ontogeny
Stein Bråten

The Social Context of Nonverbal Behavior
Edited by Pierre Philippot, Robert S. Feldman, and Erik J. Coats

Communicating Emotion
Sally Planalp

Feeling and Thinking
Edited by Joseph P. Forgas

For a list of titles in the First Series of Studies in Emotion and Social Interaction, see the page following the index.

Metaphor and Emotion

Language, Culture, and Body in Human Feeling

Zoltán Kövecses

Eötvös Loránd University

CAMBRIDGE
UNIVERSITY PRESS

& Editions de la Maison des Sciences de l'Homme
Paris

AHQ4860

PUBLISHED BY THE PRESS SYNDICATE OF THE UNIVERSITY OF CAMBRIDGE
The Pitt Building, Trumpington Street, Cambridge, United Kingdom
and EDITIONS DE LA MAISON DES SCIENCES DE L'HOMME
54 Boulevard Raspail, 75270 Paris Cedex 06, France

CAMBRIDGE UNIVERSITY PRESS
The Edinburgh Building, Cambridge CB2 2RU, UK   http://www.cup.cam.ac.uk
40 West 20th Street, New York, NY 10011-4211, USA   http://www.cup.org
10 Stamford Road, Oakleigh, Melbourne 3166, Australia
Ruiz de Alarcón 13, 28014 Madrid, Spain

© Maison des Sciences de l'Homme and Cambridge University Press 2000

First published 2000

Printed in the United States of America

Typeface Palatino 10/13 pt.   *System* DeskTopPro$_{/UX}$ [BV]

A catalog record for this book is available from the British Library.

Library of Congress Cataloging in Publication Data

Kövecses, Zoltán
Metaphor and emotion : language, culture, and body in
human feeling / Zoltán Kövecses.
p.   cm. – (Studies in emotion and social interaction. Second
series)
Includes bibliographical references and index.
ISBN 0-521-64163-2
1. Language and emotions.   2. Emotions and cognition.
3. Emotions – Sociological Aspects. I. Title.   II. Series.
BF582.K68   1999 2600
152.4 – dc21   99-24187
                                                                              CIP

ISBN 0 521 64163 2 hardback
ISBN 2 7351 0833 3 hardback (France only)

For the boys and Zsuzsi

Contents

Preface   *page* xi

1   Language and Emotion Concepts   1
2   Metaphors of Emotion   20
3   Emotion Metaphors: Are They Unique to
    the Emotions?   35
4   Events and Emotions: The Subcategorization
    of Emotions   51
5   The Force of Emotion   61
6   Emotions and Relationships   87
7   Folk Versus Expert Theories of Emotion   114
8   Universality in the Conceptualization of
    Emotions   139
9   Cultural Variation in the Conceptualization of
    Emotion   164
10 Emotion Language: A New Synthesis   182

References   201
Author Index   211
Subject Index   213
Metaphor and Metonymy Index   216

Preface

In a widely read and influential book on the neurobiology of the emotions, Joseph LeDoux (1996) draws the following conclusion:

> Emotions evolved not as conscious feelings, linguistically differentiated or otherwise, but as brain states and bodily responses. The brain states and bodily responses are the fundamental facts of an emotion, and the conscious feelings are the frills that have added icing to the emotional cake. (p. 302)

In a way, the present book can be seen as a response to these conclusions. While I am convinced by many of LeDoux's claims, including the idea that emotions did not evolve as conscious feelings, I cannot accept the second part of his conclusion. This is not only because I come to the emotions from a more humanistic perspective than he does, but also because the evidence I will present in the chapters to follow tells me that "conscious feelings" play a much more important role in human emotions than LeDoux appears to attach to them.

Conscious feelings are often expressed in or, indeed, are shaped by language, and thus the study of language can reveal a great deal about them. Of course, one must have the appropriate kind of linguistics to say anything interesting about emotions and emotional feelings. LeDoux bases his claims on an unsatisfactory kind of linguistics, in which emotion language consists only in literal emotion words, such as *fear, anxiety, terror, apprehension*, that classify and refer to a preexisting emotional reality (the brain states and bodily responses). This can only lead to an oversimplification of the many subtle ways in which emotion and language interact. Obviously, LeDoux, a neurobiologist, cannot be expected to provide us with a linguistics that provides further insight into the nature of the relationship between emotion and emotion language. In this book I regard providing what I take to be the appropriate kind of linguistics for the job at hand as the main methodological contribution to the study of emotion.

Once we give up simplistic views of emotional language, a whole new "world" of emotional feelings unfolds before us. Emotion language will not be seen as a collection of literal words that categorize and refer to a preexisting emotional reality, but as language that can be figurative and that can define and even create emotional experiences for us. Does this new approach mean that I want to discard the body from a study of emotions? I do not intend to do anything of the sort. On the contrary, I want to bring together three threads of emotion research into a coherent whole that avoids the weaknesses of each pursued separately. The three threads include the research done on how the human body behaves in an emotional state, the research on how cultural and social factors influence and shape emotional experiences, and the research on emotional language from a cognitive linguistic perspective. In other words, my major goal is to provide a new synthesis in the study of emotion, that is, to bring together language, culture, and body in such a way that we get a relatively complete and integrated account of emotional phenomena in human beings.

In the process of creating this synthesis, several issues in the study of emotion and emotion language will have to be clarified. These include, but are not limited to, the following: What is the relationship between the objectively measurable responses of the body in emotion and the subjectively felt emotional experiences of people as described by language? In a way, this is perhaps the major issue pursued in this book and can be seen as a rephrasing of the "body-language" issue just mentioned. Second, what is the relationship between culture and the conceptualization of emotion through language? In other words, does the conceptualization of emotions vary with radically different cultures? Or, is it universal? Or, is it both at the same time? If it varies, as we can reasonably expect to be the case, is the variation without constraint? Third, how are the emotions organized in our conceptual system? Are they organized as an overarching unitary system or as separate systems? This is a highly interesting question, because, as we will see, there is a certain incongruence here between what some neurobiologists (such as LeDoux) suggest for the emotions and what our linguistic analysis tells us about the conceptualization of emotions. We can further ask in this regard whether this incongruence is a predictable and systematic difference between emotions as pertaining to the brain and body, on the one hand, and emotional feelings as conceptualized by organisms having consciousness and language, on the other. Fourth, how can we place in the mind emotions as described on the basis of language? How is emotion related to rational thought and morality in our conceptual system? Do they form separate systems in our naive view of the mind, or are they somehow unified, as can be determined from linguistic evidence?

As can be seen from the way I have stated some of the major concerns of this book, my basic interest in the emotions is threefold: (1) How do we talk about the emotions in English and other languages? (2) What folk theories of the emotions do these ways of talking reveal about particular emotions and emotion in general? And (3) how do these folk theories relate to other "neighboring" folk theories (such as that associated with human relationships) and scientific theories of emotions? In other words, I have to state up front that, strictly speaking, I do not have a theory of emotions myself. The theory of emotion I arrive at is not mine in the sense that it was not my intention to construct, and so have not constructed, another expert or scientific model of emotion that can be claimed to be "true" of emotions and that can be falsified by others. What I attempt to present here is what I take English and other languages to reveal about the emotions and to offer these folk conceptualizations of emotions based on language. On the one hand, this is accomplishing very little, compared to the many large-scale and comprehensive scientific models that supposedly reflect the "true" nature of emotion; on the other, it is accomplishing quite a lot, considering that emotion language deals with many important facets of emotion and thus provides a complex picture of emotion, as well as considering that it is this rich picture unfolding from language that corresponds to what human beings consciously feel when they experience an emotion. If we want to see what our "conscious feelings" involve, we have to take our language and our folk theories about the emotions seriously.

Although I believe that this book raises many important issues concerning the nature and role of human feelings in the emotions, I do not claim that it raises all of them (or even that it can always satisfactorily deal with the ones that it does raise). One such issue is the causal and functional aspects of emotion in the larger context of human action and cognitive functioning. The approach that I am advocating here can say little about this aspect of emotion, and I do not feel it is necessary or worthwhile for my purposes to go into it at all. Others have done this job and I accept and respect their work (see, e.g., Frijda, 1986; Leventhal and Scherer, 1987; Oatley and Johnson-Laird, 1987). I will only discuss this line of work when it bears directly on issues having to do with emotion language.

Some of the questions raised here will get answered only toward the end of the book; some others will be answered as we go along. The first chapter offers an overview of recent theories of emo..on language and raises some further issues in connection with the study of emotion from a linguistic point of view. Chapters 2, 3, and 4 introduce the key findings of cognitive linguistics as they relate to the emotions. In particular, they emphasize the figurative nature of emotion language and, more important, the metaphorical character of our folk models of emotion. Chapter 5 offers the key theme in our folk theoretical thinking about emotions, the idea that we view emotions as forces that turn a "rational" self into an "irrational" one. We will find a single master metaphor (namely, the metaphor EMOTIONS ARE FORCES) that organizes much of our thinking about emotion. Chapter 6 contrasts this finding with the case of human relationships, such as love, marriage, and friendship. I will show that there are major systematic differences between the metaphorical conceptualization of emotions and that of human relationships.

Chapter 7 provides a discussion of the nature of folk models that structure emotion concepts and argues that they are inherently metaphorical, not literal as currently claimed by Naomi Quinn. Another issue the same chapter deals with is how the folk models of emotion are related to expert or scientific theories of emotion. This leads us to the question whether all scientific theorizing can be regarded as a version of folk psychology. Chapters 8 and 9 attempt to answer the question whether the conceptualization of emotions as revealed through language is universal or culture-specific. The answer is based on a detailed investigation of several unrelated languages (English, Chinese, Japanese, Hungarian, Wolof, Zulu, etc.). Finally, chapter 10 pulls together the various threads in the discussion of the several issues and offers a synthesis in which language (conceptualization), body, and culture naturally come together in a unified account of human emotion.

What is the relationship between this book and my previous work on emotion? The short answer is that the present work is *not* a summary of what I have done before (e.g., Kövecses, 1986, 1988, 1990). On the contrary, this book throws a different light on several issues that I have dealt with in earlier publications and it raises several new issues that perhaps I should have dealt with before but have not. Overall, the main difference between my previous work and this study is that in this book the emphasis is on emotions in general and the larger issues connected with them, and not on particular emotion concepts. There have been many new developments in both cognitive linguistics and emotion research in recent years, and I have attempted to make use of these developments here. For example, Leonard Talmy's work on the role of "force dynamics" in language and conceptualization led me to the new idea that much of the language and conceptualization of emotions can be described in force dynamic terms (hence the master metaphor EMOTION IS FORCE), rather than in terms of individual and independent conceptual metaphors. As will be seen, this new approach has important implications for the study of emotional feelings. I have also learned a great deal from critiques of my earlier work. In this book, I respond to challenges by Naomi Quinn, Anna Wierzbicka, and others. Hopefully, the result is a new, more refined, and more convincing view of human emotion and the way we talk about it.

In bringing this book to its final form, I have received a great deal of encouragement, help, and constructive criticism from Keith Oatley, Ray Gibbs, and Csaba Pléh. Their comments on a previous version were extremely helpful. Encouragement for the project also came from Julia Hough of Cambridge University Press. In addition, she provided me with all the moral, emotional, and material assistance that an author could wish for.

George Lakoff gave me his generous support throughout this project, and long before it. I am also indebted to his 1996 Metaphor class at UC Berkeley for reading the manuscript and providing many valuable suggestions concerning both examples and content. I also had some of the best students one can have at home in Budapest, who discussed many aspects of this book with me in several courses. Especially valuable suggestions came from Szilvia Csábi, Zsuzsanna Bokor, Orsolya Lazányi, Judit Szirmay, and Mónika Pacziga. Szilvia Csábi also gave me invaluable assistance in producing the final typescript.

Several Americans have helped me collect linguistic material for this book. Cheryl Chris, Lars Moestue, Joseph Vargo, and Ted Sablay conducted dozens of interviews for me with other native speakers of American English. The students in my 1996 Language of Emotion seminar at the University of Nevada at Las Vegas gave me many good ideas and patiently helped me clarify thoughts that were just being worked out at the time.

Gary Palmer was the first reader of an early manuscript. I have learned a great deal from our discussions of each chapter. His ideas are present in several parts of this book. Len Talmy gave me valuable feedback on the chapter dealing with force dynamics and John Taylor provided helpful comments on my discussion of Zulu emotion language.

Needless to say, I am grateful to all these people.

December 1998
Budapest

1. Language and Emotion Concepts

This chapter describes some aspects of emotion language that have not yet received a great deal of attention but are clearly important in the study of emotion concepts. Most important of these is the role of figurative language in the conceptualization of emotion. Do metaphor and other figurative language matter at all in how we think about the emotions? Do metaphors simply reflect a preexisting, literal reality, or do they actually create or constitute our emotional reality? Is it of any consequence that speakers of English use expressions like *boiling with anger, being swept off one's feet, building a relationship*, and *being madly in love*?

I will suggest that it is of serious consequence. If we are not clear about why people engage in this way of talking, we cannot really understand why lay people categorize the emotions as passions, while some experts categorize them as states and others as actions; if we do not pay a great deal of attention to figurative language, it is impossible to see precisely how the lay view of emotion differs from the lay view of human relationships or that of rational thought or morality; if we do not examine this kind of language, we will never understand why we have the theories of emotion in psychology, philosophy, and anthropology that we do; and if we do not analyze this kind of language in cultures other than our own, we will never find out whether the way we think about our emotions is shared (and, if it is, to what extent) by speakers of other languages. I will contend that metaphor, and figurative language in general, does matter in all of these issues, and crucially so.

But in order to see in precisely what ways metaphor matters in all this, we have to clarify first what we mean by the language of emotion; second, what the competing theories of emotion language and

1

emotion concepts are; and third, what the more specific issues are that emerge in connection with emotion language. The survey to follow is divided into three sections: (1) words and emotion, (2) meaning and emotion, and (3) some issues that inevitably arise in the study of everyday conceptions of emotion.

As is obvious from the goals above, I will not deal with certain important aspects of emotion language and emotional implications of language in general. I will have nothing to say about the syntactic, phonetic, and pragmatic properties of this language, although a great deal of high-quality work is being done in all these fields (see, e.g., Iván Fónagy's extremely interesting work, such as Fónagy, 1981, on the relationship between emotion and human sound systems).

Words and Emotion

When they deal with emotion language, many scholars assume that this language simply consists of a dozen or so words, such as *anger, fear, love, joy,* and so forth. I will challenge this view in this section and claim that this is just a small fraction of our emotion language. I will briefly discuss the most general functions and organization of emotion-related vocabulary, and then focus attention on a large but neglected group of emotion terms.

Expression and Description

A first distinction that we have to make is between expressive and descriptive emotion words (or terms or expressions). Some emotion words can *express* emotions. Examples include *shit!* when angry, *wow!* when enthusiastic or impressed, *yuk!* when disgusted, and many more. It is an open question whether all emotions can be expressed in this way, and which are the ones that cannot and why. Other emotion words can *describe* the emotions they signify or that "they are about." Words like *anger* and *angry, joy* and *happy, sadness* and *depressed* are assumed to be used in such a way. We should note that under certain circumstances descriptive emotion terms can also "express" particular emotions. An example is *"I love you!"* where the descriptive emotion word *love* is used both to describe and express the emotion of love.

The categories of descriptive and expressive emotion terms are analogous to Searle's (1990) categories of assertive and expressive speech acts, in that descriptive terms have an assertive function and expressive terms often constitute expressive speech acts.

In this work, I will be concerned only with that part of the emotion lexicon that is used "to describe" emotional experience. As we will see below, this is a much larger category of emotion terms than the one that "expresses" emotions.

Basic Emotion Terms

Within the category of descriptive emotion words, the terms can be seen as "more or less basic." Speakers of a given language appear to feel that some of the emotion words are more basic than others. More basic ones include in English *anger, sadness, fear, joy,* and *love.* Less basic ones include *annoyance, wrath, rage,* and *indignation* for anger and *terror, fright,* and *horror* for fear.

Basicness can mean two things (at least, loosely speaking). One is that these words (the concepts corresponding to them) occupy a middle level in a vertical hierarchy of concepts (in the sense of Rosch, 1975, 1978). In this sense, say, *anger* is more basic than, for example, *annoyance* or *emotion. Anger,* because it is a "basic-level" emotion category, lies between the superordinate-level category *emotion* and the subordinate-level category of *annoyance.* This is depicted in Figure 1.1.

The other sense of "basicness" is that a particular emotion category can be judged to be more "prototypical" (i.e., a better example) of emotion than another at the same horizontal level (again, "prototypical" in the sense of Rosch, 1975, 1978). This horizontal level coincides with the basic level of the vertical organization of concepts. For example, *anger* is more basic in this sense than, say, *hope* or *pride,* which, in the previous sense, are on the same level (see Figure 1.2).

These organizations of emotion terms have been extensively studied in the past decade for English (e.g., Fehr and Russell, 1984; Shaver,

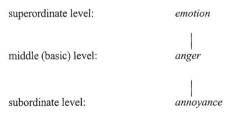

superordinate level:	*emotion*
middle (basic) level:	*anger*
subordinate level:	*annoyance*

Figure 1.1. Levels of emotion terms in a vertical hierarchy

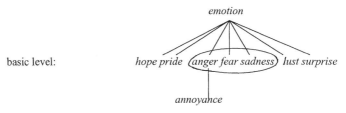

Figure 1.2. Prototypical vs. nonprototypical emotion terms on the horizontal level of conceptual organization. (The circle indicates that, e.g., *anger, fear,* and *sadness* are better examples of emotion terms than *hope, pride, surprise,* and *lust.*)

Schwartz, Kirson, and O'Connor, 1987). Cross-cultural research along these lines is just beginning. Using a methodology borrowed from Fehr and Russell (1984), Frijda, Markan, Sato, and Wiers (1995) arrive at five general and possibly universal categories of emotion in 11 languages. These basic emotion categories include happiness, sadness, anger, fear, and love. Smith and Tkel-Sbal (1995) investigate the possibility that emotion terms are prototypically organized in the Micronesian language of Palau, and Smith and Smith (1995) attempt to do the same for Turkish.

Metaphor and Metonymy

There is another kind of emotion-related term, the group of figurative terms and expressions. Since figurative terms also describe (and do not primarily express) emotions, this is a subgroup within descriptive terms. This subgroup may be larger than the other two groups combined. Here, unlike the previous group, the words and expressions do not literally "name" particular kinds of emotions, and the issue is not how basic or prototypical the word or expression is. The figurative words and expressions that belong in this group denote various *aspects* of emotion concepts, such as intensity, cause, control, and so forth. They can be metaphorical and metonymical. The metaphorical expressions are manifestations of conceptual metaphors in the sense of Lakoff and Johnson (1980). Conceptual metaphors bring two distant domains (or concepts) into correspondence with each other. One of the domains is typically more physical or concrete than the other (which is thus more abstract). The correspondence is established for the purpose of understanding the more abstract in terms of the more concrete. For example, *boiling with anger* is a linguistic example of the very productive conceptual metaphor ANGER IS A HOT FLUID (cf. Lakoff and

Kövecses, 1987; Lakoff, 1987; Kövecses, 1986, 1990, 1995a), *burning with love* is an example of LOVE IS FIRE (cf. Kövecses, 1988), and *to be on cloud nine* is an example of HAPPINESS IS UP (cf. Kövecses, 1991b). All three examples indicate the intensity aspect of the emotions concerned.

Linguistic expressions that belong in this large group can also be metonymical. Conceptual metonymies, unlike conceptual metaphors, involve a single domain, or concept. The purpose of metonymy is to provide mental access to a domain through a part of the same domain (or vice versa) or to a part of a domain through another part in the same domain (for more explanation of the nature of metonymy, see Kövecses and Radden, 1998). Thus, metonymy, unlike metaphor, is a "stand-for" relation (i.e., a part stands for the whole or a part stands for another part) within a single domain. Emotion concepts as wholes are viewed as having many parts, or elements. For instance, one part or element of the domain of anger is to be upset, and one part or element of the domain of fear is an assumed drop in body temperature. Thus, linguistic examples for these two emotion concepts include *to be upset* for anger and *to have cold feet* for fear. The first is an instance of the conceptual metonymy PHYSICAL AGITATION STANDS FOR ANGER, while the second is an example of the conceptual metonymy DROP IN BODY TEMPERATURE STANDS FOR FEAR (see Kövecses, 1990).

A special case of emotion metonymies involves a situation in which an emotion concept B is part of another emotion concept A (see, e.g., Kövecses, 1986, 1990, 1991a, 1991b). In cases like this, B can metonymically stand for A. This can explain why, for instance, the word *girlfriend* can be used of one's partner in a love relationship. Since love (A), at least ideally, involves or assumes friendship (B) between the two lovers, the word *friend* (an instance of B) can be used to talk about an aspect of love (A).

We can represent the three types of emotion language in Figure 1.3. Of the three groups identified (expressive terms, terms literally denoting particular kinds of emotions, and figurative expressions denoting particular aspects of emotions), the group of figurative expressions is the largest by far, and yet it has received the least attention in the study of emotion language. Figurative expressions are deemed completely uninteresting and irrelevant by most researchers, who tend to see them as epiphenomena, fancier ways of saying some things that could be said in literal, simple ways. Further, the expressions in group one are usually considered literal. Given this, we can understand better why the expressions in group three received scant attention. If one

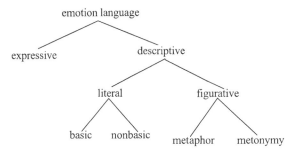

Figure 1.3. Summary of types of emotion language

holds the view that only literal expressions can be the bearers of truth and that figurative expressions have nothing to do with how our (emotional) reality is constituted, there is no need to study "mere" figurative language. However, there is also an increasing number of scholars who do not accept this view of the function of language in how human beings create their emotional realities (see, e.g., Baxter, 1992; Duck, 1994; Gibbs, 1994; Holland and Kipnis, 1995; Kövecses, 1990).

Meaning and Emotion

The isolation and description of emotion language is just the beginning in the process of uncovering the significance of this language in human conceptualization. The more difficult problem is to deal with the question of meaning. The issue of what constitutes the meaning of emotion words is a hotly debated topic in several disciplines – from psychology through anthropology to philosophy. There are several distinct views that scholars have offered in an attempt to characterize emotional meaning.

The "Label" View

The label view of emotional meaning maintains that the meaning of emotion terms is simply an association between a label, like the words *anger* and *fear*, plus some real emotional phenomena, like physiological processes and behavior. This view is the simplest lay view of emotional meaning. It is based on the folk theory of meaning in general according to which meaning is merely an association between sounds (forms) and things. This understanding of meaning in general also forms the basis of a scientific theory of emotion. Schachter and Singer (1962) proposed that emotion involves three things: a label, plus something (emotionally) real, plus a situation. This view is an improvement on the simplest lay view. However, they both exclude the possibility that emotion terms can have much conceptual content and organization. But, as several studies indicate (see, e.g., Wierzbicka, 1995; Shaver et al., 1987; and Kövecses, 1990, among others), emotion terms have a great deal of conceptual content and structure.

The "Core Meaning" View

It is customary in semantics to distinguish between core (denotative, conceptual, cognitive, etc.) and peripheral (connotative, residual, etc.) meaning (see, e.g., Lyons, 1977). What characterizes core meaning is a small number of properties or components that are taken to define a category in an adequate manner. This means, in this view of meaning, that core meaning should be capable of minimally distinguishing between the meaning of any two words; that is, by virtue of the smallest possible number of components. Since, in this view, the major function of definitions is systematic differentiation of meaning, the more important kind of meaning, the kind of meaning that really matters, is typically thought to be core meaning, while peripheral meaning is viewed as less important in giving the meaning of words and expressions. (For a more detailed discussion, see Kövecses, 1990, 1993a). Peripheral meaning or connotation is usually seen as being made up of various social, situational, or affective properties – any properties that are not taken to contribute to the cognitive content of words in a significant way. Connotations are assumed to vary from person to person and from culture to culture. However, according to some researchers, like Osgood (1964), certain connotations are universal: namely, the general meaning dimensions of evaluation (good vs. bad), activity (fast vs. slow), and potency (strong vs. weak).

The core meaning view of emotion categories typically assumes the idea that emotional meaning is composed of *universal* semantic primitives. A leading proponent of this view is Wierzbicka (see, e.g., Wierzbicka, 1972, 1995). For example, she defines the English emotion and *anger* in the following way: "X feels as one does when one thinks that someone has done something bad and when one wants to cause this person to do something he doesn't want to do" (1972, p. 62). This definition makes use of some universal semantic primitives, such as

THINK, DESIRE, WANT, BAD, GOOD, CAUSE, DO, and so forth. One of the major points of Wierzbicka's approach is that it is a mistake to think of emotion words in particular languages, such as English, as being universal (e.g., Wierzbicka, 1986, 1992a, 1995). Thus, for example, the English word *emotion* is anything but universal; it does not seem to exist even in languages otherwise closely related to English (Wierzbicka, 1995). What is universal instead, Wierzbicka maintains, are the semantic primitives that make up the conceptual content of particular emotion words in particular languages. (Because Wierzbicka's work also fits another group, her views will be discussed further in a later section.)

In one respect, however Wierzbicka's approach is not very representative of the core meaning view. In defining an emotion, one uses universals to make a clause that describes a scene or scenario: "X feels as one does when. . . ." In a typical core meaning theory, the mere presence or absence of the primitives is defining and there is no syntax that governs their construction as concepts. But in Wierzbicka, syntax matters because the semantic universals are combined in contingent clauses to construct scenes and scenarios ("X feels as one does when one thinks that . . .").

To take another example of the core meaning view, Davitz (1969) characterizes the meaning of the English emotion word *anger* as being composed of HYPERACTIVATION, MOVING AGAINST, TENSION, and INADEQUACY. These (and other) components, or clusters, of meaning are derived from linguistic data produced by speakers of English. The clusters are taken to be capable of successfully distinguishing each emotion word in English. Furthermore, it is suggested that the same clusters can be applied to the study of emotion concepts in other cultures (such as Ugandan).

The "Dimensional" View

Emotional meaning is also viewed as being constituted by values on a fixed set of dimensions of meaning. Solomon (1976), for example, postulates 13 dimensions that are sufficient to describe any emotion. These include DIRECTION, SCOPE/FOCUS, OBJECT, CRITERIA, STATUS, EVALUATIONS, RESPONSIBILITY, INTERSUBJECTIVITY, DISTANCE, MYTHOLOGY, DESIRE, POWER, and STRATEGY. The definitions of emotion concepts make use of all or some of these dimensions. The core meaning and dimensional views are not always easy to distinguish. Thus, according to Frijda the dimensions that apply to a given emotion provide a "component profile" that uniquely characterizes an emotion (Frijda, 1986, pp. 217–219). Researchers working in the dimensional approach attempt to eliminate a major alleged pitfall of the "core meaning" view in general: the large gap between emotional meaning and emotional experience. For example, de Rivera (1977) states that "there is bound to be a tension between these two poles – the one insisting that the investigator be faithful to experience, the other requiring the sparse elegance of precise relations between a few abstract constructs" (p. 121). Clearly, de Rivera is aware of a gap between emotional meaning as defined in terms of "a few abstract constructs" (i.e., semantic components and dimensions) and the totality of emotional experience, that is, complex experience of people who are in particular emotional states. Another well-known advocate of the dimensional approach is Frijda (1986). Frijda distinguishes among even more dimensions (26 altogether). Obviously, the aim is to reduce the meaning-experience gap.

The "Implicational" View

While the "core meaning" and "dimensional" views are based on the core meaning in general, the implicational view takes connotative meaning as its main point of departure. In the words of a major figure: "To study what something means is to study what it entails, implies, or suggests to those who understand it" (Shweder, 1991, p. 244). For example, according to Shweder, the sentence "One of my grandparents was a surgeon" suggests that my grandfather was a surgeon and the sentence "She is your mother" implies that she is under an obligation to care about your health (pp. 244–245). As these examples suggest, for Shweder, meaning is connotative meaning, not denotative meaning. It is the periphery, rather than the core, that counts in this view of meaning.

Shweder relativizes this approach to emotional meaning. One of his examples is *anger*. Shweder writes: "Anger suggests explosion, destruction, and revenge" (p. 245). As we will see in the discussion of yet another view of emotional meaning, these properties of anger, together with others, will show up in the representation of the meaning of *anger*.

The particular version of the connotative view of meaning that Shweder endorses is the nonuniversalist one. Unlike Osgood (1964),

Shweder believes, with anthropologists in general, that connotative meaning, and in particular emotional meaning, varies considerably from culture to culture. Making reference to work by several anthropologists, Shweder (1991) writes:

> Emotions have meanings, and those meanings play a part in how we feel. What it means to feel angry . . . is not quite the same for the Ilongot, who believe that anger is so dangerous it can destroy society; for the Eskimo, who view anger as something that only children experience; and for working-class Americans, who believe that anger helps us overcome fear and attain independence. (p. 245)

Thus, in Shweder's view the connotative meaning of anger varies cross-culturally. This is a tack that is the opposite of the one taken by Osgood (1964) whose interest lies in what is universal about connotative meaning.

Heider (1991) took a connotative approach in his study of Minangkabau (Sumatra) and Indonesian terms for emotions. Heider discovered clusters of synonyms for emotion terms. We are here regarding synonyms as a kind of verbal connotation. He constructed lists of over 200 emotion terms in each language and obtained synonyms from 50 Minangkabau, 50 Minangkabau Indonesian, and 50 Indonesian subjects for each term in the list. By drawing lines from each term to all its synonyms in each language, he was able to draw extensive maps of the lexical domain of emotion. Heider (1991, p. 27) suggested that each of the clusters of similar words "correspond[s] best to what we mean by 'an emotion.' " Those who think in terms of a small number of basic emotions might be surprised by Heider's discovery of "some forty clusters" with each having ties to "only one or two other clusters" (1991, p. 28). Heider also studied emotion prototypes, as discussed in the following section.

The "Prototype" View

In the section on "Words and Emotion," I mentioned that some emotion words are more prototypical than others. There the question was: What are the best examples of the category of *emotion*? As we saw, the best examples of the category in English include *anger, fear, love,* and others. We can also ask: What are the best examples, or cases, of *anger, fear,* and *love,* respectively? Obviously, there are many different kinds of anger, fear, and love. When we try to specify the structure and content of the best example of any of these lower-level categories, we are working within the "prototype" view of emotional meaning as it relates to individual basic-level categories. This view has produced some intriguing results. Heider (1991), for example, found that anger is less of a focal emotion in Indonesian than it is in English. Sadness and confusion, on the other hand, are more central emotions in Indonesian than in English.

The structure of emotion concepts is seen by many researchers as a script, scenario, or model (e.g., Fehr and Russell, 1984; Shaver et al., 1987; Rimé, Philippot, and Cisalono, 1990; Wierzbicka, 1990, 1992b; Heider, 1991; Lakoff and Kövecses, 1987; Kövecses, 1986, 1988, 1990; Rosaldo, 1984; Ortony, Clore, and Collins, 1988; Palmer and Brown, 1998, etc.). For example, Lakoff and Kövecses (1987) describe *anger* as a sequence of stages of events: (1) cause of anger, (2) anger exists, (3) attempt at controlling anger, (4) loss of control over anger, (5) retribution. That is, anger is viewed as being conceptualized as a five-stage scenario. Fehr and Russell (1984) characterize *fear* in the following manner:

> A dangerous situation occurs suddenly. You are startled, and you scream. You try to focus all your attention on the danger, try to figure a way out, but you feel your heart pounding and your limbs trembling. Thoughts race through your mind. Your palms feel cold and wet. There are butterflies in your stomach. You turn and flee. (p. 482)

In other words, we have the unfolding of a variety of events that are temporally and casually related in certain specifiable ways. The particular *sequence* of events make up the structure of the prototypical concept of any given emotion, like fear, while the particular *events* that participate in the sequence make up the content of the concepts.

One particularly interesting example of the scenario approach is that of Ortony et al. (1988), who define 22 emotion types. These are defined in terms of their eliciting conditions and independently of language. Examples of such types include being displeased about the prospect of an undesirable event, being pleased about the disconfirmation of the prospect of an undesirable event, and being displeased about the confirmation of the prospect of an undesirable event (p. 173). Their theory involves an element of appraisal: Events may be desirable or undesirable; actions may be praiseworthy or blameworthy; and objects may be appealing or unappealing.

Ortony et al. (1988) argue that they have the best of two worlds: a theory that is culture-free and applies universally, but nevertheless allows for culturally defined variation in emotional experience:

> At least at the meta-level, we feel comfortable that we have a theory based on culturally universal principles. These principles are that the particular classes of emotions that will exist in a culture depend on the ways in which members of a culture carve up their world. (Ortony, et al., 1988, p. 175)

But this position is not as relativistic as it may at first appear because all cultures must carve along the same joints as defined by the researchers: The particular classes of emotions allowed to any culture are presumably limited to the 22 types in their theory.

Ortony et al. (1988) believe it is wrong to start with language in the investigation of emotions. They regard it as a separate enterprise to investigate "the way in which emotion words in any particular language map onto the hypothesized emotion types" (p. 173). If we compare their approach to the characterization of anger offered by Lakoff and Kövecses (1987), we can see that the eliciting conditions would have to be subsumed entirely within stage one, "cause of anger." The emotion language pertaining to the subsequent four stages would not map directly onto the emotion types proposed in the psychological approach of Ortony et al. Thus, the psychological approach would ignore much of the conceptual content that can be discovered by the inspection of emotion language. On the other hand, their approach might provide leads for a more fine-grained linguistic analysis of stage one. This suggests that the two approaches could complement each other to the benefit of both.

Sometimes the prototype approach is combined with some other view of emotional meaning. For example, Wierzbicka (1990) states:

> The definition of an emotion concept takes the form of a prototypical scenario describing not so much an external situation as a highly abstract cognitive structure: roughly, to feel emotion E means to feel as a person does who has certain (specifiable) thoughts, characteristic of that particular situation. (p. 361)

As can be seen, this definition combines the "core meaning" approach with the prototype approach. The "(specifiable) thoughts" are constituted by the semantic primitives WANT, BAD, DO, SOMEONE, and others.

In the "prototype" approach, two kinds of views can be distinguished: the literal and the nonliteral conceptions of emotion. For example, Shaver et al. (1987) and Wierzbicka (1990) apparently do not think that metaphorical and metonymical understanding play a role in the way emotion concepts are understood and constituted. Others, however, believe that metaphorical and metonymical understanding does play a role. Some of these researchers disagree about the exact nature of this role (see, e.g., Holland, 1982; Quinn, 1991; Geeraerts and Grondelaers, 1995). Despite the disagreements, however, many believe that metaphors are important. Authors from a variety of disciplines, such as Averill (1974, 1990), Averill and Kövecses (1990), Baxter (1992), Duck (1994), Holland and Kipnis (1995), Quinn (1987, 1991), Lakoff and Kövecses (1987), Lakoff (1987), Kövecses (1986, 1988, 1990, 1991a, 1991b, 1993b, 1994b, 1995a, 1995b), discuss the role and possible contribution of conceptual metaphors and metonymies to the conceptualization of emotional experience.

Finally, in a variety of publications I have suggested (see Kövecses, 1986, 1988, 1990, 1991a, 1991b) that many emotions, such as love, fear, and happiness, have not just one, but several prototypical cognitive models associated with them (i.e., they each have multiple prototypes). That is, the proposal is that several members (or cases) can acquire the status of "best example" within an emotion category. This is because, given a category with several members, one member can be typical, another can be salient, a third can be ideal, and so on. (On metonymic models such as these, see Lakoff, 1987.)

The "Social-Constructionist" View

Several scholars take emotion concepts to be social constructions. For example Lutz (1988) gives the following account of *song* (roughly corresponding to anger) in Ifaluk:

1. There is a rule or value violation.
2. It is pointed out by someone.
3. This person simultaneously condemns the act.
4. The perpetrator reacts in fear to that anger.
5. The perpetrator amends his or her ways.

As can be seen, this model is considerably different from the one associated with the English word *anger*. To account for the difference, Lutz claims that this model of Ifaluk *song* is a social-cultural construction whose properties depend on particular aspects of Ifaluk society and culture. For example, while the view linked with the English word *anger* emphasizes properties of anger that relate to individuals, the view linked with *song* highlights the essentially social nature of this emotion concept. To account for the difference, Lutz claimed that this model of Ifaluk *song* is a socio-cultural construction whose properties depend on particular aspects of Ifaluk society and culture.

The social-constructionist view of emotion concepts is also based, at least in the work of its leading proponents (like Lutz and Averill), on the notion of prototype. The structure of most emotion concepts is seen as a highly conventionalized script from which deviations are recognized and linguistically marked in any given culture. Where the explicitly social-constructionist views differ from other prototype-based but nonconstructionist approaches is in their account of the content of emotion concepts.

The "Embodied Cultural Prototype" View

The account of *song* can be seen as diametrically opposed to that of *anger* as discussed by Lakoff and Kövecses (1987). Lakoff and Kövecses claim that to the degree that the metaphors (especially the AN-GER IS A HOT FLUID metaphor) that constitute anger are motivated by physiological functioning (e.g., increased body heat), the concept will be motivated by the human body, rather than being completely arbitrary, being just a social-cultural product.

In this work I will propose that it is necessary to go beyond both the view that the concept of anger is simply motivated by human physiology and the view that it is simply a social construction. I will suggest that it is *both* motivated by the human body *and* produced by a particular social and cultural environment. That is, I will attempt to reconcile the two apparently contradictory views (see chapters 8, 9, and 10). In this way, social constructions are given bodily basis and bodily motivation is given social-cultural substance.

Some Issues in the Study of Emotion Language

There are several issues that emerge from the foregoing discussion. I will mention only some of them, those that I find particularly important in the study of emotion concepts and emotional meaning and that will be explored further in this study.

The "Validity" Issue

Given our survey, one of the most important issues that arises is this: Which one of the views above *really* or *best* represents our everyday conception of emotion? Is it the "label" view, the "core meaning" view, the "dimensional" or some other view, or a combination of several of these? This is a tough question, and it seems that at the present time we have no reliable criteria to decide which of the views listed above is the one that can be considered a psychologically valid representation of emotion concepts. Although we have no direct evidence on the basis of which to favor any of the ways of representing emotional meaning, work in cognitive science in general suggests that prototypical cognitive models are our best candidates. "Prototype" views seem to offer the greatest explanatory power for many aspects of emotional meaning. These views, it will be remembered, come in at least two major versions: social-constructionist and experientialist (i.e., bodily based, in the sense of Lakoff, 1987, and Johnson, 1987). In my view, the two complement each other, and I will suggest a certain "marriage" between these rival theories.

The Universality of Emotion Prototypes

As several anthropologists and psychologists have argued (especially Berlin and Kay, 1969, and Rosch, 1975, 1978), focal colors appear to be universal. Is this also the case for the emotions? That is, is the prototype (the central member) for emotion X in language L a prototype (a central member) in other languages as well? Evidence that we have so far seems to indicate that it is not. The constructionists (like Harré and Lutz) argue that it is only natural that this is not the case, while others (like Russell, 1991) argue that prototypical scripts, or at least large portions of them, are the same across languages and cultures. Wierzbicka (1995) maintains, with the constructionists, that emotion prototypes are different cross-culturally, but the semantic primitives with which these differences are expressed can be, and are, universal.

It can also be suggested that what is universal are some general structures within the emotion domain, corresponding, as Frijda et al. (1995) put it, to an "unspecified positive emotion" (the happiness/joy range), an "unspecified negative emotion" (the sadness range), "an emotion of strong affection" (the love range), "an emotion of threat" (the fear range), and an angerlike range. However, the prototypical or focal members of the basic emotion categories (or ranges) in different languages tend to be different to varying degrees (compare Ifaluk *song* with English *anger*). This situation seems to be unlike the situation for color. In color, the focal members of particular colors are exactly the same across languages. In emotion, the "focal" members of basic emotion categories in different languages differ from each other to varying degrees – despite the fact that the same general basic emotion categories exist in possibly all languages and cultures. In the final chapters, I will make some suggestions concerning some of the details of cross-cultural similarities and differences.

The Universality of Conceptual Tools

So far we have seen a variety of conceptual tools or elements that scholars utilize in their attempts to provide a cognitive representation of emotional meaning. These include semantic primitives (components), connotative properties, dimensions of meaning, scripts or scenarios, and conceptual metaphors and metonymies. The question arises: Which of these conceptual elements are universal? Again, authors disagree. Lakoff (1987) and Johnson (1987) suggest that none of these are. Instead, what is universal, they argue, are certain basic image schemas, as these arise from certain fundamental bodily experiences. In this work, I will take this general direction. However, others, like Wierzbicka (1995), suggest that there is a small set of universal semantic primitives with the help of which all concepts (including emotion concepts) in all languages can be adequately described and defined.

Are Emotion Metaphors Unique to the Emotions?

As research so far has established, there is a large number of metaphors, or more precisely metaphorical source domains, that speakers of English use to understand their emotions, like anger, love, fear. These include HOT FLUID, FIRE, DANGEROUS ANIMAL, OPPONENT, BURDEN, NATURAL FORCE, etc. Why do speakers need all these different metaphors? And even more important, is this set of metaphorical source domains unique to the understanding of emotions or does it overlap with the source domains that people use to understand other experiences? (See chapter 3 for a discussion.) What is at stake here is the issue of whether we have a conceptual system from which the emotions "carve out" a unique part or not. My answer to this will be both yes and no. I will claim that at one level of generality, at the level where the specific conceptual metaphors cited above work, the emotions are not conceptualized in terms of a unique set of metaphors. However, I will claim that at another level there is something like a unique conceptualization of emotions. Drawing on Len Talmy's (1988) work on force dynamics, I will isolate an extremely general "master metaphor" for emotion that I will call the EMOTION IS FORCE metaphor (see chapter 5). I will show that most of the specific-level metaphors are merely instantiations of this generic-level metaphor. The FORCE metaphor will be shown to have several important consequences for the study of emotion. Given the FORCE metaphor, we will see that (1) it is impossible to conceptualize most aspects of the emotions in other than metaphorical terms; (2) this is a universal way of understanding emotion (see chapter 8); and (3) we can systematically contrast the domain of emotion with that of human relationships, like friendship, love, and marriage (see chapter 6).

The Role of Metaphor and Metonymy

Lakoff and Johnson (1980) argued that many everyday metaphors are conceptual in nature, that is, they are not mere words used in a non-literal sense. Rather, metaphors are conceptual devices used for important cognitive jobs. One of these is that metaphors can actually "create," or constitute social, cultural, and psychological realities for us. What is the role of conceptual metaphor in emotion concepts in a given culture? The more specific issue is this: Are the conceptual metaphors constitutive of the cultural models associated with emotions or do they simply reflect them? In a recent debate and based on data concerning the American conception of marriage, Quinn (1991) proposes that the latter is the case. Here again, I will take the opposite tack and argue in chapter 7, on the basis of the prevalent "unity" metaphor for love and marriage, that conceptual metaphors, together with other factors, can contribute to how abstract concepts are constituted. However, as Holland (personal communication) suggests, this "either/or" view of the role of metaphor might not be the best way of looking at the issue. Moreover, it seems closer to the truth to believe that some metaphors have the capacity to constitute reality, while others do not. Which ones do and which ones don't can only be decided on the basis of detailed future research.

The same issue arises in connection with scientific or expert theories of emotion. Are the metaphors used in scholarly discussions "merely explanatory, pedagogical" devices, or do the metaphors actually constitute the theories? Soyland (1994), for one, argues that the latter is the case. I will return to this question in chapter 7.

"Lay Views" Versus "Scientific Theories"

What is the relationship between everyday emotion concepts (as revealed in conventional language use) and scientific conceptions of emotion? That is, how are lay and scientific theories of emotion related? This is an issue that, among others, Parrott (1995) addresses in an explicit way in relation to the lay "heart–head" and the corresponding expert "emotion–cognition" distinction.

More generally, assuming that there *is* a relationship and that the relationship can be either strong or weak (somewhat on the analogy of distinct interpretations of the Sapir-Whorf hypothesis), we can imagine four theoretical possibilities (with several additional in-between cases not specified here):

1. folk conception determines expert theory
2. folk conception influences expert theory
3. expert theory determines folk theory
4. expert theory influences folk theory

In the strong version, "determines" is intended in the sense of "leads to, produces." In the weak version, "influences" covers such disparate cases as "constrains," "builds on," or "makes it natural and popular."

Given this admittedly ad hoc classification, we can look at specific instances in emotion research and try to identify the specific relation that might obtain between a given lay view and a given expert theory. In some publications (e.g., Averill and Kövecses, 1990; Kövecses, 1991a), Averill and I make some preliminary observations concerning some of these possibilities. For instance, I point out (1991a) how a number of expert theories of love build and focus on various aspects of the language-based folk model of love. The nature of the relationship between lay and expert theories in psychological domains, such as the domain of emotion, is a hotly debated topic today, as indicated by several recent collections of articles that bear on this question, such as those by Siegfried (1994) and Russell, Fernández-Dols, Manstead, and Wellenkamp (1995). I will explore this issue at some length in chapter 7.

Subcategorizing Emotions

Indeed, what are the emotions? Do we subcategorize them as states, events, actions, or passions? Is the psychologist right who says they are states, or the lay public that says they are passions? Can they be thought of as actions at all? And most intriguingly, how can we find out? Recently, George Lakoff (1990, 1993) proposed that much of our understanding of states, events, actions, and activities is structured by what he calls the "Event Structure" metaphor. To shed some light on these issues, I will make use of this complex metaphor to see the extent of the overlap between the domain of emotions and the event system in chapter 4.

These are the issues that I wish to address in subsequent chapters. However, before we plunge into deep water, it will serve us well to see which English emotion concepts have been studied so far from a cognitive semantic perspective and what the results are. This will provide us with a good foundation in the discussion of the issues introduced above and in comparing English with other languages. I will survey some of the results for English in chapter 2, while languages other than English will be examined in chapters 8 and 9.

2. Metaphors of Emotion

In this chapter I wish to survey and summarize the research that has been done on metaphorical aspects of emotion concepts in English in the past decade or so. (The research on figurative emotion language in other cultures will be presented in chapters 8 and 9.) I will limit myself to the presentation of results that have been acquired by using a cognitive linguistic framework within the tradition that was established in the 1980s and early 1990s by the work of such figures as George Lakoff (Lakoff and Johnson, 1980; Lakoff, 1987; Lakoff and Turner, 1989), Ronald Langacker (1987, 1991), Mark Johnson (Johnson, 1987, 1993), Mark Turner (1987), Eve Sweetser (1990), Ray Gibbs (1994), and others. Clearly, it is this framework that takes figurative (metaphoric and metonymic) language most seriously in the study of human conceptual systems.

The emotion concepts that have received attention from a variety of scholars in this tradition include anger, fear, happiness, sadness, love, lust, pride, shame, and surprise. I take this set to be a fairly representative sample of emotion concepts. Many of them are proto-typical emotion concepts and occur on most lists of "basic emotions" (e.g., anger, fear, happiness, sadness), and some of them such as love and surprise, represent at least arguable cases of basic emotions. In regard to their cognitive status as linguistic categories in a vertical hierarchy of concepts, they are all basic-level categories.

The focus in this chapter will be predominantly on conceptual metaphor, since I will claim that metaphor not only pervades the language people use about the emotions, but also that it is essential to the understanding of most aspects of the conceptualization of emotion and emotional experience. Several questions arise in connection with the use of such metaphorical language: (1) Is such language actually used by people, and if it is, to what extent? (2) Who coins this language? Does it come from poets, novelists, or ordinary people? (3) Does this language change with time? I will attempt to address each of these questions in the present chapter.

The survey below is also crucial in order to see some of the directions in which the study of metaphorical language can lead us and to see some of the possibilities that the research that has been done so far can open up. Let us begin the survey with anger.

Anger Metaphors

Anger is perhaps the most studied emotion concept from a cognitive semantic point of view. Kövecses (1986) and Lakoff and Kövecses (1987) found a number of metaphorical source domains that characterize anger. Some further ones can be added to those source domains, such as AN ANGRY PERSON IS A FUNCTIONING MACHINE and ANGER IS A SOCIAL SUPERIOR. Below is a list of the main metaphorical source domains for the concept in English, with one or more linguistic examples illustrating each conceptual metaphor (consisting of a target and a source domain):

ANGER IS A HOT FLUID IN A CONTAINER: She is *boiling with* anger.
ANGER IS FIRE: He's doing a *slow burn*. His anger is *smoldering*.
ANGER IS INSANITY: The man was *insane with* rage.
ANGER IS AN OPPONENT IN A STRUGGLE: I was *struggling with* my anger.
ANGER IS A CAPTIVE ANIMAL: He *unleashed* his anger.
ANGER IS A BURDEN: He *carries* his anger *around* with him.
ANGRY BEHAVIOR IS AGGRESSIVE ANIMAL BEHAVIOR: Don't *snarl at* me!
THE CAUSE OF ANGER IS TRESPASSING: Here I *draw the line*.
THE CAUSE OF ANGER IS PHYSICAL ANNOYANCE: He's *a pain in the neck*.
ANGER IS A NATURAL FORCE: It was a *stormy* meeting.
AN ANGRY PERSON IS A FUNCTIONING MACHINE: That really *got* him *going*.
ANGER IS A SOCIAL SUPERIOR: His actions were completely *governed* by anger.

These metaphorical source domains address various aspects of the concept of anger. For example, the FUNCTIONING MACHINE metaphor focuses on the angry person, PHYSICAL ANNOYANCE and TRESPASSING on the cause of anger, AGGRESSIVE ANIMAL BEHAVIOR on the angry behavior, OPPONENT on the aspect of control, and so forth. Now the conceptual metaphor that seems to be the central one for anger is ANGER IS A HOT FLUID IN A CONTAINER. Its centrality derives from two sources: One is that the container metaphor captures many different aspects of the concept of anger. The other is that it is highly elaborated both in terms of its metaphorical entailments and its conventionalized vocabulary. The idea of the centrality of this metaphor in our folk theories of emotion in general was dealt with in some detail elsewhere (Kövecses, 1990).

Who creates the kind of metaphorical language exemplified above? It can be safely suggested that most of this language is the normal, conventional way of talking about anger in English. The language derives from certain metaphorical ways of conceptualizing the experience of anger. But how do other users of English who are regarded as the most "creative" ones comprehend anger? Can't it be that they are the ones that provide "ordinary speakers" with this metaphorical language and imagery? The answer seems to be that even the most creative speakers employ similar conceptualizations (see Gibbs, 1994), though the language they use may be different from that of ordinary speakers. To demonstrate this, let us take the ANGER IS A HOT FLUID IN A CONTAINER metaphor. A good poetic example in which a similar conceptualization occurs is provided by Adrienne Rich's poem "The Phenomenology of Anger," quoted in full by Gibbs (1994, p. 8). In the poem, anger is talked about as "acetylene" that "ripples" from the body and is "released" on the "enemy." When we understand the poem, we activate in our minds one of the most conventional metaphors for anger: ANGER IS A HOT FLUID IN A CONTAINER. This is a perfectly everyday metaphor that we see in such everyday linguistic examples as *"boiling* with anger," *"making one's blood boil," "simmer down," "blowing your stack,"* and many others. In Rich's poem, the hot fluid gets elaborated as acetylene and the passive event of explosion is replaced by directing the dangerous substance of acetylene at the target of anger. When Rich modifies the hot fluid and turns it into a dangerous substance, she performs the (unconscious) act of elaborating on an everyday metaphor. A large part of the intuitive appeal of the poem derives from our (possibly unconscious) recognition of this familiar and completely mundane metaphorical view of anger. In the cognitive process of elaboration, the poet elaborates on an existing element of the source in an unusual way. It seems then that much of our language of anger is based on normal, conventional ways of understanding anger. Creative speakers (such as poets), however, often deviate from these entrenched ways. In this section, we have dealt with only one example, but there are many similar cases. They point to the same conclusion: that emotion metaphors as used by poets are based on everyday conventional metaphors. Gibbs (1994), following Lakoff and Turner (1989), puts the more general point in the following way:

> My claim is that much of our conceptualization of experience is metaphorical, which both motivates and constrains the way we think creatively. The idea that metaphor constrains creativity might seem contrary to the widely held belief the metaphor somehow liberates the mind to engage in divergent thinking.

Fear Metaphors

I described the metaphors for the concept of fear in *Emotion Concepts* (1990). They include the following:

FEAR IS A FLUID IN A CONTAINER: The sight *filled* her *with* fear.

FEAR IS A HIDDEN ENEMY: Fear slowly *crept up on* him. He was *hounded by* the fear that the business would fail. The thought continued *to prey on* her mind.

FEAR IS A TORMENTOR: My mother was *tormented* by fear.

FEAR IS A SUPERNATURAL BEING: He was *haunted* by fear.

FEAR IS AN ILLNESS: Jill was *sick with* fright.

FEAR IS INSANITY: Jack was *insane with* fear.

THE SUBJECT OF FEAR IS A DIVIDED SELF: I was *beside* myself with fear.

FEAR IS AN OPPONENT IN A STRUGGLE: Fear *took hold of* me.

FEAR IS A BURDEN: Fear *weighed heavily on* them.

FEAR IS A NATURAL FORCE: She was *engulfed* by panic.

FEAR IS A SOCIAL SUPERIOR: His actions were *dictated* by fear.

Fear appears to be characterized by both very general emotion metaphors, such as FLUID IN A CONTAINER, OPPONENT, BURDEN, and very specific metaphors. The group of specific metaphors includes HIDDEN ENEMY and SUPERNATURAL BEING. I will take up the issue of the generality and specificness of emotion metaphors in the next chapter.

The FLUID IN A CONTAINER metaphor is not a central way of understanding fear in English. One interesting characteristic of the concept is that it is constituted by a large number of conceptual metonymies, such as DROP IN BODY TEMPERATURE, PHYSICAL AGITATION, INCREASE IN RATE OF HEARTBEAT, and many others. The physiological aspect of the concept is greatly elaborated in language. I will not analyze these in the present work, but a more or less complete understanding of fear is impossible without taking these metonymies into account. The metonymies by themselves, however, do not constitute a sufficiently rich conceptual structure for the concept. That is primarily provided by the metaphors, no matter how bland and unspecific they are. The question of how metaphors in general provide that structure will be discussed in the next three chapters.

By the concept of the DIVIDED SELF, I mean a source domain in which there is a canonical person. The canonical person consists of a self and a body, and they are related in such a way that the body contains the self. The DIVIDED SELF as a metaphorical source domain suggests that the self that is normally inside the body container moves outside it. This happens when the person loses control, in our case, over his or her emotions.

Happiness Metaphors

The list of metaphorical source domains that follows is taken from Kövecses (1991b) and Lakoff and Johnson (1980).

HAPPY IS UP: We had to cheer him *up.*

HAPPINESS IS BEING OFF THE GROUND: I am *six feet off the ground.* I was so happy *my feet barely touched the ground.*

HAPPINESS IS BEING IN HEAVEN: That was *heaven on earth.*

HAPPY IS LIGHT: She *brightened* up at the news.

HAPPINESS IS VITALITY: He was *alive* with joy.

HAPPY IS WARM: That *warmed* my spirits.

HAPPINESS IS HEALTH: It made me *feel great.*

A HAPPY PERSON IS AN ANIMAL THAT LIVES WELL: He was happy as *a pig in shit.* He looks like *the cat that got the cream.*

HAPPINESS IS A PLEASURABLE PHYSICAL SENSATION: I was *tickled pink.*

HAPPINESS IS A FLUID IN A CONTAINER: He was *overflowing with* joy.

HAPPINESS IS A CAPTIVE ANIMAL: His feelings of happiness *broke loose.* She couldn't *hold back* her feelings of happiness.

HAPPINESS IS AN OPPONENT IN A STRUGGLE: He was *knocked out!* She was *overcome by joy.*

HAPPINESS IS A RAPTURE/HIGH: I was *drunk with* joy.

HAPPINESS IS INSANITY: They were *crazy with* happiness.
HAPPINESS IS A NATURAL FORCE: He was *swept off his feet*.

Here again, we find some very general metaphorical source domains, such as CAPTIVE ANIMAL, OPPONENT, INSANITY, and so forth. The concept of happiness is also characterized by a number of more limited source domains, including UP, LIGHT, RAPTURE/HIGH. It seems to have some very specific ones as well, such as AN ANIMAL THAT LIVES WELL and PLEASURABLE PHYSICAL SENSATION.

In the next chapter, I will argue that we have to distinguish the source domains of UP, on the one hand, and BEING OFF THE GROUND and BEING IN HEAVEN, on the other, despite the apparent similarity of UPNESS found in these source domains. I will also suggest that the "hot" part of the emotion heat-scale needs to be distinguished from the "warm" part, which characterizes happiness. As will be seen in chapter 9, there is some cross-cultural justification for this decision as well.

A central aspect of the concept of happiness involves evaluation. I will suggest in the next chapter that it is the notion of positive evaluation that lends the concept its special flavor (see also Kövecses, 1991b).

Sadness Metaphors

Metaphors for sadness were analyzed from a cognitive linguistic perspective by Barcelona (1986). He identified the following source domains, which I present here with some modifications:

SAD IS DOWN: He *brought* me *down* with his remarks.
SAD IS DARK: He is in a *dark* mood.
SADNESS IS A LACK OF HEAT: Losing his father *put his fire out*; he's been depressed for two years.
SADNESS IS A LACK OF VITALITY: This was *disheartening* news.
SADNESS IS A FLUID IN A CONTAINER: I am *filled with* sorrow.
SADNESS IS A PHYSICAL FORCE: That was a *terrible blow*.
SADNESS IS A NATURAL FORCE: *Waves* of depression *came over him*.
SADNESS IS AN ILLNESS: She was *heart-sick*. Time *heals* all sorrows.
SADNESS IS INSANITY: He was *insane with* grief.
SADNESS IS A BURDEN: He *staggered under* the pain.
SADNESS IS A LIVING ORGANISM: He *drowned* his sorrow in drink.
SADNESS IS A CAPTIVE ANIMAL: His feelings of misery *got out of hand*.

SADNESS IS AN OPPONENT: He was *seized by* a fit of depression.
SADNESS IS A SOCIAL SUPERIOR: She was *ruled* by sorrow.

In addition to some more specific metaphorical source domains, we find the usual general ones. The specific source domains mostly have to do with negative evaluation of the concept of sadness and, as such, form the opposites of several of the source domains for happiness.

Love Metaphors

I have studied metaphors of love in my *The Language of Love* (1988), in which I also drew on Lakoff and Johnson's (1980) work. Most of the metaphors that I found coincide with Baxter's results, who studied them from a psychological point of view (Baxter, 1992). Her work will be further discussed in the chapter on relationships. The conceptual metaphors for love that make themselves manifest in everyday language use are the following:

LOVE IS A NUTRIENT: I am *starved for* love.
LOVE IS A JOURNEY: It's been *a long, bumpy road.*
LOVE IS A UNITY OF PARTS: We're *as one.* They're *breaking up.* We're *inseparable.* We *fused together.*
LOVE IS CLOSENESS: They're very *close.*
LOVE IS A BOND: There is a close *tie* between them.
LOVE IS A FLUID IN A CONTAINER: She was *overflowing with* love.
LOVE IS FIRE: I am *burning* with love.
LOVE IS AN ECONOMIC EXCHANGE: I'm *putting more into* this than you are.
LOVE IS A NATURAL FORCE: She *swept* me *off my feet.*
LOVE IS A PHYSICAL FORCE: I was *magnetically drawn to* her.
LOVE IS AN OPPONENT: She tried to *fight* her feelings of love.
LOVE IS A CAPTIVE ANIMAL: She *let go of* her feelings.
LOVE IS WAR: She *conquered* him.
LOVE IS SPORT/A GAME: He *made a play for* her.
LOVE IS A DISEASE/AN ILLNESS: I am *heart-sick.*
LOVE IS MAGIC: He was *enchanted.*
LOVE IS INSANITY: I am *crazy about* you.
LOVE IS A SOCIAL SUPERIOR: She is completely *ruled* by love.
LOVE IS RAPTURE/A HIGH: I have been *high on* love for weeks.
THE OBJECT OF LOVE IS APPETIZING FOOD: Hi, *sweetie-pie.*

THE OBJECT OF LOVE IS A SMALL CHILD: Well, *baby*, what are we gonna do?
THE OBJECT OF LOVE IS A DEITY: Don't *put* her *on a pedestal*. He *worships* her.
THE OBJECT OF LOVE IS A VALUABLE OBJECT: You're my *treasure*!

As can be readily seen, the concept of love is perhaps the most highly "metaphorized" emotion concept. I will claim that this is possibly due to the fact that it is not only an emotion, but a relationship as well. As such, it also partakes of metaphorical source domains that typically characterize human relationships (see chapter 6).

One conceptual metaphor for love that has escaped the attention of scholars interested in the metaphorical conceptualization of love is THE OBJECT OF LOVE IS A POSSESSED OBJECT. The reason for this may be that this source domain is very natural and obvious for most of us when talking about the loved one; this naturalness and obviousness does not make it even appear a metaphor. The examples are well known; let's just look at two: "You are *mine* and I am *yours*," "I won't let anyone *take* you from me."

The central idea, and hence the central metaphor, in the love system is the notion of UNITY, at least judged by the number of various metaphorical entailments of and lexical elaborations on such source domains as UNITY OF TWO COMPLEMENTARY PARTS, BOND, and CLOSENESS. However, there seems to be an interesting discrepancy here between my suggestions and Baxter's (1992) findings. Baxter's interviews, as far as I can tell on the basis of her examples, did not show up anything significant about the UNITY-related aspects of love. One reason for this may be that the highly conventionalized and traditionally used expressions that have to do with UNITY do not form a part of the vocabulary of Baxter's subjects, who were young college students in the early 1990s. Young college students may be at a stage of their lives in which their relationships are transitory and superficial rather than lasting and deeply felt. (But in a set of interviews conducted by Ted Sablay in 1996, another set of American college students did come up with the UNITY metaphor in their conceptualization of romantic love. See chapter 7.)

The discussion of the love metaphors above allows us to return to another of our three questions in the introduction: Do the metaphors for the emotions change with time? The short answer is that most of them are stable through time; that is, we have had them in some linguistic form for a long time. These metaphors have been character-ized by the same conceptual structure or "scaffolding" through time, while the linguistic examples making them manifest may have changed with time. As an illustration of the point, let us take a look at the conception of love according to which LOVE IS A UNITY OF TWO COMPLEMENTARY PARTS. This conceptual metaphor has been with us for a long time and was made famous and popular by Plato. In the *Symposium*, Aristophanes says that Zeus had cleft people in two be-cause of their hubris, and love is a yearning to be reunited with one's missing part. As we saw above, the UNITY metaphor is still with us today; even college students "live by" it. The metaphor has also been popular throughout the centuries between Plato's time and our own. As an example, consider the poem of the 17th-century American poet, Anne Bradstreet, entitled "To My Dear and Loving Husband."

> If ever two were one, then surely we.
> If man were loved by wife, then thee;
> If ever wife was happy in a man,
> Compare with me, ye women, if you can.
> I prize thy love more than whole mines of gold
> Or all the riches that the East doth hold.
> My love is such that rivers cannot quench,
> Nor ought but love from thee, give recompense.
> Thy love is such I can no way repay.
> The heavens reward thee manifold, I pray.
> Then while we live, in love let's so persevere
> That when we live no more, we may live ever.

Much of the understanding of this poem appears to be based on fa-miliar, conventional metaphors of love, including LOVE IS A UNITY (as in "She is my *better half*" and "We're *inseparable*"), LOVE IS AN ECO-NOMIC EXCHANGE (as in "I'm *putting more* into this than you are"), and LOVE IS A NUTRIENT (as in "I'm *sustained* by love"). All of these are made use of in the poem:

> If ever two were one, then surely we. – LOVE IS A UNITY
> Thy love is such I can no way repay. – LOVE IS AN ECONOMIC EXCHANGE
> My love is such that rivers cannot quench, – LOVE IS A NUTRIENT

As the first line of the poem shows, the author conceives of love as a unity between two parts. The particular linguistic expression that makes this idea manifest may be unique ("If ever *two were one*, then surely we."), but the conceptual structure of the metaphor (i.e., the correspondences between love and the unity of the parts that make it up) remain the same through the ages.

Lust Metaphors

Lakoff and I collected examples of metaphors used for the comprehension of lust or sexual desire. What we found was reported in Lakoff (1987). The metaphors include:

LUST IS HUNGER: She's sex-*starved*.
LUST IS A VICIOUS ANIMAL: You bring out the *beast* in me.
LUST IS HEAT: I've got the *hots* for her.
LUST IS PRESSURE INSIDE A CONTAINER: Her whole body *exploded* in passion.
LUST IS INSANITY: You're driving me *insane*.
A LUSTFUL PERSON IS A FUNCTIONING MACHINE: She *turned* me *on*.
LUST IS A GAME: I couldn't *get to first base* with her.
LUST IS WAR: She was his latest *conquest*.
LUST IS A PHYSICAL FORCE: She *knocked* me *off my feet*.
LUST IS A NATURAL FORCE: There were *waves* of passion.
LUST IS A SOCIAL SUPERIOR: He's completely *ruled* by lust.

Lakoff and I found these conceptual and linguistic metaphors scattered throughout a variety of sources, including informal conversations, magazines, movies, pop literature, et cetera. This explains why some of the examples may appear forced and without context. The unsystematic character of gathering data inevitably leads one to ask: Who actually uses these linguistic metaphors in a natural way, and are all these conceptual metaphors equally common in natural usage? These are extremely important questions in the enterprise I am advocating. Without answering them, we cannot get a sense of the reality of this kind of metaphorical emotion language for certain communities of speakers.

In response to this challenge, two students of mine, Tina Gummo in Las Vegas and Szilvia Csábi in Budapest have done a systematic survey of conceptual metaphors relating to lust in English (Csábi, 1998). An obvious domain to look for lust metaphors is romance fiction. Gummo and Csábi read several romance novels and collected over 400 metaphoric and metonymic linguistic examples. Then we tried to categorize these examples according to source concepts. This was done independently by each of us. In our final product (a list of conceptual and linguistic metaphors), we only kept those linguistic examples on which all three of us agreed. This resulted in a little over 370 linguistic examples altogether. Table 2.1 summarizes our findings. First the source domains are given, then the approximate number of linguistic examples found for the source concept, and finally some linguistic examples. Only those conceptual metaphors and metonymies are presented that manifested themselves in at least 5 linguistic examples in our corpus.

Table 2.1 represents the findings of an admittedly informal survey. Nevertheless, it helps us make several important observations. First, there is a large community of speakers of English (romance fiction writers and readers) that makes extensive use of this kind of figurative language. For them, linguistic metaphors and metonymies such as the ones given above provide the normal ways of talking about lust. Second, the large number of figurative linguistic expressions (roughly 400) found in the survey can be seen as manifestations of a much smaller number of conceptual metaphors and metonymies (roughly 20). Third, the conceptualization of lust by these speakers is couched predominantly in two metaphorical source domains: fire/heat and hunger/eating. The emphasis on these particular source domains may distinguish this category of speakers from speakers of other communities (see Csábi, 1998).

Pride Metaphors

I have dealt with the concept of pride in two studies (Kövecses, 1986, 1990). The metaphors that emerged are as follows:

PRIDE IS A FLUID IN A CONTAINER: The sight *filled* him with pride.
PRIDE IS A SUPERIOR: Her self-esteem did *not let* her do it.
PRIDE IS AN ECONOMIC VALUE: Don't *underestimate* yourself.
CAUSING HARM TO A PROUD PERSON IS CAUSING INJURY TO SOMEONE: His pride was *injured*.
CAUSING HARM TO A PROUD PERSON IS CAUSING PHYSICAL DAMAGE TO A STRUCTURED OBJECT: That *put a dent* in his pride.

Pride is a concept that is conceptualized metaphorically to only a small degree. The metaphorical source domains above characterize "balanced" forms of pride, as opposed to such prototypes as vanity or conceit (see Kövecses, 1990). These latter are comprehended

Table 2.1. *Metaphors and Metonymies for* LUST

Metaphors	No. of Ex's	Linguistic Examples
FIRE/HEAT	65	She yielded to his *fiery* passion. She felt that her very being would demolish in the *heat*. He *kindled* her body into savage excitement.
HUNGER/EATING	50	He prepared *to satisfy* their sexual *hunger*. He *fell to* her like a *starved* man might *fall to food*. Her *appetites* were hot and uninhibited.
ANIMAL BEHAVIOR/ WILDNESS	25	She was a *tigress*. He moved *with animal ferocity*. He hadn't been able *to hold back*.
WAR	21	She *lost the battle*. He *took* her mouth *in a preliminary conquest*.
INSANITY	20	She had turned him into a *raving maniac*. He enticed them both in the direction of *madness*.
NATURAL FORCE	19	She felt the *flood*. He was *drowning in* his own desire.
RAPTURE	18	He gave her a *drugging* kiss. His presence *made* her *dizzy with* pleasure.
OPPONENT	17	He *struggled against* his lust. Her body joined forces with his, *demolishing her control*.
PAIN/TORMENTOR	16	He devoured her lips with the insatiable hunger that had been *torturing* him. His touch *tormented* her.
CONTAINER	15	She *depleted* him, *exhausted* every secret *reserve* of passion. Her passion *exploded*.
UNITY/BOND	12	Their bodies collided and *merged into one fiery entity*. They *united* in the end.
POSSESSED OBJECT	10	She wanted him *to let* him *have* her. He *possessed* her body. She *took* him.
PHYSICAL FORCE	10	The brush of his fingers sent amazing *jolts of electricity* shooting up her leg. There was no denying the *power* of his sexual *magnetism*.
GAME/PLAY	9	"I'm not *playing your games*," she said. He *played with* her body.
MAGICIAN	7	Their lovemaking had been *magic*. She *broke the spell* he *weaved around* her.
TRICKSTER	5	She wanted *to lure* him into her bed. She *bewitches* men.
SOCIAL SUPERIOR	5	He was *overpoweringly* male. She was *driven by* lust.

(*continued*)

Table 2.1 *(continued)*

Metonymies	No. of Ex's	Linguistic Examples
BODY HEAT	25	His masculinity *made her body go hot.* He *went hot all over* just to think about it.
PHYSICAL AGITATION	17	A hot *shiver* went through her. His body *shook from* the fever.
INTERFERENCE WITH ACCURATE PERCEPTION	6	She *lost her ability to think.* He was rendered *senseless* by his uncontrollable, fiery desire for her.

through some further highly specific source domains, such as THE CONCEITED PERSON IS UP/HIGH and BIG (e.g., *"Get off your high horse"*) for conceit and VANITY IS AN INDULGENT PERSON (e.g., "He was *basking in* the praises") for the concept of vanity.

Shame Metaphors

In presenting the major metaphorical source domains for shame, I rely on work by Holland and Kipnis (1995) and Pape (1995). In listing the metaphors, I will not distinguish between the related concepts of shame and embarrassment, though the two are clearly distinct. The concept of shame will be used throughout. The source domains that these authors identified include:

A SHAMEFUL PERSON IS A PERSON HAVING NO CLOTHES ON: I felt so *naked*; so *exposed.* I was *caught with my pants down.*
SHAME IS A FLUID IN A CONTAINER: The memory *filled* him with shame.
SHAME IS AN ILLNESS: He *suffered* much embarrassment in his youth.
SHAME IS A DECREASE IN SIZE: I felt *this big.*
SHAME IS HIDING AWAY FROM THE WORLD: I wanted to *bury my head in the sand.* I wished the *ground would just swallow me up.*
A SHAMEFUL PERSON IS A DIVIDED SELF: I tried to *regain my composure.*
A SHAMEFUL PERSON IS A WORTHLESS OBJECT: I felt like *two cents waiting for change.*
SHAME IS PHYSICAL DAMAGE: I was *shattered.*
SHAME IS A BURDEN: Guilt was *weighing him down.*

As can be seen, the conceptualizations of "unbalanced" forms of pride contrast with those of shame: UP/HIGH and BIG contrast with DECREASE IN SIZE and INDULGENT PERSON contrasts with BLOCKING OUT THE WORLD. There is also a difference in the self's value of himself or herself. Although pride and shame share the source domain PHYSICAL DAMAGE, it applies to the emotion in pride and to the person in shame.

The central metaphor for shame according to Holland and Kipnis (1995) is HAVING NO CLOTHES ON. This is not a general metaphor for emotions, but it is clearly important for understanding shame. One would think that it is more like a conceptual metonymy than a metaphor. I will argue in the next chapter that it is both.

Surprise Metaphors

The language and metaphors of surprise were studied by Kendrick-Murdock (1994). Her results indicate that most of our understanding of surprise comes from three metaphorical source domains:

SURPRISE IS A PHYSICAL FORCE: I was *staggered* by the report.
A SURPRISED PERSON IS A BURST CONTAINER: I just *came apart at the seams*.
SURPRISE IS A NATURAL FORCE: I was *overwhelmed* by surprise.

Let us observe just two points. First, obviously, the BURST CONTAINER metaphor is not highly typical of surprise, but it highlights a very important aspect of surprise, namely, that the surprised person temporarily loses control over himself or herself. The BURST CONTAINER metaphor captures this particular aspect of the concept. Second, not surprisingly, surprise is the least metaphorically comprehended concept on our list. The reason possibly is that surprise is not a socially very complex phenomenon, and, consequently, there is not a great amount of conceptual content to be associated with it.

Conclusion

To conclude this chapter, we found that the emotion concepts under investigation are comprehended via a large number of conceptual metaphors, ranging from 3 (surprise) to 24 (love). As the analysis of lust showed, lust metaphors characterize and define a real community of speakers of English (romance fiction fans). We assume that all the metaphors we found for particular emotions characterize similar categories of speakers, although the conceptual metaphors themselves may be more or less productive and central for these speakers (as was the case with the FIRE and HUNGER metaphors for lust). The size of these groups or categories of speakers may vary from small (just a few people) through extensive (like romance fiction fans) to the entire community of speakers of English. Furthermore, generalizing from the example of anger, I assume that roughly the same conceptual metaphors characterize ordinary speakers and "creative" speakers. This suggests that the figurative linguistic expressions that speakers use to talk about their emotions derive from a largely shared conceptual system. Finally, as the example of the UNITY metaphor for love indicates, conceptual metaphors may have stability over time. This does not, however, mean that the particular linguistic manifestations of the conceptual metaphors will always remain the same; instead, the particular expressions are likely to change as a result of, for instance, new cultural, technical, and scientific developments.

There are two inevitable questions that arise in connection with the discussion of the metaphorical source domains identified above: (1) Are these source domains specific to the emotions? (2) Is there a higher-level conceptual organization to them? I will attempt to answer the first question in the next two chapters and will take up the second in chapter 5.

3. Emotion Metaphors
Are They Unique to the Emotions?

The general issue I wish to raise in this chapter can be put in the following way: Are there any metaphorical source domains that are specific, or unique, to the emotions? In other words, the question is whether the source domains of emotion metaphors have application outside the concept of emotion or only inside it. This is an important question to ask because it has bearings on how we conceive of the structure of our conceptual system. What is at issue is whether we understand an abstract domain (like emotion) in a unique way (e.g., in the case of emotion, by means of source concepts that are specific to emotion), or whether we understand it through source concepts that are shared also by other (nonemotional) domains in their conceptualization.

The focus of this chapter will be on what I have called elsewhere the "scope of metaphor" (Kövecses, 1995c, n.d.). This notion is intended to capture an aspect of conceptual metaphor that has not been given sufficient attention thus far, namely, the idea that the source domains of conceptual metaphors do not have unlimited applications. That is, particular source domains seem to apply to a clearly identifiable range of target concepts. I will make use of this notion in relation to the emotions.

When we ask whether the source domains of emotion are specific to the domain of emotion, we are really asking four questions: Are the metaphorical source domains of emotions specific to one emotion; are they specific to a subset of emotions; are they specific to all emotions; or do they extend beyond the domain of emotion? Obviously, to answer our questions in an adequate way, we would have to examine all the metaphors of all emotion concepts. This examination has not yet been done, and it will possibly take years for the interested community of scholars to produce these results.

Nevertheless, we can begin to answer the questions in a tentative manner. In this chapter, I will look at the nine emotion concepts and the metaphorical source domains that we saw in the previous chapter: anger, fear, happiness, sadness, love, lust (sexual desire), pride, shame, and surprise. As a tentative answer to our questions, I will suggest that most of the source domains associated with these emotion concepts are *not* specific to emotion concepts, but have wider application. In addition, I will claim that there are some metaphorical source domains associated with the emotion concepts mentioned above that do appear to be specific to the emotions. I will also attempt to give an explanation of why this is the case.

Source Domains and the Emotions to Which They Apply

In the previous chapter, we saw which emotion concepts are associated with which metaphorical source domains. Now we are in a position to make generalizations about the application of the particular source domains to target emotion concepts. We will have to take each of the source domains that were found in the previous chapter and check with which target emotion concept(s) they occur.

Source Domains That Apply to All Emotion Concepts

There are metaphorical source domains that apply to all emotion concepts. I did not even bother to list these in the previous chapter, because they are so general. Since we want to be able to talk about the existence of all emotions, we have, for this purpose, such metaphors as the EXISTENCE OF EMOTION IS PRESENCE HERE ("All feelings *are gone*"), EXISTENCE OF EMOTION IS BEING IN A BOUNDED SPACE ("She was *in* ecstasy"), and EXISTENCE OF EMOTION IS POSSESSION OF AN OBJECT ("She *has* a lot of pride"). And since people also want to talk about an increase or decrease in the intensity of their emotions, they will employ the EMOTION IS A LIVING ORGANISM metaphor ("His fear *grew*").

Source Domains That Apply to Most Emotion Concepts

The source domains that apply to most but not all emotions tend also to be more specific in their metaphorical imagery than those that apply to all.

Container. In many ways, this is the major metaphorical source domain for emotions. It seems to occur with all the emotions we have looked at above. The container image defines an "inside–outside" perspective for the human body. This seems to be a near-universal way of conceptualizing the body in relation to the emotions. ("Near-universal" means that the conceptualization can be found in many unrelated languages in the world). Consequently, emotions in many cultures throughout the world are seen as occurrences inside the body. (This topic will be further explored in chapter 8.) The container image schema also defines a large and varied set of metaphorical implications for the comprehension of emotion in general (see Kövecses, 1990).

Natural Force and Physical Force. It is not always easy to distinguish physical forces from natural ones. We can perhaps suggest that natural forces constitute a subcase of physical forces.

The idea and image of a natural force (like wind, storm, flood) seems to be present in the conceptualization of many emotions. When in an emotional state, we often describe ourselves and others as being *overwhelmed, engulfed, swept off our feet,* and so on (especially in the case of the "strong" emotions).

Physical forces can also take a variety of forms. They include such physical phenomena as heat, attraction of bodies, abrupt physical contact between bodies, and the like. Perhaps with the exception of pride and shame, all the emotion concepts described in the previous section make use of physical force as a source domain.

Social Superior. The source domain of social superior appears to apply to most of the emotion concepts under consideration. Anger, fear, love, and pride can definitely take it. "Social superior" is understood here as the social equivalent of physical–natural forces. In our survey, it has not been found with happiness, sadness, shame, and lust, but it is easily conceivable with these emotions as well. However, it is unlikely to occur with surprise, which is a short-lived, transitory event, unlike the habitual state captured by the social superior metaphor in its application to the other emotions.

Opponent, Captive Animal, Insanity. These source domains seem to have a similar distribution to that of social superior, that is, they are shared by roughly the same emotion concepts. Of the nine emotion concepts we have investigated, only three do not seem to take these metaphorical images: pride, shame, and surprise.

Divided Self. The concept of divided self as explained in the previous chapter appears in the conceptualization of most of the emotions under study. In addition to the cases shown in chapter 2, it also applies to happiness and anger ("He was *beside* himself with happiness/anger"). However, it does not seem to apply to pride and its application to surprise is debatable ("She was *beside* herself with surprise"?).

Burden. The emotion concepts that clearly take burden as a metaphorical image are anger, fear, sadness, and shame (guilt). The ones that do not seem to take it include happiness, pride, and surprise. It is imaginable that love and lust can make use of it in some of their nonprototypical applications (i.e., negative instances of love and lust).

Illness. The source domain of illness applies primarily to emotions that are considered "negative." These emotion concepts include fear, sadness, (unrequited) love, and shame. Thus, the distribution of this source domain comes close to that of burden.

Source Domains That Apply to Some Emotions

There are source domains associated with the emotion concepts under consideration here that are less general than the ones mentioned above; they do not apply to most emotions, but they apply to at least two.

Heat/Fire. The image of heat/fire, in the sense of "hot," can be found in anger, (romantic) love, and lust. It may be applicable to shame ("She was *burning with* shame/embarrassment"?). Note, however, that the fully conventionalized expression for shame "My cheeks were *burning*" is, strictly speaking, a metonymy (body heat for shame) on which a metaphor is built (we can call this "metaphorical metonymy"). Heat/fire does not seem to occur as a source domain with happiness, sadness, pride, and surprise.

For reasons that will become clear later, I find it useful and legitimate to draw a distinction between "heat–cold" and "warm–cold" as metaphorical source domains of emotions. The element of heat can be combined with the CONTAINER image (plus the image of emotion as

FLUID) to yield the composite image of HOT FLUID IN A CONTAINER (see Lakoff and Kövecses, 1987).

Warm–Cold, Light–Dark, Up–Down, Vitality–Lack of Vitality. The metaphorical source domains of "warm–cold," "light–dark," "up–down," and "vitality–lack of vitality" seem to behave in a uniform way, in that they apply to happiness and sadness only. In Australian English, one can be dark at someone, but this relates to the assumed darkening (reddening) of the face in anger and so it is a metonymy (darkness/ reddening of the face for anger).

Economic Value. The source domain of economic value applies to pride and shame. In pride, the subject of the emotion may assign either a high (too much pride) or a low (too little pride) value to himself or herself, whereas in shame the value is low. Incidentally, unlike pride and shame, in respect the subject of emotion assigns a high value to the object of respect (see Kövecses, 1990).

Nutrient/Food, War, and Game. This is a set of seemingly disparate source concepts. What is common to them is the desire to obtain an object (corresponding either to an emotion or the object of an emotion). Their application seems to be limited to love and lust.

Machine, Animal Aggression, and Hunger. These source domains can be found in the conceptualization of anger and lust. The machine metaphor appears in such examples as "That *got* her *going*," which can be thought of as both an anger and lust metaphor. In the case of anger, hunger appears as part of the "vicious animal" metaphor (see Lakoff and Kövecses, 1987). Lakoff (1987) discusses these interesting parallels in the American understanding of anger and lust.

Rapture/High and Hidden Object. The concepts of rapture/high and hidden object are used to understand the emotion concepts of happiness and love.

Magic, Unity, Journey. These metaphorical source domains characterize love and lust. As the survey reported in chapter 2 shows, not only love but also lust can take magic and unity as its source. However, journey was not given in the same survey because it only occurred in two or three examples (as in "She *neared the peak* of ecstasy"). On the other hand, in love the journey metaphor is extremely productive (as in "We're *stuck*," "This was a *long and bumpy road*"). This indicates that the journey metaphor is marginal but present in the comprehension of lust. A possible reason for the importance of the journey metaphor in love and its marginal status in lust and other emotions will be offered in chapter 6.

Physical Damage. Physical damage is used in the conceptualization of pride and shame, two obviously related emotions. (For a detailed examination of the relationship between the two, see Holland and Kipnis, 1995.) Physical damage is intended here in the sense of visible damage as a result of one physical object knocking into another (as in one car making a dent in another).

Source Domains That Apply to One Emotion

As our survey in chapter 2 shows, some of the metaphorical source domains occur with only a single emotion concept. I will simply list these below, together with the emotion to which they apply.

TRESPASSING, PHYSICAL ANNOYANCE – ANGER
HIDDEN ENEMY, SUPERNATURAL BEING – FEAR
BEING OFF THE GROUND, BEING IN HEAVEN, AN ANIMAL THAT LIVES
  WELL, PLEASURABLE PHYSICAL SENSATION – HAPPINESS
HAVING NO CLOTHES ON, DECREASE IN SIZE, BLOCKING OUT THE
  WORLD – SHAME

As a conclusion to this section, it seems fair to suggest that most of the metaphorical source domains are shared by several emotion concepts, but there are some that appear to be specific to particular emotion concepts. This raises the issue of which ones are shared and which are specific, and why. I will return to this question in a later section.

Aspects of Emotion Concepts

So far I hope to have established that most source domains are not specific, or unique, to particular emotion concepts. In order to see whether these source domains are limited to the general category of emotion or whether they extend beyond it, we have to examine the aspects of emotion concepts that the shared source domains focus on.

Existence

As was mentioned above, some of the metaphors (or rather, source domains) have as their main focus the "existence" of emotion. That is, there are metaphors whose task is to express whether an emotion exists or does not exist. The major conceptual metaphors with this function include:

EXISTENCE OF EMOTION IS PRESENCE HERE
EXISTENCE OF EMOTION IS BEING IN A BOUNDED SPACE
EXISTENCE OF EMOTION IS POSSESSING AN OBJECT
THE EXISTENCE OF EMOTION IS THE FUNCTIONING OF A MACHINE

While the first three metaphors are very general and apply to all emotion concepts, the FUNCTIONING (MACHINE) metaphor has limited application (to anger and lust).

These metaphors clearly extend beyond the domain of emotion. They are a part of what Lakoff (1993) calls the "Event Structure" metaphor, an extremely general metaphor in our conceptual system. The "Event Structure" metaphor applies to states of all kinds, including emotional states. (In the next chapter, I will discuss the Event Structure metaphor in detail.) Thus the metaphors above are the standard ways of conceptualizing the existence or nonexistence of emotional states. Whether the FUNCTIONING MACHINE is a part of this system is a question that I cannot undertake to answer here.

Intensity

Intensity is a further aspect of emotion concepts that is highlighted by several metaphors. The prototypical emotion concepts are regarded as highly intense states. The metaphorical source domains that focus on this aspect include CONTAINER, HEAT/FIRE, LIVING ORGANISM, and NATURAL/PHYSICAL FORCE. Given these source domains and given that intensity is their main focus, we get the general metaphors:

INTENSITY OF EMOTION IS AMOUNT/QUANTITY (OF SUBSTANCE IN A CONTAINER)
INTENSITY OF EMOTION IS HEAT
INCREASE IN THE INTENSITY OF EMOTION IS GROWTH
INTENSITY OF EMOTION IS STRENGTH OF EFFECT (OF FORCE)

Thus, for example, to be *full of* emotion indicates more intensity of emotion than to be emotionally *drained*. In the former case there is more substance in the container than in the latter.

Again, the metaphors have application beyond the domain of emotion. We can present them in this more general usage in the following way:

INTENSITY IS AMOUNT/QUANTITY

INTENSITY IS HEAT

INCREASE IN INTENSITY IS GROWTH

INTENSITY IS STRENGTH OF EFFECT

Here are some examples to demonstrate the "nonemotional" application of these metaphors: "I appreciate it *very much*" (amount), "*to blaze away* at something" (fire/heat), "the sudden *growth* of the economy" (growth), and "The country was *hit hard by* the flood" (effect). In all of these cases, it is intensity that is the focus of the metaphor.

Passivity

Although the NATURAL/PHYSICAL FORCE metaphor also participates in capturing the aspect of intensity, its primary focus is on the notion of passivity. In our naive, or folk, understanding of the world, the passivity of emotional experience is regarded as the criterial feature of emotion (hence the word *passion*, originally meaning "suffering," a kind of passive experience). Hence emotions are viewed as happening to us. This is reflected in the metaphor:

THE PASSIVITY OF EMOTIONAL EXPERIENCE IS THE PHYSICAL EFFECT OF NATURAL/PHYSICAL FORCES

More generally again, any kind of passive experience is understood in terms of this metaphor. Thus the more general metaphor would be something like this:

PASSIVE EXPERIENCES ARE THE PHYSICAL EFFECTS OF FORCES

The main use of this metaphor is in situations where there is an entity that is conceptualized as being affected by another (a force) in a one-sided or unidirectional manner, as in the example "Communism was *swept away by* the storms of history."

Control

Many of the source domains we have seen above have "control" as
their target within the domain of emotion. They include NATURAL/
PHYSICAL FORCE, OPPONENT, CAPTIVE ANIMAL, FLUID IN A CONTAINER,
INSANITY, MAGIC, SUPERIOR, INCOMPLETE OBJECT, RAPTURE/HIGH. Control is a complex notion that, in the realm of emotion at least, can be
broken down into three parts, or stages: attempt at control, loss of
control, and lack of control. Given these stages, the source domains
tend to focus on different stages: attempt at control, loss of control,
and lack of control (with possible overlaps):

Focus on Attempt at Control:
ATTEMPT AT EMOTIONAL CONTROL IS TRYING TO OVERCOME AN OPPO-
NENT
ATTEMPT AT EMOTIONAL CONTROL IS TRYING TO HOLD BACK A CAP-
TIVE ANIMAL
ATTEMPT AT EMOTIONAL CONTROL IS TRYING TO SUPPRESS FLUID IN A
CONTAINER
ATTEMPT AT EMOTIONAL CONTROL IS TRYING TO KEEP A COMPLETE
OBJECT TOGETHER

Focus on Loss of Control:
LOSS OF EMOTIONAL CONTROL IS LOSS OF CONTROL OVER A STRONG
FORCE

Focus on Lack of Control:
LACK OF EMOTIONAL CONTROL IS INSANITY
LACK OF EMOTIONAL CONTROL IS MAGIC
LACK OF EMOTIONAL CONTROL IS RAPTURE/HIGH
LACK OF EMOTIONAL CONTROL IS A SUPERIOR
LACK OF EMOTIONAL CONTROL IS A DIVIDED SELF

Here again, the metaphors appear not to be specific to the domain of
emotion. In the source domains above we have literal forces (like a
captive animal, hot fluid in a container, a superior) or entities that are
metaphorically conceptualized as forces (insanity or magic). This observation makes it possible for us to reformulate the emotion-specific
metaphors above. The more general "control-related" metaphors
would be as follows:

ATTEMPT AT CONTROL IS STRUGGLE WITH FORCE
LOSS OF CONTROL IS LOSS OF CONTROL OVER FORCE

LACK OF CONTROL IS LACK OF CONTROL OVER FORCE
A PERSON IN CONTROL IS A CANONICAL PERSON
A PERSON OUT OF CONTROL IS A DIVIDED SELF

Due to these very general metaphors, one can be said to *struggle with* mathematics and *fight a losing battle against* gaining weight. These and many other examples show that the metaphorical source domains used in the understanding of the control aspect of emotion are not unique to the domain of emotion, but form a part of a much larger system that includes the emotion domain.

"Positive–Negative" Evaluation

Emotions can be judged to be "positive" or "negative." This is the most general dimension along which the emotions are classified. Emotions that are viewed as "negative" in some sense are partially understood as ILLNESS, hence the metaphor

NEGATIVE EMOTIONS ARE ILLNESSES

Emotional relationships can also be judged according to whether they are functioning or not functioning (in the sense of fulfilling their purpose). Thus, one can talk of *a sick* or *a healthy* relationship. This suggests that the sense of "negativity" may arise from "nonfunctionality." "(Non)-functionality" is understood as ILLNESS/HEALTH outside the domain of emotion. Accordingly, one can talk about a *sick/healthy* mind, society, or economy.

There are additional source domains that focus on this aspect of emotion concepts: up–down, light–dark, warm–cold, valuable–nonvaluable. Interestingly, these source domains only apply to happiness–sadness, pride–shame, and affection–indifference, which are inherently positive or negative. Emotions like anger, fear, romantic love, lust, and surprise are not conceptualized as inherently good or bad, although they may make use of the hot–cold (but not the warm–cold) schema.

The metaphors involving these source domains have a wider scope than the domain of emotion. Good things in general (like life) are metaphorically UP, LIGHT, WARM, and VALUABLE, while bad things (like death) are DOWN, DARK, COLD, and maybe also NONVALUABLE. (For a discussion of some of these cases, see Lakoff and Johnson, 1980.)

Difficulty

Many emotions (e.g., anger, fear, sadness, shame) are viewed as diffi-cult states to cope with for the subject of emotion. This is the aspect of emotion concepts that the source domains of burden focuses on. This yields the metaphor

EMOTIONAL DIFFICULTIES ARE BURDENS.

More generally, any kind of difficulty is conceptualized as a burden, yielding

DIFFICULTIES ARE BURDENS.

Thus when we say "This exam places a terrible *burden on* me," or "This teacher is *bearing down on me,*" we have to do with a linguistic (and nonemotional) example of this general metaphor.

Desire/Need

The notion of desire appears in emotion concepts in two ways. In the first, there is some desire on the part of the subject of emotion to perform an action, where the action is "spurred" by or is a result of the emotion itself. This is what we find in anger and lust. In the other, the desire consists of having the emotion. Thus, we *hunger for* love, but we do not hunger for anger, though our anger can be said to be *insatiable.* Let us jointly call these cases "emotional desire." This is conceptualized metaphorically as hunger. Hence the metaphor

EMOTIONAL DESIRE IS HUNGER.

But just as in the previously discussed cases, the more general meta-phor is

DESIRE IS HUNGER,

which is a metaphor whose scope extends beyond the emotion do-main, unless, of course, desire is viewed as a special kind of emotion.

Nonphysical Unity

The unity metaphor has a wide scope of application outside the emo-tion domain (love and lust). It extends to a variety of nonphysical unities such as religious, psychological, social, and so forth. One can *unite with* God and we can talk about the *unity* of body and mind. This is based on the general metaphor

NONPHYSICAL UNITY IS PHYSICAL UNITY.

The unity metaphor for love and lust is a special case of this metaphor.

Progress

This source domain does not apply to most of the emotion concepts under investigation. However, in addition to love and (marginally) to lust, journey as a source applies to many activities outside the emotion domain (as in "We aren't *getting anywhere* with this project"). The main dimension on which the journey metaphor focuses seems to be progress with respect to a goal. This yields the general metaphor

PROGRESS IS MOVEMENT TO A DESTINATION (IN A JOURNEY).

We will return to the discussion of the journey metaphor in the next chapter.

Harm

We have seen that the source domain of physical damage applies primarily to two emotion concepts: pride and shame. However, we can also see it in other emotion concepts, such as anger (e.g., "He *burst with* anger") and love (e.g., "She *got burned* again"), and even surprise (e.g., "When he heard the news, he *came apart at the seams*"). Thus the metaphor that is at work in these cases is

EMOTIONAL HARM IS PHYSICAL DAMAGE.

One kind of emotional harm is loss of control. This explains some of the overlap with metaphors of loss of control. In general, the concept of harm (or nonliteral negative effects) is understood in terms of physical damage, hence the general metaphor

NONPHYSICAL HARM IS PHYSICAL DAMAGE.

This shows up in the nonemotional sentence "The strike caused *inestimable damage* to the country."

Aspects of Emotion and Wierzbicka's Semantic Universals

In the light of the discussion in the previous section, it seems that we have a set of aspects, or dimensions, for characterizing emotion concepts in general: existence, intensity, passivity, control, evaluation, difficulty, desire, and harm. (As we just saw, the dimension of progress is not typical of the emotions.) These can be regarded as the target domains proper of the source domains that have been identified in relation to the emotion concepts under study.

At this point, it is interesting to compare these aspects of emotion concepts with Wierzbicka's universal "semantic primitives." Wierzbicka (1995) suggests that there are 16 kinds of such primitives, including "mental predicates," "action, event, movement," "existence, life," "evaluators," and "intensifier, augmentor." There seems to be some correspondence between these kinds of universal semantic primitives and the aspects of emotion concepts I described in this section.

Wierzbicka's mental predicates include "want" and "feel." "Want" can be seen as corresponding to my "desire," while "feel" corresponds to the category of "emotion." Wierzbicka's action, event, movement includes the three primitives "do," "happen," and "move." We can take "happen" to correspond to my "passivity" aspect. The primitives "there is, live" for existence, life may be regarded as the counterpart of my "existence" dimension. The evaluators "good" and "bad" have the obvious function of my "positive–negative evaluation." Finally, Wierzbicka's intensifier category has "very, more," which can be seen as corresponding to the aspect of "intensity." Thus, it seems that there is a clear set of correspondences between Wierzbicka's categories of semantic primitives and the aspects of emotion that are focused on by emotion metaphors: five categories of sematic primitives (mental predicates; action, event, movement; existence, life; evaluators; and intensifier) have matching counterparts in aspects of emotion concepts that have been identified above.

The importance of this, as far as I can see, is that the aspects of emotion concepts discovered on the basis of conceptual metaphors used in English are not limited to the conceptual system of speakers of English. Instead, assuming that Wierzbicka is right, it seems that the aspects of emotion concepts may have universal application.

What is equally interesting is to see what is missing from Wierzbicka's system but present in the system I have outlined. There appear to be three aspects that do not have easily recognizable counterparts among Wierzbicka's primitives: "control," "difficulty," and "harm." I can offer no explanation for why this is the case. One may conjecture, though, that if the other aspects have universal application, then these latter three must as well. It would be worth trying to see whether "control," "difficulty," and "harm" could be added to the list of universal semantic primitives or, alternatively, whether they should be viewed as parts of the Western (Anglo-American) conception of emotion. This second alternative seems viable, given the general Western emphasis on controlling emotion and regarding the emotions as things that are harmful to the proper functioning of the Western ideal of a rational person.

Emotion-Specific Source Domains

Now we have to take up the issue of whether there are any source domains that are specific to particular emotion concepts. There are source domains that seem to be both specific to a particular emotion and limited to the emotion domain. These include

> for ANGER: TRESPASSING, PHYSICAL ANNOYANCE;
> for FEAR: HIDDEN ENEMY, SUPERNATURAL BEING;
> for HAPPINESS: BEING OFF THE GROUND, AN ANIMAL THAT LIVES WELL, PLEASURABLE PHYSICAL SENSATION;
> for SHAME: HAVING NO CLOTHES ON, DECREASE IN SIZE, BLOCKING OUT THE WORLD.

For example, trespassing leads to anger, dancing about (in being off the ground) indicates happiness, and decrease in size shows that a person is ashamed or embarrassed. How can we account for the emotion-specificity of these source domains? My suggestion is that the specificity of the source domains derives from two factors. Some of them have to do with causes of emotion, whereas some of them have to do with effects of emotion. Both the causes and the effects in question appear to be unique to a given emotion. Thus, for example, it can be suggested that given the metaphor SHAME IS HAVING NO CLOTHES ON, having no clothes on is a potential cause for shame and it is typically associated with shame. Or, to take another example, dancing and jumping up and down (but not stomping your feet) is typically associated with joy/happiness and it is seen as a result or effect of this emotion; hence the metaphor HAPPINESS IS BEING OFF THE GROUND (which is not an evaluative metaphor, unlike the "up" metaphor).

More generally, we can say that emotions can be, and are, comprehended via both their assumed typical causes and their assumed typical effects. When this happens, we can get emotion-specific metaphorical source domains. Here are some of the emotion-specific metaphors deriving from assumed typical causes and effects of particular emotions:

Emotion Is a Cause of That Emotion:
ANGER IS TRESPASSING
ANGER IS PHYSICAL ANNOYANCE
FEAR IS A HIDDEN ENEMY
FEAR IS A SUPERNATURAL BEING
A HAPPY PERSON IS AN ANIMAL THAT LIVES WELL
HAPPINESS IS A PLEASURABLE PHYSICAL SENSATION
SHAME IS HAVING NO CLOTHES ON

Emotion Is an Effect of That Emotion:
HAPPINESS IS BEING OFF THE GROUND
SHAME IS A DECREASE IN SIZE
TO BE ASHAMED IS TO BLOCK OUT THE WORLD

Although the particular source domains are unique to particular emotion concepts, the cognitive mechanism of understanding a state-event (in this case an emotion state-event) in terms of its cause or effect is fairly general (see Kövecses, 1991b, 1994b). The nature of this process is essentially metonymic (see Kövecses and Radden, 1998; Radden and Kövecses, in press; Kövecses, 1998).

Conclusions

We began with the question of whether there are any source domains that are unique to the conceptualization of the emotion domain. The general conclusion I would like to offer is that most source domains of emotion metaphors are not specific to the domain of emotion, though some are. In this sense, my answer to the question "Are there any emotion-specific metaphors?" would have to be a qualified "no." Indeed, we have found that most of the source domains of emotion concepts have a scope of application that extends beyond the domain of emotion. These nonspecific source domains are parts of very general metaphorical mappings whose range of application covers large portions of our conceptual system. (Here I have not investigated the issue of precisely how large these portions are.)

This has the important theoretical implication that, at least in cases like the domain of emotion, we do not understand abstract domains in unique ways, that is, by making use of a set of metaphors specific to a given abstract domain. Instead, we seem to build up an abstract domain from "conceptual materials" that we make use of in other parts of our conceptual system as well. For example, we employ metaphors for "control" in whatever domain that requires it (either inherently or because we conceptualize it as such). In the chapter on relationships, I will make the same general claim in relation to the concept of friendship.

Nevertheless, some emotion source domains do seem to be specific both to particular emotion concepts and to the emotion domain. I suggested that this occurs when, by means of a regular metonymic process, we understand an emotion concept via its cause or effect.

4. Events and Emotions
The Subcategorization of Emotions

Emotions are commonly categorized in two major ways. Chiefly in scholarly writing, emotions are viewed as a subcategory of states, as opposed to events; thus, psychologists and some others often talk about emotional states. On the other hand, laymen and early scholars think of emotions as a subcategory of passions, as opposed to actions. Indeed, the question arises: Are the emotions subcategories of states, passions, events, or actions, or any combination of these? As it happens, we can find proponents for each of the four ways of categorizing emotions. For example, some anthropologists consider emotions as events (e.g., Lutz, 1988), while some philosophers, like Solomon and Fromm, view them as actions, rather than passions (e.g., Solomon, 1976; Fromm, 1956). It seems, however, that these latter subcategorizations are outside the mainstream ways of classifying emotions.

It is in this light that it becomes important to examine the details of the subcategorization of emotion in the most natural folk theory, namely, language. The language on the basis of which I will consider the nature of the subcategorization of emotion is English. If emotions are simply "states," we cannot expect any overlap between metaphors for events and metaphors for emotions; and if emotions are "passions," as opposed to actions, action metaphors should not be found among metaphors for emotions. Curiously, however, there seem to exist both event and action metaphors for emotions, thereby supporting the two "minority" views of emotion mentioned above (which is not to say that, e.g., Fromm saw the actionlike character of love in precisely the same sense as this is suggested in the folk theory we are describing).

My main goal in this chapter is to examine the extent of the overlap, if any, and the nature of the relationship between metaphors of emotion and what Lakoff (1990, 1993) calls the "EVENT STRUCTURE metaphor."

The Event Structure Metaphor and Emotions

Lakoff (1990) characterizes the EVENT STRUCTURE metaphor in English in the following way. Events in general, including changes of states, actions, activities, et cetera, are understood metaphorically in terms of physical movement, physical force, and physical space. The main aspects or components of events include states, change, cause, purpose, means, difficulty, progress, and some others. It is these abstract concepts to which the notions of physical space, force, and motion apply, yielding conceptual metaphors that enable speakers to get a clearer understanding of them. Let us now see if the EVENT STRUCTURE metaphor overlaps with emotion metaphors in English at all. The submetaphors of the EVENT STRUCTURE metaphor as identified by Lakoff include:

STATES ARE LOCATIONS
CHANGES ARE MOVEMENTS
CAUSES ARE FORCES
ACTION IS SELF-PROPELLED MOTION
PURPOSES ARE DESTINATIONS
MEANS (OF CHANGE OF STATE/ACTION) ARE PATHS (TO DESTINATIONS)
DIFFICULTIES ARE IMPEDIMENTS TO MOTION
EXPECTED PROGRESS IS A TRAVEL SCHEDULE
EXTERNAL EVENTS ARE LARGE, MOVING OBJECTS
LONG-TERM, PURPOSEFUL ACTIVITIES ARE JOURNEYS

In the EVENT STRUCTURE metaphor, states in general are conceptualized as physical locations or bounded regions in space. States are a part of EVENT STRUCTURE because events often involve entities changing from one state to another. Thus, given the submetaphor STATES ARE LOCATIONS within the EVENT STRUCTURE metaphor, speakers of English will use sentences such as "I am *in* trouble" to talk about states, where the key word to show this metaphor is *in*, which has as its primary reference physical bounded regions in space, such as rooms, tubs, and so forth. Similarly, one of the most natural ways of referring to emotional states is by making use of this metaphor. Thus, in English we say "I'm *in* love," "He's *in* a rage," and "She's *in* depression." In general, scholars and laymen alike speak of a person *being in an emotional state*, as was noted above.

The notion of change is viewed as physical movement into or out of bounded regions. Thus in English we find sentences such as "The patient *went into* a coma." The same submetaphor applies to the emotions, when we speak of someone *entering* a state of bliss, falling *in* love, or flying *into* a rage.

Events have a causal aspect. Causes are metaphorical forces within event structure. This is what enables speakers of English to use verbs such as *drive, send, push, keep,* and so on, to talk about causes in sentences like "Circumstances *drove* him to commit suicide," "I *pushed* him *into* washing the dishes," and "What *kept* you *from* suing them?" The same and additional verbs can be found in descriptive statements about the emotions; for example, "The news *sent* the crowd *into* a frenzy," "His depression *drove* him to commit suicide," "Fear *ruled over* her," and "Love *makes* the world go *round.*"

Actions are intentionally produced events, and they are conceptualized metaphorically as self-propelled movements. For example, we can say that a person *goes on* with what he is doing, that he or she *went back to* sleep, that he or she exercised *to* the point of exhaustion. Here we do not seem to find any natural counterparts in the metaphorical conceptualization of emotions in English. The linguistic example that comes closest to the submetaphor ACTIONS ARE SELF-PROPELLED MOTIONS is something like "I *worked* myself *up into* a rage," where the word *work* implies deliberation or intention. However, *work* is not a motion verb itself (though the words *up* and *into* are particles expressing motion, but they simply indicate change of state).

A subclass of events is associated with purpose, and purposes are commonly viewed as metaphorical destinations. Thus we get the submetaphor PURPOSES ARE DESTINATIONS, an example of which could be "We aren't *getting anywhere* (with this project)." The same sentence could be used of a marriage or a love relationship (as shown in Lakoff, 1993).

An aspect of change and action is the deliberate use of some means (of change of state or action). The submetaphor MEANS ARE PATHS cannot be naturally extended to the conceptualization of emotions. Thus, although we can say things like "He went from fat to thin *through* an intensive exercise program," it would not be easy to find the description of some emotional experience as deliberately achieved *through* some means. A possible situation where this might occur is one in which a person seeks psychiatric help, as a result of which he can claim to have achieved some emotional feeling *through* training.

But clearly, this would be a nonordinary application of the EVENT STRUCTURE metaphor.

According to the next submetaphor DIFFICULTIES ARE IMPEDIMENTS TO MOTION. In talking about a project, one can say "We have *to get around* this problem," where a difficult problem is seen as an impediment. In the EVENT STRUCTURE metaphor, five different kinds of impediment to motion are recognized:

Blockages: He *got over* his divorce. He's trying *to get around* the regulations.
Features of the terrain: He's *between a rock and a hard place*. It's been *uphill* all the way.
Burdens: He's *carrying quite a load*. He's *weighed down* by a lot of assignments.
Counterforce: Quit *pushing* me *around*. She's *holding* him *back*.
Lack of energy source: I'm *out of gas*. We're *running out of steam*.

This aspect of EVENT STRUCTURE applies to the emotions when the emotions are viewed as something difficult, something to cope with, given a larger context. In this case, we get sentences such as "He *got over* his anxiety," "She's *weighed down* by her sadness," or "He's *held back* by his anger in life."

A further aspect of activities is progress. This is conceptualized as a travel schedule, yielding the submetaphor EXPECTED PROGRESS IS A TRAVEL SCHEDULE. A nonemotional example would be: "We're *behind schedule* on this project." This metaphor also applies to love relationships, and so a lover could say "We've *made a lot of headway* in recent months" or "We're just *spinning our wheels*."

Long-term, purposeful activities themselves are metaphorically conceived as journeys; hence the submetaphor LONG-TERM, PURPOSEFUL ACTIVITIES ARE JOURNEYS. One can be *at a crossroads* both as regards a project and a love relationship. Similarly, both a project and a love relationship can be described as *a long, bumpy road*.

In EVENT STRUCTURE, events are conceptualized as large, moving objects. This has three special cases:

External Events Are Large, Moving Objects
1. Things: *Things are going against* me these days.
2. Fluids: The *tide* of events . . . The *flow* of history . . .
3. Horses: *Wild horses* couldn't make me go.

It is debatable whether this submetaphor applies to the emotions. One can think of cases of emotion language that seem somewhat similar to the examples above:

1./2. She was *moved*. I was *transported*. He got *carried away*.
3. He *held back* his anger.

As we will see, these examples can be accounted for by evoking a different conceptual metaphor (EMOTIONAL RESPONSES ARE OTHER-PROPELLED MOTIONS). We'll come back to the issue later.

The Degree of Overlap Between Events and Emotions

We have seen that metaphors of emotion overlap with the EVENT STRUCTURE metaphor; many submetaphors of EVENT STRUCTURE are applicable to the emotions as well. We can now address the issue of the degree of the overlap. What I would like to do is point out the generalizations that emerge from the comparison of statements and descriptive phrases about emotions with those about events. Let us turn to the details.

First, the metaphors for emotions coincide with the "state" part of the EVENT STRUCTURE metaphor. As we saw above, there is clear evidence in three such cases (the single-line arrow indicates "corresponds to"):

1. State (Entity) → Bounded Region.
   The emotional state of a person corresponds to a bounded region.
2. Change (Entity, State$_1$; Entity, State$_2$) → Motion.
   The state of a person changes from a nonemotional state to an emotional one. This change is conceptualized as motion.
3. Cause (Change [Entity, State$_1$; Entity, State$_2$]) → Force.
   The change from a nonemotional to an emotional state is caused by an entity or an event. This cause of emotion is seen as a physical force. In the most prevalent folk theory of emotion, the cause of emotion is believed to lead to an emotion; or to put the same idea in a schematic way (where the double-line arrow indicates "causes, leads to":

Cause of Emotion (Entity/Event) ⇒ Emotion

Second, as regards the "action" part of the EVENT STRUCTURE metaphor, we find much less, and much less clear, overlap. As we have seen, the following submetaphors do not, or hardly, apply to the emotions.

ACTION IS SELF-PROPELLED MOTION
PURPOSES ARE DESTINATIONS
MEANS (OF CHANGE OF STATE/ACTION) ARE PATHS (TO DESTINATIONS)
DIFFICULTIES ARE IMPEDIMENTS TO MOTION
EXPECTED PROGRESS IS A TRAVEL SCHEDULE
LONG-TERM, PURPOSEFUL ACTIVITIES ARE JOURNEYS

As we saw, DIFFICULTIES ARE IMPEDIMENTS TO MOTION does apply to some extent, but this does not make the conceptualization of emotions "actionlike." It only suggests that some emotions, like fear, anxiety, anger, et cetera, can be thought of as difficult to cope with in one's life. ACTION IS SELF-PROPELLED MOTION and MEANS ARE PATHS do not seem to apply at all. The reason is obvious: In the folk understanding, emotions are predominantly not actions but passions, and the use of ordinary language reveals this. But then why is it that the other four submetaphors mentioned above appear to be used of the emotions? It should be noticed that they appear to be applicable only to love, marriage, and some other relationships, which may have a purposive component. Couples in love and marriage may set goals that they want to achieve. However, there are no such explicit goals associated with emotions such as anger, fear, happiness, pride, and so forth. These latter emotions are assumed *to happen* to people (and love of course shares this property with them – as shown by the phrase *fall in love*), while love may also have a clear purposive aspect (which the other emotions do not share with love). To the extent that love can be associated with long-term goals, it can be regarded as an activity on a par with something like working on a project. This explains why both will have goal-based metaphors in common.

Third, as Lakoff, Espenson, and Goldberg point out (in the *Master Metaphor List*, 1989), the ACTION IS SELF-PROPELLED MOTION and the CAUSES ARE FORCES submetaphors have two joint metaphorical entailments. One is CONTROL OVER ACTION IS CONTROL OVER SELF-PROPELLED MOTION. If action is motion and causes are forces, then control over action is control over motion. For example, one can say that "She *held* him *back* in his endeavors" or that "She *has* her fiancé *on a short leash*," where both sentences indicate control over action. We can find counterparts of statements like these in the emotion domain as well: "He *held back* his anger," "He *unleashed* his anger," or "She *let go of* her feelings." Here the emotion terms *anger* or *feelings (of love)* stand metonymically for certain emotional acts on the part of the person in the emotional state of anger or love. It is the particular acts or events associated with particular emotions that are controlled by the subject of emotion and that are metaphorically conceived as motion and their control as control over motion. The control of emotional acts or events as control over motion is conscious and is intended by the subject of emotion in the examples above. The important point is that in these cases there is a clear "action" aspect to the emotions, in that the emotions may involve conscious control of certain acts or events. This aspect of emotions is conceptualized by means of the more general EVENT STRUCTURE metaphor.

According to Lakoff and his colleagues, a second metaphorical entailment of ACTION IS SELF-PROPELLED MOTION and CAUSES ARE FORCES is that DESIRES THAT CONTROL ACTION ARE EXTERNAL FORCES THAT CONTROL MOTION. Linguistic examples of this entailment are the sentences: for liking, "The coat *pulled* me *into* the store," and for love, "She *attracts* me *irresistibly*." Here desires are viewed as external forces that control one's emotional actions. However, in contrast to the previous case, the desire as a force exerts its influence on the subject of emotion, who in turn experiences the effect of the desire as force. That is, the desire that controls (emotional) action is not intended by the subject of emotion. Thus, here we have a case of the conceptualization of emotion as something closer to passion than to action.

Fourth, there are many phrases in English that describe emotional experiences that involve verbs of motion. Examples of such verbal phrases include *swept away, moved, blown away, transported, carried away*, and others. Why is this so? Given the EVENT STRUCTURE metaphor, we get a fairly straightforward explanation. The picture that has emerged so far is that emotions are assumed to lead to certain behavioral responses that the self undergoes. In this scheme, emotion itself becomes a cause relative to the response it produces. Thus the emotion is conceptualized as a force and the effect of the emotion, that is, the behavioral responses, as the effects of the force. As we saw above, in EVENT STRUCTURE actions are viewed as self-propelled movements. Given this, it makes sense that emotional responses, that is, caused events (as opposed to intended actions), should be conceptualized not as self-propelled but as *other*-propelled motions. This would account for the use of the motion verbs mentioned above to describe emotional responses. Thus, in this case the EVENT STRUCTURE submetaphors apply to emotions in the following way:

EVENT STRUCTURE
  EMOTION STRUCTURE
CAUSES ARE FORCES
  EMOTIONS ARE PHYSICAL FORCES
CAUSED EVENTS ARE OTHER-PROPELLED MOTIONS
  EMOTIONAL RESPONSES ARE OTHER-PROPELLED MOTIONS

This use of motion verbs in the conceptualization of emotion indicates that emotional responses are regarded as events that the self undergoes. In other words, in the folk theory emotions are not simply states but also very clearly events.

Finally, the submetaphor of EVENT STRUCTURE, EXTERNAL EVENTS ARE LARGE, MOVING OBJECTS does not seem to apply to the emotions. The reason is that emotions are assumed to be internal – not external – phenomena in the folk theory under discussion. Hence the metaphor for external events cannot apply.

The Subcategorization of Emotion

The submetaphors of the EVENT STRUCTURE that do apply to the emotions suggest that the emotions are subcategorized in several ways in the most prevalent folk theory of emotion; they are states, events, actions, and passions. Elsewhere (Kövecses, 1990), I suggested that this folk theory of emotions can be characterized as a five-stage scenario, or cognitive model, as shown below:

Cause (Cau)→ Emotion (Emo)→ Control (Con)→ Loss of Control (LoCon)→ Behavioral Response (BeRe)

Emotion is a change of state from a nonemotional state (the "state" aspect) to an emotional one. The emotion is assumed to affect the self (the "passion" aspect). The self may try to control emotional behavior (the "action" aspect). The self may respond to the emotion by undergoing emotional behavior, rather than acting as a willful agent (the "event" aspect).

We can see in Figure 4.1 how the submetaphors of the EVENT STRUCTURE metaphor converge on this scenario. However, this diagram and

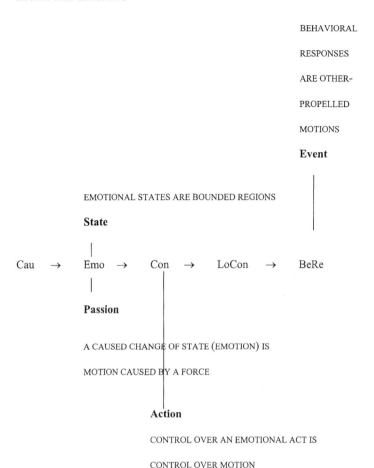

Figure 4.1. The EVENT STRUCTURE metaphor, emotion metaphors, and the subcategorization of emotion

the preceding discussion do not do justice to the concept of passion. Passion is not accounted for fully, and it cannot be, on the basis of the comparison with the EVENT STRUCTURE metaphor alone. Since EVENT STRUCTURE is not concerned with the concept of passion, we cannot expect the comparison to tell us more about passion than what it did: it is a caused change of state. Obviously, there is more to passion than this. The complexity of passion involves at least two more metaphors that we did not examine in the chapter: EMOTION IS INSANITY and DESIRE IS HUNGER. The first captures the "irrational" "uncontrolled" aspects of passion, while the second the "intense, forceful action" that it can lead to (as in *"insatiable* anger"). These complexities concerning the passions will be taken up in more detail in the next chapter.

Conclusion

The EVENT STRUCTURE metaphor reveals some of the most common conceptual metaphors that apply to states, events proper (i.e., unintended events), actions, and activities, on the one hand, and their various components, such as cause, change, et cetera, on the other. By examining the extent to which this general metaphor applies to the emotions, we uncovered the several ways in which emotion is subcategorized. Based on this examination, it appears that we think and talk about the emotions as states, events, actions, and passions all at the same time. This is possible because the folk theory of the emotions represented as a five-stage cognitive model has several aspects to it and these distinct aspects lend themselves to all of these subcategorizations.

5. The Force of Emotion

In studies of emotion concepts from a cognitive linguistic perspective (including my own previous work), it is typical to find analyses in which emotion concepts are described as being characterized by a number of distinct and unrelated conceptual metaphors. This book challenges the validity of this view and offers a new way of looking at emotion concepts and the metaphors that characterize them.

We saw in the previous chapter that emotions are commonly conceptualized as causes that lead to certain behavioral responses. Because in the EVENT STRUCTURE metaphor CAUSES ARE FORCES, it is natural to conceptualize emotions as forces that bring about certain responses, or effects. In fact, this seems to be the predominant conception of emotions in Western cultures. But as we will see in chapter 8, the FORCE metaphor can be found in several non-Western cultures as well. Furthermore, this is a metaphor that applies to all basic (and many nonbasic) emotions. For all these reasons, it plays a very important role in how we think about the emotions in general.

There are two points I would like to make and stress in this chapter. One is that most of the well-known metaphors of emotion (such as FIRE, OPPONENT, NATURAL FORCE) seem to be instantiations of a single underlying "master metaphor": EMOTION IS FORCE. The other is that these metaphors instantiate the generic-level metaphor in very different ways, capturing very different aspects of emotional experience. Both of these points are significant for the study of emotion language because, given the first, we can see a degree of coherence in the conceptual organization of the emotion domain that has not been pointed out so far. This underlying coherence behind the conceptual metaphors makes it possible for us to see the precise ways in which the emotion domain is conceptualized in a systematically different way from other "neighboring" generic-level domains, such as rational thought. Given the second claim, we can get an idea of the details and richness of the conceptualization of emotion – without losing sight of its deep underlying coherence.

The Force Schema

The EMOTIONS ARE FORCES metaphor has as its source domain the FORCE schema. There is considerable agreement among scholars that this schema is one of the basic image schemas that structures the conceptual system. This is how Leonard Talmy (1988), who studied it most extensively, characterizes the schema:

> The primary distinction that language marks here is a role difference between the two entities exerting the forces. One force-exerting entity is singled out for focal attention – the salient issue in the interaction is whether this entity is able to manifest its force tendency or, on the contrary, is overcome. The second force entity, correlatively, is considered for the effect that it has on the first, effectively overcoming it or not. (p. 53)

Based on this characterization, Talmy isolates the following factors in the force schema:

Force entities:
    Agonist
    Antagonist
Intrinsic force tendency:
    toward action
    toward rest (inaction)
Resultant of the force interaction:
    action
    rest (inaction)
Balance of strengths:
    the stronger entity
    the weaker entity

If we apply these factors to the concept of emotion, we get the following generic-level mappings:

Force Agonist (FAgo) → Emotion Agonist (EmAgo)
Force Antagonist (FAnt) → Emotion Antagonist (EmAnt)
FAnt's force tendency → EmAnt's force tendency

FAgo's force tendency → EmAgo's force tendency
FAgo's resultant state → EmAgo's resultant state

I will take the entity that manifests a force tendency toward inaction to be the Agonist and the entity that exerts force on the Agonist and typically overcomes it to be the Antagonist. As a result of the interaction, the Agonist will typically cease to be inactive and will produce a response. Typically, though not exclusively, the Agonist is instantiated by the rational self that is or will be emotional, while the Antagonist is instantiated by the cause of emotion or the emotion itself. Correspondingly, the Agonist's typical force tendency in the emotion domain is to remain unaffected by the Antagonist, whereas the Antagonist's force tendency is to cause the Agonist to change. As we will shortly see in Table 5.1 below, however, there are some significant exceptions to these generalizations.

The question that immediately arises is, of course, precisely how the set of mappings above applies to the emotion domain. As we will see, there are numerous ways in which this abstract force schema can

Table 5.1. *The Agonist and Antagonist in Emotion Metaphors*

Source Domains	Agonist	Antagonist
I.		
INTERNAL PRESSURE	self	emotion
OPPONENT	self	emotion
WILD ANIMAL	self	emotion
SOCIAL SUPERIOR	self	emotion
NATURAL FORCE	self	emotion
TRICKSTER	self	emotion
INSANITY	self	emotion
FIRE	self	emotion
II.		
HUNGER1	self	desire for emotion
HUNGER2	emotional self	insatiable desire
PHYSICAL AGITATION1	self	cause of emotion
PHYSICAL AGITATION2	body	emotion
BURDEN	self	emotional stress
III.		
PHYSICAL FORCE	self	cause of emotion

apply to the concept of emotion. We can get such specific-level instantiations of the generic-level EMOTION IS FORCE metaphor as EMOTION IS INTERNAL PRESSURE, EMOTION IS A NATURAL FORCE, EMOTION IS FIRE, EMOTION IS A BURDEN, and so forth.

To give some structure to the discussion, we can think of these more specific metaphors as focusing on basically two parts of the most general notion of the Western folk theory of emotion:

(1) a cause leads to emotion and (2) emotion leads to some response.

Thus some metaphors have primarily to do with the part "cause ⇒ emotion" ("That *kindled* my ire"), while others with the part "emotion ⇒ response" ("He was *overcome* by passion"). That is, not only can emotion itself be conceptualized as a cause (and hence a force) that produces certain responses, but also the cause of emotion, the event or object that leads to emotion in the first place. In this sense, then, the *cause* of emotion is even more naturally and obviously thought of as a cause, and hence a force, than emotion itself. Moreover, some metaphors will be shown to play some role in the conceptualization of *both* parts of the skeletal emotion scenario just sketched.

To give the reader an initial sense of the analyses to follow, Table 5.1 shows how two factors of Talmy's abstract force schema, the Agonist and the Antagonist, are instantiated in the many specific-level metaphors of emotion. Group "I" indicates that the metaphorical source domains focus on the "emotion ⇒ response" part of the scenario; group "II" indicates that the source domains can take either "emotion ⇒ response" or "cause ⇒ emotion" as their focus; and group "III" indicates that the focus is on the "cause ⇒ emotion" part.

I will start the analysis with those specific-level metaphors that are used to conceptualize primarily the second part of the scenario (emotion ⇒ response), then I will look at those that seem to focus on both parts, and finally attention will be paid to those that focus on the first part of the skeletal emotion scenario (cause ⇒ emotion). However, it should be kept in mind that this structure is used only to give some order to the discussion of the metaphors.

Many of the conceptual metaphors of emotion that have been identified so far in the literature (see chapter 2 and also, e.g., Lakoff and Johnson, 1980; Lakoff, 1987; Kövecses, 1986, 1988, 1990) are specific-level instantiations of the generic-level EMOTION-AS-FORCE metaphor. In other words, the claim is that we can account for a large portion of the conceptualization of emotion in a coherent way if we assume the existence of the general-level EMOTION IS FORCE metaphor. Just as important, however, I also wish to show that all of the specific-level metaphors instantiate the generic-level one in a different way, addressing several distinct aspects of emotion. This is why we have an extremely rich understanding of the concept of emotion in the language-based folk model.

Specific-Level Metaphors Focusing on "Emotion-Response"

Let us begin the survey and the reanalysis of specific-level emotion metaphors with perhaps the best known and most studied metaphor for emotion EMOTION IS PRESSURE INSIDE A CONTAINER (see, e.g., Kövecses, 1990, chap. 9).

Emotion Is Internal Pressure Inside a Container. In the case of the emotions, the generic-level FORCE schema can be found in the more specific version of PRESSURE. The "internal pressure" metaphor assumes two further metaphors: PEOPLE ARE CONTAINERS (FOR THE EMOTIONS) and EMOTION IS A SUBSTANCE IN A CONTAINER. The specific container for emotion is the human body and the specific substance is typically a fluid or a gas.

Now let us see how the generic-level EMOTION IS FORCE metaphor is instantiated in this complex special case:

Source: INTERNAL PRESSURE

1. *Agonist*: the container-entity that is affected by the pressure.
2. *Antagonist*: the substance with pressure inside the container.
3. *The intrinsic force tendency* of the Antagonist: substance-pressure on the container.
4. *The intrinsic force tendency* of Agonist: the container-entity resists the pressure.
5a. *The resultant action* due to a stronger Antagonist's force: the substance goes out of the container.
5b. *The resultant inaction* due to a stronger Agonist's resistance: the substance does not go out of the container.

Target: EMOTION

1. *Agonist*: the rational self.
2. *Antagonist:* the emotion.

3. *The intrinsic force tendency* of the Antagonist: the emotion causing the self to respond.
4. *The intrinsic force tendency* of the Agonist: the rational self attempts not to respond.
5a. *The resultant action* due to the emotion's force: the self responds.
5b. *The resultant inaction* due to Agonist's resistance: the self does not respond.

Given these instantiations, we can explain the source-to-target mappings between the FORCE and EMOTION domains in the following way: In this metaphor complex, the level of the emotion substance may go up inside the container; if it does, the substance creates perceivable pressure on the container; the pressure may increase to the point that the substance goes out of the container. In other words, when there is very little substance in the container, the pressure is low and thus emotion is at a low intensity; when the substance rises, this corresponds to an increase in emotional intensity; the pressure itself corresponds to the emotion causing the self to respond; the pressure's bringing about an effect corresponds to the emotion's leading to a response; and the substance going out of the container corresponds to some external behavior (response) by the self, or, alternatively, the substance not going out of the container corresponds to the lack of response.

We can make this clearer by laying out the mappings for this specific-level metaphor as follows:

the substance with pressure	→	the emotion
the pressure on the container	→	the emotion causing the self to respond
the intensity of the pressure	→	the intensity of the emotion
the container-entity affected by the pressure	→	the self affected by the emotion
the substance going out of the container	→	the response of the self caused by the emotion
the substance not going out of the container	→	lack of response by the self

The particular type of force dynamic pattern that this set of mappings represents is what Talmy calls the "shifting force dynamic pattern." In such a pattern, there occurs a shift in the balance of strengths between the Antagonist and Agonist.

Due to the causal relationship between the emotion and the action-response, emotions are seen as motivations relative to the action-response. That is, in this scheme the emotion is seen as an internal motivation for action (i.e., to respond). The motivation is conceptualized as an internal force, while the action produced is viewed as the external effect of this internal force. The greater the intensity of internal pressure, the greater is the degree of motivation to respond emotionally. Thus, we can add the following to the mappings above:

internal pressure	→	motivation for action
external effect of the force	→	action (response) caused by the emotion
the intensity of the internal pressure to bring about an effect	→	the intensity of the motivation to respond emotionally

If the intensity of internal pressure increases beyond a point, this brings about an effect on the body-container; that is, an emotional response is carried out. The effect (i.e., the action) may be prevented by not letting the substance go out of the body-container. (More will be said about this aspect later.) In other words:

attempting to keep the substance inside	→	attempting to control the emotional response

If, however, the self is unable to keep the substance inside the container, the external effect on the container takes place: An emotional response is performed. This may happen in two ways: either by the container overflowing or by the container exploding.

These two possibilities call for a refinement in Talmy's system, in that we have to recognize *two kinds of action* on the Agonist's part. When the container overflows, we get uncontrolled but nonviolent emotional responses; when it explodes, we get uncontrolled violent responses, such as in the case of anger:

the overflowing of the container	→	uncontrolled nonviolent response
the explosion of the container	→	uncontrolled violent response

The "milder," or romantic, emotions (like affection and sadness) are conceptualized as "overflowing" the container, whereas the more "violent" emotions are viewed as "exploding" out of the body-container. However, this only applies in the typical cases; sometimes a "violent" emotion may be conceptualized as producing a nonviolent response (e.g., "He was *brimming/overflowing* with rage") and a "nonviolent" emotion may be seen as leading to a relatively violent response (e.g., "She felt like she was going *to burst* with joy"). Nonetheless, it would be strange, at least in English, to talk about someone *exploding* with joy, where explosion is associated with deliberately causing damage to others in a violent way.

To handle a further elaboration of this metaphor, we can continue to use Talmy's system with a further modification: We can talk about the *resultant action of the resultant* action. That is, we get a chain of resultant actions, which are in fact the entailments of the metaphorical source domain (as explained by Lakoff and Kövecses, 1987). The damage to the container and/or things/people nearby that is caused by the explosion is the social, psychological damage caused by the uncontrolled violent behavior to the self and/or other people who are involved in the situation:

the damage caused by the   → the social damage caused by
    explosion   the violent response

A crucial aspect of this metaphorical reasoning is the "point beyond which" emotional control cannot be maintained. This point on the intensity scale of the container-entity's resistance to internal pressure corresponds to the notion of "emotional tolerance," that is, the self's emotionality or disposition to emotional behavior.

However, it is not claimed that all external emotional responses are internally motivated. When this is the case, we do not have the conceptualization of emotions as internal forces (internal pressure) but simply as substances in the body-container. Thus the container may have a little or a lot of a substance in it or it may be empty or full, but the emotional responses of the self will not be seen as "caused" by an internal force (which is not to say that, in some instances, a weaker external force cannot be exerted, as in "My respect for her *kept* me *from* reporting the fraud"). This is characteristic of the less prototypical, weaker emotions, such as respect or less intense forms of otherwise "stronger" emotions.

Emotion Is an Opponent. The emotions are also conceptualized as opponents in a struggle. There are a number of linguistic examples to show this:

Table 5.2. EMOTION IS AN OPPONENT

Metaphorical Mapping	Agonist's Force Tendency	Antagonist's Force Tendency	Resultant Action
Source	*Opponent 1* opponent 1's attempt to resist opponent 2	*Opponent 2* opponent 2's attempt to cause opponent 1 to give in to his force	either opponent 2 wins or opponent 1 wins
Target	*Rational self* self's attempt to try to maintain control	*Emotion* the emotion causing the self to lose control	self either loses or maintains control

Source: Opponent in a struggle.
Target: Emotion.

He was *seized by* emotion.
He was *struggling with* his emotions.
I was *gripped by* emotion.
She was *overcome by* emotion.

The struggle takes place between the self and an emotion as opponents. The self first is in control of the emotion, but then the emotion causes the self to respond, that is, to lose control. The self attempts to maintain control over the emotion. Thus the struggle is an attempt for emotional control. There are two outcomes to the struggle: winning or losing. Table 5.2 shows the instantiation of the generic EMOTION IS FORCE metaphor through the concept of opponent. In this metaphor it is assumed that it is better to maintain rational control than to give in to the emotions. This is why the rational self applies a counterforce in an attempt to control the causal force of the emotion.

Emotion Is a Wild Animal. The WILD ANIMAL metaphor is a special case of the OPPONENT metaphor and thus inherits most of its mappings. In the WILD ANIMAL metaphor the struggle is between a master and an animal that tries to get away from the master. It is in this sense that the master and the animal are "opponents," as shown by the examples:

Table 5.3. EMOTION IS A WILD ANIMAL

Metaphorical Mapping	Agonist's Force Tendency	Antagonist's Force Tendency	Resultant Action
Source	*Master* to hold animal back	*Animal* to get away from master	either animal gets away or master holds it back
Target	*Rational self* to try to maintain emotional control	*Emotion* to exert force on self to lose control	self either loses control or maintains it

Source: Opponent in a struggle.
Target: Emotion.

His emotions *ran away* with him.
She *kept* her emotions *in check*.
He *couldn't hold back* his feelings.

Table 5.3 shows some shared mappings. Obviously, the struggle between the master and the animal corresponds to the struggle for emotional control. The animal is trying to get away but is held back by the master. In attempting to get away, it exerts a force on the master. Corresponding to this force is the emotion's force to cause the self to lose emotional control. The effect of the animal's force can be the performance of an unintended emotional response on the part of the self, which is metaphorically conceptualized as UNINTENDED ACTION IS OTHER-PROPELLED MOTION. This is based on the metaphor EVENTS ARE MOVEMENTS in EVENT STRUCTURE (see chapter 3).

Emotion Is a Social Force. Emotions can also be viewed as social forces. Of these, the most commonly used version is EMOTION IS A SOCIAL SUPERIOR metaphor. Let us look at some examples:

He is *ruled by* anger.
She is *driven by* fear.
His whole life is *governed by* passion.
Your actions are *dictated by* emotion.

According to this metaphor, the emotion, that is, the social superior, has control over the rational self. The social force of the superior cor-

Table 5.4. EMOTION IS A SOCIAL FORCE

Metaphorical Mapping	Agonist's Force Tendency	Antagonist's Force Tendency	Resultant Action
Source	*Social inferior*	*Social superior*	inferior does what superior wants him to do
Target	*Irrational self*	*Emotion*	self has no control and acts according to emotion

Source: Social superior.
Target: Emotion.

responds to the control that the emotion has over the self. The social effect of the superior on the self is the emotional effect of the emotion on the self (see Table 5.4).

In this case of the application of force dynamics, there is no longer any struggle between the superior and the inferior forces. This is shown in the table by leaving empty the boxes that correspond to the Antagonist's and the Agonist's force tendencies. The superior social force, that is, the emotion, controls the inferior one, that is, the irrational self (which was a rational self before the struggle). It is this resulting state that is shown in the diagram.

The overall result is that this metaphor primarily applies to a person whose behavior is controlled by emotion, not by reason. Thus, the idea that this particular metaphor adds to the conception of emotion is that it is a way of conceptualizing habitual tendencies, or dispositions, not so much momentary states or actions. A superior has long-term control over an inferior, whose behavior is determined by the superior over a long period of time. Thus the metaphor predominantly describes a certain kind of person ("an *emotional* one"), rather than an emotional event, as most of the FORCE metaphors we have seen so far do.

Emotion Is a Natural Force. Natural forces, like floods, wind, and so forth, are viewed as extremely forceful and as affecting physical objects with a great impact. Physical things can't help but undergo their effects. Here are some linguistic examples that reflect this conceptualization for the domain of emotion:

Table 5.5. EMOTION IS A NATURAL FORCE

Metaphorical Mapping	Agonist's Force Tendency	Antagonist's Force Tendency	Resultant Action
Source	*Physical object* to keep being the same	*Natural force* to cause an effect in physical object	physical object undergoes effect in a passive way
Target	*Rational self* to continue to behave as before the emotion	*Emotion* to cause the self to respond to emotion	self responds to the emotion in a passive way

Source: Natural force.
Target: Emotion.

I was *overwhelmed*.
I was *swept off my feet*.

As the second example indicates, one of the effects of a natural force on an entity may be that it moves the entity from one location to another. We described this in the previous chapter as the CAUSED EVENTS ARE OTHER-PROPELLED MOVEMENTS metaphor. The instantiation of the metaphor can be seen in Table 5.5. Obviously, only the passions or very intense forms of other emotions are conceptualized this way. By "inertia" the self's tendency is to continue to behave in the same way; that is, to continue not to get under the influence of the emotion force.

The object affected by the natural force can't help but undergo the impact of the force; in the same way, a person experiences emotion in a passive and helpless way. This is the single most important property of emotion in the folk theory.

Emotion Is a Mental Force. This metaphor comes in several versions. The mental force may be a force coming from a human or a drug. If it comes from a human source, it is EMOTION IS A MAGICIAN and EMOTION IS A TRICKSTER (or DECEIVER). Both of these are capable of deceiving a person; that is, they have the intellectual power to change one's beliefs about the world – either by magic or by a trick. The MAGICIAN metaphor is probably limited to romantic love, and we will not discuss it

Table 5.6. EMOTION IS A MENTAL FORCE

Metaphorical Mapping	Agonist's Force Tendency	Antagonist's Force Tendency	Resultant Action
Source	*Normal person* to continue to be undeceived	*Trickster* to attempt to deceive a person	trickster deceives normal person
Target	*Rational self* to continue to be rational	*Emotion* to make the rational self irrational	emotion makes self irrational

Source: Trickster (deceiver).
Target: Emotion.

further here. The TRICKSTER (or DECEIVER) metaphor seems to be much more general, in that its application may extend to any emotion. We can begin the analysis of this metaphor with some examples:

Our emotions often *fool* us.
His emotions *deceived* him.
She was *misled* by her emotions.

In addition, a person in an emotional state is commonly seen as incapable of "higher" mental functioning. This can be expressed by sentences such as "His emotions *clouded* his judgment." Language use such as this assumes the instantiation and mappings shown in Table 5.6.

As can be seen, the normal person is identified with the rational self that as a result of the trickster-emotion's tricks becomes irrational. The emotion's force tendency is to make the rational self see the world in a distorted way, while the rational self's tendency is to remain rational. Eventually, however, the trickster (or deceiver) deceives its victim, and correspondingly the emotion makes the rational self irrational. In other words, the self who is in an emotional state is depicted by this metaphor as being irrational.

Emotion Is Insanity. The element of irrationality can also be found in the INSANITY metaphor:

He is *mad* with desire.
I was *crazy* with emotion.

However, as the examples indicate, this metaphor also suggests more: Intense emotion is a state of the ultimate lack of control. While in the case of the TRICKSTER/DECEIVER metaphor the rational self becomes irrational in a limited situation (in his judgment of the aspect of the world relative to the emotion), in the case of the INSANITY metaphor the rational self is completely incapacitated cognitively as well as in terms of behavior; he loses all control.

In the INSANITY metaphor, emotion is an unspecified intense psychological force that can produce insanity. In the source domain of the metaphor, a normal person becomes insane as a result of this intense psychological force. Consequently, it would be more precise to restate the EMOTION IS INSANITY metaphor as THE EFFECT OF AN INTENSE EMOTIONAL STATE IS INSANITY Table 5.7 offers a more formal description of the INSANITY metaphor. Another major difference between the TRICKSTER and the INSANITY metaphors is that the latter applies only to very intense emotions (the passions, such as anger, fear, love), while the former can apply to any emotion.

The irrationality resulting from intense emotions need not be as intense as suggested by the INSANITY metaphor. A milder form of irrationality can be found in the metaphor EMOTION IS RAPTURE, as exemplified by expressions like *"drunk* with emotion" or *"intoxicated* with passion." Here emotion is viewed as some kind of alcoholic beverage capable of affecting a person's intellectual abilities in adverse

Table 5.7. EMOTION IS INSANITY

Metaphorical Mapping	Agonist's Force Tendency	Antagonist's Force Tendency	Resultant Action
Source	*Normal person* to remain normal	*Intense psychological force* to cause insanity in normal person	normal person becomes insane
Target	*Rational self* to remain rational	*Emotion* to cause self to become irrational (i.e., to lose all control)	rational self becomes irrational

Source: Insanity.
Target: Emotion.

ways. This metaphor shares the mappings of the INSANITY metaphor, but it also adds something to it. Many emotional states are viewed not only as irrational but also as "pleasant" states, a metaphorical projection that comes from conceptualizing emotions as an intoxicating beverage. Thus we have the additional mapping:

the assumed pleasantness of → the pleasantness of the
   being drunk   emotional state

Obviously, this mapping only applies to "positive" emotions, such as love or happiness, and can account for examples like "being *high on love*" or "having a *delirious* feeling."

In general, emotions are viewed as mentally incapacitating phenomena. The specific "mental incapacities" involve in addition to the ones above: INABILITY TO SPEAK and INABILITY TO THINK. We can take these to be special cases of the very general metonymy, according to which MENTAL INCAPACITIES STAND FOR EMOTION.

Emotion Is Fire/Heat. This specific-level force metaphor can be illustrated by the following examples:

He was *on fire* with emotion.
She was *consumed* by passion.
The events *kindled* several emotions in him.
I am *burning* with emotion.
They were *hot* with passion.

It is the prepositions *with* and *by* that indicate that there is *causal* link between certain emotional responses and emotion as fire (Radden, 1998); responses are seen as being caused by emotion itself. The FIRE metaphor "straddles across" both parts of the emotion schema; that is, both "emotion ⇒ response" and "cause of emotion ⇒ emotion." The expression *kindle* has to do with latter. However, most of the examples above have to do with the "emotion ⇒ response" aspect of the concept of emotion. To account for them, consider how the source and target domains of this metaphor instantiate the generic-level force metaphor for emotion (see Table 5.8).

The Antagonist's force tendency is to cause the person in an emotional state to undergo the effects of the emotion, such as becoming energized, dysfunctional, et cetera. On the other hand, the Agonist's force tendency is to remain unchanged, that is, not to undergo the effects of the emotion. However, the usual resultant action is that the

Table 5.8. EMOTION IS FIRE/HEAT

Metaphorical Mapping	Agonist's Force Tendency	Antagonist's Force Tendency	Resultant Action
Source	*Thing burning* to remain unchanged by fire	*Fire* to cause thing to undergo effects of fire	thing burning is changed by fire
Target	*Person in emotional state* to remain unchanged by emotion	*Emotion* to cause person to undergo effects of emotion	person's behavior changed by emotion

Source: Fire.
Target: Emotion.

person in an emotional state does change, that is, becomes energized, becomes dysfunctional, and so forth.

Intensity in general is commonly conceptualized as heat (see chapter 3). Thus many states and actions that have an intensity aspect are comprehended via the concept HEAT. The "hot" emotions include anger, romantic love, desire, sexual desire. Thus, one can *be hot* with anger, romantic love, and sexual desire. These emotions are seen as very intense and energized states.

A mapping not shown above is that various degrees of heat correspond to various degrees of intensity of emotion and lack of heat corresponds to lack of emotion. Given the latter, the mappings also account for the "opposites" of emotions, such as emotional calmness, indifference, lack of desire, et cetera. In addition, the mappings indicate that the emotions characterized here include both the "passions" and the "milder" kinds of emotion, such as affection, sadness, and the like. These emotions are conceptualized at a lower level of heat (e.g., warmth for affection) and hence are not seen as forces. Correspondingly, it is by virtue of being conceptualized as "hot" that certain forms of anger, romantic love, and sexual desire are conceived of as passions. But there are other reasons as well.

The heat can make the object hot. As previously, the physical force, that is, here the heat-force, corresponds to the emotion. The question is: What specifically is the intrinsic force tendency of the heat-force in the source domain and what is the force tendency of the emotion in the target? High degrees of heat ("hotness") produce an energized state in the object-person. The "hot" emotions are all viewed as being very intense states, in which the self is highly energized, that is, is in a state of readiness to act in intense ways. One linguistic example of this is when we say that a person is *hot to trot*, where *to trot*, a motion verb, indicates intense activity, a meaning that derives from, or is motivated by, the EVENT STRUCTURE metaphor, in which ACTIONS ARE SELF-PROPELLED MOVEMENTS.

But the particular effect of the heat-force may also be damage to the thing burning, that is, damage to the self. In the same way as the object becomes dysfunctional as a result of exposure to uncontrolled fire (high degrees of heat), so does the self as a result of uncontrolled intense emotion. This can be seen in expressions like *be burned up, be consumed,* and so forth, where the intense physical response of the thing corresponds to the damage to the self, where the damage results from the self's inability to control the emotion.

Another characteristic of the FIRE metaphor is that the fire may cause damage not only to the object on fire but also to another object. This can happen when the fire is intentionally directed at a target by the self. The fire in this case is inside the object-container. In other words, the FIRE and the PEOPLE AS CONTAINER metaphors are combined; the fire is inside the person as a container who directs it at another *(breathe fire)*. The damage to another object is the damage to the other person.

The example of *breathing fire* is based on a mapping that is inherited from a more general mapping in the FLUID IN A CONTAINER metaphor: externalization of the internal force is the response taking place. This response constitutes deliberate aggressive behavior.

Metaphors Focusing on Both Parts of the Emotion Schema

The metaphors discussed in this section have a double focus; they can instantiate both the initial and the final parts of the emotion scenario.

Emotion Is a Physiological Force. What can be viewed as "physiological forces" are also used to conceptualize the emotions. These come in several kinds: hunger, thirst, illness, and agitation.

EMOTION IS HUNGER/THIRST
I'm *starved for* affection.
His anger was *insatiable.*

As was noted in chapter 3, the hunger for food corresponds to the desire for either the emotion (e.g., affection) or the action associated with the emotion (e.g., an act of retribution in anger). The version in which an emotion is "insatiable" usually forms a part of the EMOTION IS A WILD ANIMAL metaphor. In this metaphor, the animal's responses may be motivated by the physiological force of hunger.

What unifies these two seemingly disparate examples is the very general mapping in the conceptual system that we saw in chapter 3:

hunger (for food)   → desire (for emotion or action)

The DESIRE IS HUNGER metaphor thus instantiates the general FORCE schema in two different ways. Let us look at the details of the difference between "desire for emotion" and "desire for emotional action." The food corresponds to emotion in the former version. When this is the case, the person who is hungry is the person who would like to but does not have the emotion. When the food corresponds to action in the latter, the wild animal that is (insatiably) hungry is the emotion itself that causes the self to perform an action.

In other words, the two versions of the HUNGER metaphor are structured by the mappings in Table 5.9. This set of mappings reflects an

Table 5.9. EMOTION IS A PHYSIOLOGICAL FORCE *(version one)*

Metaphorical Mapping	Agonist's Force Tendency	Antagonist's Force Tendency	Resultant Action
Source	*Person* for the (non-hungry) person not to want food	*Hunger (for food)* to cause the person to want food	hunger makes person go get food
Target	*Self* for the (desireless) self not to want emotion	*Desire (for emotion)* to cause self to want to have emotion	desire causes self to have emotion

Source: Hunger.
Target: Emotion.

Table 5.10. EMOTION IS A PHYSIOLOGICAL FORCE *(version two)*

Metaphorical Mapping	Agonist's Force Tendency	Antagonist's Force Tendency	Resultant Action
Source	*Wild animal* animal (without insatiable appetite) eats "just enough"	*Insatiable appetite (for food)* insatiable appetite makes animal keep eating food	animal with insatiable appetite keeps eating
Target	*Emotional self* emotion (without insatiable desire) does not cause self to keep acting on emotion	*Insatiable emotional desire* insatiable emotional desire causing self to keep acting on emotion	self with insatiable emotional desire keeps acting on emotion

Source: Hunger.
Target: Emotion.

instantiation of the generic-level force schema that is very different from the instantiations we have seen so far. The major difference seems to be that the emotion instantiates neither the Agonist nor the Antagonist. What is at issue is the desire for emotion. Naturally, this version only applies to "positive emotions" like affection and love.

However, in the other application of the schema (in which one's emotion is *"insatiable"*), the concept of emotion does instantiate the Agonist. Let us look at the details in Table 5.10.

The correspondence that is new relative to the instantiations given above is

"the food → the action response."

This is because "food" does not instantiate either the Agonist or the Antagonist. However, it is clearly a part of the elements that get mapped onto the emotion domain, although outside the FORCE schema as limited to the five elements (such as Agonist, force tendency of Antagonist, etc.) that we are working with here. Since most emotions, both "positive" and "negative," are associated with particular actions, version 2 of the metaphor can apply to most emotions.

In the general FORCE schema, one of the elements of the schema is "the effect of the force" on the entity affected by it. Now we can ask how this is realized in the HUNGER metaphor. In version 2 it seems to be the gratification of the animal's hunger, corresponding to the performance of some action associated with the emotion. In version 1, it is also the gratification of one's hunger, corresponding to having the desired emotion.

In sum, the same general FORCE schema is employed differentially in the case of the HUNGER metaphor, but at the same time the generic structure of the schema is preserved in both versions.

Emotion Is Physical Agitation. Similar to the HUNGER metaphor, this metaphor also comes in two versions. Version 1 has as its scope the "cause ⇒ emotion" part of the emotion scenario, while version 2 has the part "emotion ⇒ response." Some linguistic examples for version 1 include (Kövecses, 1990):

The speech *stirred* everybody's feelings.
I am all *shook up*.
She was all *worked up*.
Why are you *upset*?
Don't get *excited*.
He was slightly *ruffled* by what he heard.
The children were *disturbed* by what they saw.

The examples are based on the instantiations in Table 5.11.

According to this application of the metaphor, emotion is a dis-

Table 5.11. EMOTION IS PHYSICAL AGITATION *(version one)*

Metaphorical Mapping	Agonist's Force Tendency	Antagonist's Force Tendency	Resultant Action
Source	*Object in state of calm* to remain calm	*External cause that can create agitation in object* to cause physical agitation in object	object is physically agitated
Target	*Rational self* to remain emotionally calm	*Cause of emotion* to produce emotional disturbance in self	self is emotionally disturbed

Source: Physical agitation.
Target: Emotion.

turbed state of mind that arises from some cause. What is the conceptual relationship among EMOTIONAL DISTURBANCE, PHYSICAL AGITATION, and EMOTION? In this case, EMOTIONAL DISTURBANCE is metaphorically understood as PHYSICAL AGITATION. However, EMOTIONAL DISTURBANCE stands metonymically for EMOTION. To put it more simply, emotion is viewed as being defined by (emotional) disturbance, and the disturbed state of mind is used to stand for emotion as a whole.

Version 2 presents a different situation both regarding scope and conceptual organization. Let us see some examples first:

I stood there *trembling* with emotion.
He *quivered all over* with emotion.
As a result of what she felt, *shivers ran up and down her spine.*
He was *quaking* in his boots.

These examples suggest bodily agitation that arises from some emotion (as again indicated by the preposition *with*) – not a disturbed state of mind as previously. Table 5.12 shows the instantiations and mappings. The verbs *tremble, quiver, shiver, quake* above are all examples of this last mapping that is concerned with the "resultant action" part of the force schema.

Unlike in version 1, here we have to do with the "emotion ⇒ response" part of the emotion scenario, where the response is agitation

Table 5.12. EMOTION IS PHYSICAL AGITATION *(version two)*

Metaphorical Mapping	Agonist's Force Tendency	Antagonist's Force Tendency	Resultant Action
Source	*Physical object to remain physically calm*	*Force that can cause physical agitation in object to cause physical agitation in object*	object is physically agitated
Target	*Person's body to remain bodily calm*	*Emotion to cause bodily agitation in body*	person is bodily agitated

Source: Physical agitation.
Target: Emotion.

arising from an emotion. Moreover, PHYSICAL AGITATION stands metonymically for EMOTION; that is, physical agitation is used to conceptualize emotion in a more direct way.

Agitation is a kind of incapacity, bodily or mental incapacity; when
it happens, the self is unable to act normally. This fits the general
metonymy in which THE INCAPACITATING EFFECTS OF EMOTION STAND
FOR THE EMOTION.

Emotion Is a Burden. A metaphor that focuses on the general evaluation of emotions is EMOTION IS A BURDEN:

She is *weighed down* by sadness.
He felt good after he *unburdened* himself.
When they left the dark forest behind, he felt *relieved*.

The external pressure caused by the burden (Antagonist) on the body-
container (Agonist) corresponds to the stress or difficulty caused by
the emotion (Antagonist) on the self (Agonist). Let's call this "emotional stress or difficulty." In this metaphor, emotional stress or difficulty causes the self to function abnormally (Antagonist's intrinsic
force tendency), while the Agonist's force tendency can be identified
as the self's tendency to function normally. Table 5.13 shows what
mappings are involved.

The Antagonist's force tendency in the source domain includes

Table 5.13. EMOTION IS A BURDEN

Metaphorical Mapping	Agonist's Force Tendency	Antagonist's Force Tendency	Resultant Action
Source	*Person* to hold the burden	*Burden* to cause physical pressure on person	person experiences physical difficulty
Target	*Self* to withstand emotional stress	*Emotion* to cause emotional stress in self	self experiences emotional difficulty

Source: Burden.
Target: Emotion.

"pressure *on* person," while in the target it is "stress *in* self." The change from *on* to *in* indicates that there is an additional metaphor underlying the mapping: namely, INTERNAL IS EXTERNAL, according to which internal states are comprehended as external events.

Notice also that the BURDEN metaphor may entail physical movement and, consequently, difficulty in action. This implication comes from the EVENT STRUCTURE metaphor. In EVENT STRUCTURE movement corresponds to action (ACTION IS MOTION).

Finally, it can be seen that the BURDEN exerts a steady or constant pressure on the self. This is in contrast to the internal force in the PRESSURIZED CONTAINER metaphor, where the internal pressure is typically momentary or lasts a short time. Correspondingly, the intrinsic force tendency of emotion (i.e., that of the Antagonist) will be momentary in the INTERNAL PRESSURE, while steady, or longer-lasting, in the BURDEN metaphor.

Metaphors Mainly Focusing on the "Cause of Emotion"

Emotion Is a Physical Force. Let us begin with some examples for the specific-level metaphors that belong to this group:

EMOTION IS A MECHANICAL FORCE; EMOTIONAL EFFECT IS PHYSICAL CONTACT
When I found out, it *hit* me *hard*.
That was a terrible *blow*.
She *knocked* me *off my feet*.

EMOTION IS AN ELECTRIC FORCE
It was an *electrifying* experience.

EMOTION IS A GRAVITATIONAL FORCE
Her whole life *revolves around* him.
They *gravitated toward* each other immediately.

EMOTION IS A MAGNETIC FORCE
I was *magnetically drawn to* her.
I am *attracted to* her.
She found him *irresistible*.
That *repels* me.

As the instantiations of the generic-level FORCE schema and its mappings in Table 5.14 indicate, these metaphors have primarily to do with the way emotions arise. I will not analyze here how these differ-

Table 5.14. EMOTION IS A PHYSICAL FORCE

Metaphorical Mapping	Agonist's Force Tendency	Antagonist's Force Tendency	Resultant Action
Source	*Physical object* to remain unaffected by force	*Physical force* to produce effect in object	object undergoes effect
Target	*Self* to remain unemotional	*Cause of emotion* to cause self to become emotional	self is emotional

Source: Physical force.
Target: Emotion.

ent specific-level metaphors each contribute to the folk conception of emotion. Instead, I will only look at what's common to the metaphorical mappings of the metaphors above. In other words, our concept of emotion is understood as physical effect produced by a cause. This makes sense because our emotions are conceptualized as responses to a situation (the cause of emotion).

We should notice about these mappings that they apply to completely different parts of our emotion scenario in the folk theory of emotion than the ones we have dealt with previously. In the cases above, we had the following picture: Emotion as Antagonist has a force tendency; the force tendency manifests itself in the self as Agonist; the result is some emotional effect on the part of the self. Schematically:

emotion – force tendency of emotion/self ⇒ self has emotion ⇒ resultant emotional effect

With the PHYSICAL FORCE metaphor, however, we have a different one: It is the cause of emotion that has the Antagonist's force tendency; the force tendency manifests itself in the self as Agonist; as a result, the self has the emotion. Schematically again:

cause of emotion – force tendency of cause of emotion ⇒ self has emotion

While the first chain is a description of what happens after an emotion has come into being, the second captures what it takes for it to come into being. The two causal chains complement each other, in that one captures what happens before an emotion comes into being, and the other captures what happens afterward. Thus, we can put them together in the following way to get a complete picture of the skeletal scenario that forms the basis of the most pervasive folk theory of emotion coded into English:

(1) cause of emotion – force tendency of the cause of emotion ⇒ (2) self has emotion – force tendency of emotion ⇒ (3) resultant effect

What is missing from this is the control-related aspects of emotion discussed above that can be placed between (2) and (3). If we place this information in the schema, we get:

(1) cause of emotion – force tendency of the cause of emotion ⇒ (2) self has emotion – force tendency of emotion ⇒ (3) self's force tendency ↔ emotion's force tendency ⇒ (4) resultant effect

This skeletal but now complete schema reveals that our basic understanding of emotion rests upon our understanding of how various forces interact with each other. Most important, the schema shows that even our most basic understanding of emotion as "cause ⇒ emotion ⇒ response" is metaphorical through and through.

Conclusion

Emotion metaphors are not isolated and unrelated specific-level metaphors, but form a large and intricate system that is organized around the generic concept of force, as analyzed by Talmy. The various emotion metaphor source domains are instantiations of the concept of force. This is a conclusion that places prior studies of emotion metaphors in a new light.

At a generic level, emotion and all the source domains share what Fauconnier and Turner (e.g., Fauconnier, 1997; Turner, 1996) would call a "generic space," which is here the space of force. This force space structures not only the particular source domains but also the concept of emotion, yielding the skeletal structure: cause of emotion ⇒ emotion ⇒ response. This provides an extremely basic structure for emotion that is metaphorical.

The conclusion to draw from all this is that there is very little about the emotions that is not metaphorically conceived. Even our most basic understanding of emotion (such as the skeletal schema identified above) is metaphorical and not literal. However, the "very little" that is nonmetaphorical is crucial in the conceptualization of the domain of emotion and constitutes the experiential basis of this large metaphor system. What exactly this experiential basis consists in will be dealt with in the chapter on the universal aspects of conceptualizing the emotions.

This conclusion about the inherently metaphorical nature of our notion of emotion undercuts Naomi Quinn's (1991) claim that cultural models for concepts like emotion and marriage are literal and that the various conceptual metaphors merely reflect such literal understandings. It may be that some of the conceptual metaphors reflect the basic cultural schemas, but these schemas, at least for the domain of emotion, are clearly inherently metaphorical from the very start. I will come back to the discussion of this issue in chapter 7.

As has been stressed in this chapter, the basic schema of emotion presented above is only a skeletal one. Many details of the schema are filled out by the conceptual contributions of the many specific-level metaphors we have described above. I will present this conceptually much richer cultural model in chapter 7, where I will discuss the relationship between folk and expert theories.

6. Emotions and Relationships

So far we have seen a wide variety of metaphors for the emotions. In chapter 2, the many specific-level metaphors for nine emotion concepts were discussed. In chapter 5, I pointed out that there is a single underlying "master metaphor" for the domain that organizes most of the diverse emotion metaphors into a coherent system. My goals in this chapter are twofold: First, I wish to uncover the specific-level conceptual metaphors that underlie the domain of human relationships, especially friendship, love, and marriage. Part of the task will be to see whether human relationships such as these are conceptualized metaphorically in the same way the domain of emotion is conceptualized. Second, the question arises whether, similar to the emotions, human relationships are also organized around a "master metaphor" such as EMOTION IS FORCE, as we saw in the previous chapter.

My main focus will be on the concept of friendship. This is because extensive studies of love and marriage have already been made using the methodology of detailed metaphor analysis (see, e.g., Quinn, 1987, 1991; Kövecses, 1988, 1991a; Baxter, 1992). However, by making use of these studies of "meaningful relationships" (Duck, 1994), we will be in a position to make some interesting generalizations concerning the issue of how the emotions and human relationships are conceptualized.

The linguistic material used for the study of friendship in this chapter comes from two sources, reflecting two methods of collecting language data. In one, 17 adults, all native speakers of American English, were interviewed about the topic of friendship. (The interviews were conducted by three native speakers of American English: Cheryl Chris, Lars Moestue, and Joseph Vargo.) The subjects were white, middle-class adults (within the age range of 19 to 57), 8 males and 9

females. All had college degrees or were attending college at the time
of the interviews. In the other method, students at Rutgers University,
in New Jersey, were assigned the task of writing any number of sentences with the word *friendship* or *friend* in them. In this way, more
than 500 sentences were collected. The analysis of friendship in the
present study is based exclusively on these two databases.

The "Communication" System

For the Americans we have talked to, friendship involves a great deal
of communication, and communication appears to be a basic property
of friendship. Communication between friends is a special case of
communication in general (as described, e.g., by Reddy, 1979).
Therefore, we can expect "friendly communication" to inherit the
metaphors of communication in general. What I will try to do in this
section is to see the extent to which this is the case and what the details
of the process are.

Communication is a multifaceted notion in the American conception of friendship. It involves such aspects as what the kinds of things
are that are communicated, how they can be communicated, and what
the communicators themselves are like. In this section, I will deal with
each of these issues under three interrelated metaphors: EXPERIENCES
ARE OBJECTS, COMMUNICATION IS SHARING (EXPERIENCE) OBJECTS, and
PEOPLE ARE CONTAINERS (FOR EXPERIENCE OBJECTS). However, these
metaphors should be regarded merely as convenient headings under
which the discussion to follow is organized. Other, equally important,
metaphors will also be presented.

Experiences as Objects

A feature of friendship that occurs frequently in the data is sharing:
"An important element for friendship is *sharing*"; "Friendship is *sharing* happiness and sadness"; and "Friendship is *sharing* deep, dark
secrets." In addition to sharing certain emotions (such as happiness
and sadness) and information (such as secrets), several other things
were mentioned. One person said that "a best friend almost *has to be
going through what you're going* through at the same time." Sharing
ideas also came up: "A friend is someone that you *can share* your ideas
with." That is, people talk about important life events, important emotions, and important ideas (including information) as something that

friends share, or are supposed to share. Events, emotions, and ideas (information) are all experiences that are commonly conceptualized as objects. This leads us to assume the existence of the metaphor EXPERIENCES ARE OBJECTS. As the examples above tell us, these experiences are to be shared in friendship. Thus in place of the general conceptual metaphor EXPERIENCES ARE OBJECTS we get the more specific SHARING EXPERIENCES IS SHARING OBJECTS that applies to friendship. Indeed, one of the most common expressions that people used in the data in connection with friendship was *sharing experiences.*

The Conduit Metaphor

Experiences can be shared either directly or indirectly. When it is shared directly, an event will, metaphorically speaking, cause people to have the same experience OBJECTS in them. In the case of indirect sharing, one person will transfer his or her experience OBJECTS to the other, as a result of which they will share the relevant experience. In other words, this latter kind of sharing is communication as based on Reddy's (1979) description of the folk theory of the communicative process. According to this model, THE MIND IS A CONTAINER, MEANINGS ARE OBJECTS, and COMMUNICATION IS SENDING. That is, communication is sending objects from one container to another along a conduit. What we described above as "sharing experiences" corresponds to a large degree to this view of communication. The mind and the person are both containers, meanings and experiences are both objects, and communication and sharing both involve the transfer of objects from one container to another.

Indirect sharing overlaps greatly or is virtually synonymous with communication in people's conception of friendship: "It's just that whole concept of *sharing the same things with each other* that the two could easily relate to and *express to each other.*" Or according to another person: "Ideal friendship. Someone you can *tell your innermost thoughts to,* someone you can *share feelings with.*" The identification of sharing with communication is most obvious in this statement: "someone that you'll *share intimate things with,* like you'll *tell things to* your best friend you'll never tell to other people." We can take (indirect) sharing to be a metaphorical consequence of the CONDUIT metaphor: Experience OBJECTS (meanings) are transferred from one container to another with the result that both containers have the same experience objects.

Persons as Containers

A special kind of communication in friendship is confiding. For many people, "A friend is one who I can confide in." Confiding seems to be based on the metaphor A PERSON IS A CONTAINER:

> We've been exchanging letters, *deeply felt* letters, where we really try to work out ideas about things and share those ideas and argue about those ideas and *dredge-up our deepest feelings* about things, I mean, I really think of this man as a confidant.

A person has a deepest part and a superficial part. The most important part of a person is the deepest part; that is where the real person "resides." Here the CONTAINER metaphor for person is combined with the IMPORTANT IS CENTRAL metaphor. What the CONTAINER metaphor assumes is that a person has two selves: a true self, corresponding to the deepest part, and a superficial self, corresponding to the superficial part. The special significance of the distinction in the conception of persons is pointed up by another metaphor in the data: LIFE IS A PLAY. People are often assumed to live their lives with the "superficial" rather than the "real self," as the following quote shows: "A friend is someone that you can share your ideas with and know that you can be at peace with them. There are *no facades, no masks*." A main advantage of friendship, as reported in the data, is that friends do not have to *"wear this mask,"* that is, they can be their "real, true selves":

> The difference between a best friend and a good friend is a great degree of honesty, complete *renunciation of facades and masks* which consequently leads to them *being themselves in a very natural way* – it's *not something contrived, or planned*; rather it's *a very natural state of being.*

The most important mapping in the LIFE IS A PLAY metaphor as regards friendship is that playing a role in a play corresponds to one's "superficial self" in life, a self that hides one's "real, true self." It is the true self that becomes visible in friendship. It is, of course, no accident that this particular mapping is most relevant to friendship. The reason is that the role, and especially its quintessential form, the mask, can be regarded as a version of the container metaphor, where it is the outermost layer of the person that covers the most significant aspects of the self.

Furthermore, when the deepest, innermost experiences are shared, the real, true self is shared. This is based on the metaphorical idea that THE REAL SELF IS (CONSTITUTED BY) ONE'S INNERMOST (EXPERIENCE) OBJECTS. The concepts of intimacy and openness are based on the PERSON AS CONTAINER metaphor: "I feel that friendship involves an *intimacy and openness.*" What intimacy and openness mean in the language of the CONTAINER metaphor is that the container that holds our experiences can be opened. If it is open, we can look inside, and the more we open it the more we can see. We can see the content that we could not see before it was open, that is, the truth, the real self. It is this real self that becomes shared by means of communication between friends. In other words, a key metaphor for friendship as regards communicating experiences in friendship is COMMUNICATION BETWEEN FRIENDS IS SHARING ONE'S INNERMOST (EXPERIENCE) OBJECTS. Given that friendship appears to involve a large amount of communication between friends as a major property, this leads to a further metaphor: FRIENDSHIP IS SHARING ONE'S INNERMOST (EXPERIENCE) OBJECTS (and its main submapping: FRIENDS ARE CONTAINERS [THAT OPEN UP TO EACH OTHER]). That is, friendship is sharing one's real self with another person.

What we found in this section is that the American conception of friendship is constituted to a considerable extent by the notion of communication. This has the effect that friendship is understood to a large degree in terms of the conventionalized metaphors for communication and its subcomponents, such as people and their experiences. Friendship assumes all the major metaphors for communication, people, and experiences: the CONDUIT metaphor and the metaphors PEOPLE ARE CONTAINERS and SHARING EXPERIENCES IS SHARING OBJECTS. What seems to be more or less specific to friendship (and some closely related domains, like love and marriage) are the nature of the experiences shared (INNERMOST EXPERIENCE OBJECTS, i.e., the real self), the way of sharing them (CONFIDING), and the intimacy that this sharing leads to (THE MORE EXPERIENCE OBJECTS ARE SHARED, THE MORE INTIMACY THERE IS BETWEEN THE TWO PEOPLE).

On the basis of the linguistic evidence presented in this section, the general conclusion that can be drawn is that communication between two friends is a prominent property of American friendship. Given this, it is not surprising that metaphors that are conventionally associated with communication in general will apply to friendship and will be prevalent in the way Americans talk about friendship. However, since communication *between friends* is a special case of communication in general, it will have some features that are, at least to some degree, specific to friendship.

The "Emotion" System

Friendship is viewed by people as being not only an interpersonal relationship but also an emotion, though a very *non*prototypical one, as some studies indicate. It is mentioned as a peripheral emotion word in a study by, for example, Storm and Storm (1987), but it is not mentioned as an emotion word in similar studies, such as those by Fehr and Russell (1984) and Shaver et al. (1987). What lends friendship something of the flavor of an emotion is that it appears to involve at least two concepts, intimacy and affection, that are more clearly members of the category of emotion. (Respect is a third such concept, but it did not appear in a metaphorically elaborated form in the data.) Now, since friendship is linked with these two emotion concepts, it will also have the metaphors that intimacy and affection are generally associated with.

We can begin with intimacy in friendship. It was mentioned in the section on communication that sharing leads to more intimacy. This makes use of the PEOPLE ARE CONTAINERS metaphor. Another metaphor used by our informants is FRIENDSHIP IS CLOSENESS, which is a special case of the fully conventionalized and very general metaphor INTIMACY IS CLOSENESS. This in turn seems to derive from the high-level metaphor AN EMOTIONAL RELATIONSHIP IS A DISTANCE BETWEEN TWO ENTITIES (like two people), which applies primarily to love and affection and an absence of these. A phrase that was frequently mentioned is *"close* friends." The word *close* points to the metaphorical distance between the two friends. The CLOSENESS metaphor occurs with great frequency in the data for friendship, which indicates the importance of intimacy in the American conception of friendship. Examples of the CLOSENESS metaphor in friendship include: "We were *tight as a glove,*" "They were *bosom* buddies," "We are *attached at the hip,*" "He was a *sidekick* of mine," "They are as *thick as thieves,*" "They are *inseparable,*" and "We were *two peas in a pod.*" Thus, in this case, there is the general metaphor AN EMOTIONAL RELATIONSHIP IS A DISTANCE BETWEEN TWO ENTITIES, where the distance is specified for intimacy as being close. Since friendship involves intimacy, it will also have the CLOSENESS metaphor.

The other emotion concept that friendship involves for many Americans is affection. This manifested itself in examples like the following: "Yeltsin and Bush have a *warm* friendship" and "Making too many requests can put a *warm* friendship permanently *on ice.*" The emotion of affection is understood in terms of warmth, and lack of affection in terms of coldness. Emotions in general are often conceptualized as temperature (see chapter 4). Thus the high-level metaphor EMOTION IS TEMPERATURE/HEAT is specified for WARMTH as the source domain of affection. Since the emotion of affection is characteristic of friendship (at least in the paradigmatic case), the AFFECTION IS WARMTH metaphor will also apply to friendship in the form of FRIENDSHIP IS WARMTH. It should be pointed out that, as we saw in the previous chapter, the emotion metaphors AN EMOTIONAL RELATIONSHIP IS CLOSENESS and EMOTION IS TEMPERATURE/HEAT constitute part of the "emotion" metaphor system. Thus, the conception of friendship relies partly on emotion metaphors.

The "State" Metaphor System

At least prototypically, to be friends with somebody is to be in a permanent state. This shows up in the conceptualization of friendship as an OBJECT. States in general are metaphorical objects. Furthermore, the state is an attributed state; we attribute friendship to others and ourselves. Attributed states are metaphorically viewed as possessed objects (Lakoff, 1993).

Friendship as a Possessed Object

Friendship is often conceptualized as a possessed object, as the following examples show:

FRIENDSHIP IS A POSSESSED OBJECT
The friendship that Kelly and I *hold* is ten years old. Julie and I *carry* our friendship through our correspondence. The *loss* of friendship is like a little part of you dying off. People who have trouble making friends have a hard time *keeping* friendship. . . . You can *possess* the "quality" of friendship.

The examples assume the following mappings:

- the people possessing the object are the friends
- possessing the object is the existence of the friendship

- the loss of the possessed object is the loss/cessation of the friendship
- keeping the object is keeping/continuation of the friendship

Thus, the main focus of this metaphor is the existence (or nonexistence) of friendship.

FRIENDSHIP IS A POSSESSED OBJECT is a special case of the higher-level metaphor ATTRIBUTES ARE POSSESSED OBJECTS. Attributes in general are commonly conceptualized as objects and the existence (or nonexistence) of attributes as objects that are possessed, lost, kept, et cetera (see Lakoff, 1993). Attributes include physical, emotional, social, and so forth, states and relationships. Here are some examples:

> ATTRIBUTES ARE POSSESSED OBJECTS
> have a headache
> have trouble
> keep cool, lose control
> lose health, keep health
> lose one's love, keep one's love
> lose speed, lose weight
> lose one's sanity
> have pride, lose respect, discard dignity
> lose wealth/fortune, gain wealth
> lose status, keep face

All of these examples have to do, in one form or another, with the existence (or nonexistence) of the attribute.

Friendship as a Bond

Attributed states are a special case of states, and attributed states include relationships. A common way to comprehend relationships is through the source domain of PHYSICAL LINKS or CONNECTIONS. Friendship is also a relationship, and as such it is conceptualized as a STRONG (PHYSICAL) BOND between two people:

> FRIENDSHIP IS A STRONG (PHYSICAL) BOND
> True friendship is a *bond that can weather the storms of life.*
> [In] real friendship somehow or other you make the other person feel and they make you feel what *connects* you is that you have this *common, heavy heavy link* in many areas, not that you were just working in the same field or what have you.

A real friendship *starts with a thread and spins into a rope*. It *gets stronger and it gets stronger* and it *spins another thread and another thread*, and with a real friendship, occasionally *one of the little threads may break but the rope is so strong*, it survives it – you know the boundaries, it's understood – but it grows.

The mappings are as follows:

- the two entities (people, etc.) are the two friends
- the physical bond between two people is the emotional bond between the two friends
- the strength of the bond is the stability of the relationship

The emotional bond between the two people is something that guarantees the stability, the enduringness of the friendship. Thus the metaphor focuses on the enduring nature of the relationship. Other positive interpersonal and emotional relationships that involve the BOND metaphor include love (Baxter, 1992), marriage (Quinn, 1987, 1991), and affection (as in a "child's *bond* with his mother"). Moreover, relationships in general are viewed as connections, links, ties, bonds, and so forth. These indicate differing degrees of strength, with "bond" being reserved primarily for strong positive human emotional relationships. In general, a very strong bond corresponds to a very stable relationship that the participants see as being lasting or permanent.

Friendship as an Economic Exchange

If two entities are in a relationship, they can interact. In friendship, the two friends are related and they do interact in many ways (communicatively, emotionally, behaviorally, etc.). Several examples suggest that people think of friendship as an interaction between two people. The resulting metaphor is (INTERACTION IN) FRIENDSHIP IS AN ECONOMIC EXCHANGE. Sentences like "Friendship is a *give and take*" occurred frequently in the corpus. They can be accounted for by the following correspondences between the source domain of an economic exchange and the target domain of interaction in the friendship:

- the parties in the economic exchange are the friends who interact with each other
- the economic exchange (i.e., paying the money and handing over the commodity) is the mutual interactions performed by the friends
- the profit gained from the exchange is the benefit gained from the interaction

- the price paid is the time and energy one has to devote to the friendship

There is important knowledge about friendship that is based on the ECONOMIC EXCHANGE metaphor:

S(ource): Economic exchanges are reciprocal.
T(arget): Friendship relationships are reciprocal.
> All friendships are rooted in *reciprocity*. Friendship is a *give and take relationship*.

S: Economic exchanges are typically based on equality.
T: Friendship relationships are typically based on equality.
> *Being reciprocal* is good in a friendship. This doesn't necessarily mean 50/50 and, yet, some people always use that. Like *partnership*, and then it gets this tinge of *50/50-ish and percentages*.

The key concept here appears to be "beneficial interaction." Interactions that are performed for the benefit of the participants are metaphorically understood as economic exchanges that produce a profit. Hence the metaphor INTERACTION IS AN ECONOMIC EXCHANGE. Thus the FRIENDSHIP IS AN ECONOMIC EXCHANGE metaphor seems to be a special case of the INTERACTIONS ARE ECONOMIC EXCHANGES metaphor. The interactions-as-economic exchanges metaphor extends beyond friendship to other relationships, including love (Kövecses, 1988; Baxter, 1992) and marriage (Quinn, 1987, 1991), and even further. For example, moral interactions are also viewed as economic exchanges (see Johnson, 1992). In addition, the interaction between man and nature is commonly thought of as a *"give and take,"* and man is often said *"to exploit"* nature. Even a conversation can be regarded as an economic exchange, as when we talk about a lively *"give and take"* of ideas. Interactions that produce a benefit can then be seen as economic exchanges with a profit. Since friendship is viewed as being characterized by the mutual interaction of the two friends that is expected to produce mutual benefits, it is not surprising that the very general mapping "an economic exchange with a profit is interaction with a benefit" applies to it.

In sum, it seems that friendship inherits some metaphors from the "State" hierarchy of which it forms a part. The metaphors it inherits are conventionally associated with the concepts above it in the hierarchy. This can be shown in Table 6.1, where capitalized words represent concepts below each other in the hierarchy, capitalized words in

Table 6.1. *Friendship and the "State" Hierarchy*

STATE	*OBJECT*	
ATTRIBUTE	*POSSESSED OBJECT*	existence
RELATIONSHIP	*BOND*	stability
INTERACTION	*ECONOMIC EXCHANGE*	benefit
FRIENDSHIP	*OBJECT*	
	POSSESSED OBJECT	
	BOND	
	ECONOMIC EXCHANGE	

italics the source domains of metaphors for the concepts in the hierarchy, and words in lowercase letters the "main meaning orientation" of the metaphor.

What we can observe in Table 6.1 is that there is a vertical hierarchy of concepts with the concept of state at the top, attributed state below state, relationship below attribute, interaction below relationship, and friendship at the bottom. The concepts above friendship have their characteristic metaphorical source domains: OBJECT for states, POSSESSED OBJECT for attributes, BOND for relationship, and ECONOMIC EXCHANGE for interaction. Now, because friendship is all of these things (that is, state, attributed state, relationship, and interaction), it will inherit these metaphors to express the general meanings the metaphors are associated with. In the state system of which friendship is a part, the concept of friendship inherits four *different* source domains from four different concepts above it.

The "Complex Systems" Metaphor

But a more complete metaphorical understanding of friendship involves other metaphors as well. These include FRIENDSHIP IS A STRUCTURED OBJECT, FRIENDSHIP IS A MACHINE, and FRIENDSHIP IS A LIVING ORGANISM. All of the source domains in these metaphors represent complex objects. As we will see, these conceptual metaphors are pervasive in the data. To account for the presence of these metaphors in the conceptualization of friendship, it seems reasonable to suppose a system of metaphors similar in nature to Lakoff's (1990, 1993) Event Structure system (see chapter 3). Since the STRUCTURED OBJECT, MACHINE, and LIVING ORGANISM metaphors take complex systems like theories, the mind, the body, society, complex interpersonal relationships and others, not events, as their target domain, we can call them the "Complex Systems" metaphor. Thus, the target domain of this metaphor is Complex Systems, while the source domain is Complex Physical Objects (like Building, Machine, Plant). In this very general metaphor we can find the following major mappings:

Target: Complex systems   Source: Complex objects

THE CREATION OF THE COMPLEX SYSTEM IS THE MAKING OF THE OBJECT

THE EXISTENCE OF THE COMPLEX SYSTEM IS THE EXISTENCE OF THE OBJECT

THE MAINTENANCE OF THE SYSTEM IS THE MAINTENANCE OF THE OBJECT

THE EFFORT WITH WHICH THE COMPLEX SYSTEM CAN BE CREATED AND MAINTAINED IS THE EFFORT WITH WHICH THE OBJECT CAN BE MADE AND MAINTAINED

THE LASTINGNESS OF THE COMPLEX SYSTEM IS THE STRENGTH OF THE OBJECT

THE FUNCTION OF THE COMPLEX SYSTEM IS THE FUNCTION OF THE OBJECT

THE FUNCTIONING OF THE COMPLEX SYSTEM IS THE FUNCTIONING OF THE OBJECT

THE PURPOSE FOR WHICH THE COMPLEX SYSTEM IS USED IS THE PURPOSE FOR WHICH THE OBJECT IS USED

THE DEVELOPMENT OF THE COMPLEX SYSTEM IS THE GROWTH OF THE OBJECT

These are mappings at the highest level. As has been mentioned above, the most common lower-level target domains of the COMPLEX SYSTEMS metaphor include society, the mind, the body, and human relationships. In other words, the metaphor takes various social, psychological, biological, and emotional domains as its focus. In the list of mappings given below, the concept ABSTRACT should be understood as referring to these social, psychological, et cetera, domains. Thus, the mappings that were elaborated in some detail above can be given in a more succinct way as follows:

CREATION IS MAKING

ABSTRACT EXISTENCE IS PHYSICAL EXISTENCE

ABSTRACT MAINTENANCE IS PHYSICAL MAINTENANCE

ABSTRACT EFFORT IS PHYSICAL EFFORT

LASTINGNESS IS STRENGTH
ABSTRACT FUNCTION IS PHYSICAL FUNCTION
ABSTRACT FUNCTIONING IS PHYSICAL FUNCTIONING
ABSTRACT PURPOSE IS PHYSICAL PURPOSE
DEVELOPMENT IS GROWTH

My suggestion will be that these mappings constitute the COMPLEX SYSTEMS metaphor. Complex Systems have interpersonal relationships as a special case. Friendship is, in turn, a special case of interpersonal relationships. Similar to Lakoff's Event Structure, the lower-level domains inherit the mappings of the higher-level ones. Thus, the mappings specified above will be inherited by the concept of friendship. The obvious constraint on the mappings in the COMPLEX SYSTEMS metaphor is that human relationships, including friendship, prototypically involve two active participants. In human relationships, this results, for example, in two creators (and makers) in the first mapping.

I will claim that complex systems take the general structure of complex entities/objects: They do not exist first and then they are made; they are made for a purpose; they have a function; they have a large number of parts that interact with each other; they require effort to make and maintain; the stronger they are the longer they last. There are also objects that are not made, but which come into existence by themselves (living organisms). They represent a subclass within the category of complex objects. Complex systems, like society, the mind, human relationships, are metaphorically understood as having these properties. I will provide linguistic evidence for these mappings in relation to a variety of target domains within the general COMPLEX SYSTEMS metaphor in the present section, but the main focus will, of course, be on how this general metaphor applies to friendship.

Friendship as a Structured Object

A metaphor that occurs most frequently in the data is the FRIENDSHIP IS A STRUCTURED OBJECT metaphor. As the examples below suggest, the structured object may be essentially three things: a building, an implement, or a machine. We begin with the "building" and "implement" versions. First let us see some examples from our corpus:

The two campers *formed* a lasting friendship. They *created* their friendship through the mail.
Even if you have another relationship with somebody else, that

wouldn't in any way intrude or *destroy* the relationship which *you built*.

Friendship is something *stable which will not go away*. Their friendship was *as strong as steel*. My mother's high school friendships are still as *strong as they were 40 years ago*.

These examples suggest the following basic source domain ontology: there are the people building the house (or making the implement), the building (or implement) itself, and the activity of building (or making). In the target domain, we have the two people who are in the process of becoming friends, the friendship itself, and the process or activity of forming the friendship. This situation gives us the following ontological mappings, or correspondences:

- the people building the house are the friends forming the friendship
- the house or building (or the object) is the friendship
- the building of the house is the forming of the friendship/the bringing into existence of the friendship
- the strength (weakness) of the building is the stability (instability) of the friendship

We have a great deal of knowledge about friendship based on these mappings:

S: Certain things can destroy the building.
T: Certain things can cause the friendship to end.
      The friendship was *shattered* due to neglect.

S: Building a house is difficult.
T: Forming a friendship is difficult.
S: It is easy to break an object.
T: It is easy to ruin a friendship.
      Friendships are *hard to make* and *easy to break*.

S: It takes a long time to build a house.
T: It takes a long time to form a friendship.
      It *takes time to build* a friendship.

S: It is hard work to build a house.
T: It is hard work to form a friendship.
S: Buildings can be strong or weak. A strong house is better.
T: Friendships can be stable or unstable. A stable friendship is better.

It *takes a lot to build a strong* friendship. We are *working on making* our friendship *stronger*.
Their friendship seems *very shaky*

As we have seen, the STRUCTURED OBJECT (BUILDING, IMPLEMENT) metaphor's main focus is on the various aspects of forming a friendship and the stability of the relationship that is formed. Marriage (Quinn, 1987, 1991) and love (Kövecses, 1988; Baxter, 1992) relationships also take this metaphor. But it extends much beyond the emotion domain. We find it in the conceptualization of argument, theories, and society. The main orientation of the BUILDING (and IMPLEMENT) metaphor seems to be the creation, the making of strong arguments, theories, and society. Arguments may be *"solid,"* may *"fall apart,"* are *"constructed,"* et cetera (Lakoff and Johnson, 1980, p. 98). Theories are also *"constructed,"* can be *"strong"* or *"shaky,"* can *"collapse"* or *"fall apart,"* and so forth. (Lakoff and Johnson, 1980, p. 46). We also *"build"* societies, which may have *"strong or weak foundations"* and may *"fall down."* All of these examples seem to be based on the mapping according to which the building of a strong physical object is the construction/creation of a strong abstract entity.

Friendship as a Machine

The MACHINE metaphor is primarily concerned with the functional aspects of friendship.

FRIENDSHIP IS A MACHINE
His friendship with Joe *was off and on.*
A friendship is so special that *to get* that (friendship) connection *going is tough.*
Honesty is vital to a *working* friendship.

The basic source domain ontology includes the people operating the machine, the machine itself, the working of the machine, and the starting and the turning off of the machine. In the target, we have the two friends, the friendship itself, and the functioning of the friendship. Here are the mappings in some detail:

- the people operating the machine are the people involved in the friendship
- the machine is the friendship

- the proper working of the machine is the proper functioning of the friendship
- the working of the machine is the functioning of the friendship
- the breakdown of the machine is the breakdown of the friendship

Again, a great deal of knowledge is derived from the mappings:

S: After a breakdown, the machine can be repaired.
T: After a breakdown, the relationship can be repaired.
   The test of friendship is something that *can be repaired*, you have to *work that out*.

S: It is possible for the machine not to work for a while and then start working again.
T: It is possible for the friendship not to function for a while and then start functioning again.
   You can *start up* after a break.

S: To keep a structured object functional requires hard work and a great deal of attention.
T: To maintain a friendship requires hard work and a great deal of attention.
   It's not just that we possess or have friends. We have *to work hard at it*. Friendship *requires a level of care and attention for its maintenance*.

S: A machine that has been in use for a long time works well without much maintenance work.
T: A long-established friendship functions well without much maintenance work.
   In the kind of friendship involving my very *long-established* friend I feel as if *I don't have to work very much. I didn't have to work at renewing anything* because it *was continuing and always was*.

According to the MACHINE metaphor, friendship is a relationship that may be functional or dysfunctional and functioning (active) or non-functioning (inactive). This metaphor also applies to love (Kövecses, 1988; Baxter, 1992) and marriage (Quinn, 1987, 1991) relationships. When the relationship is functional *and* it is functioning, it can do the things it is supposed to do: help people solve their problems, help people help each other, allow people to enjoy each other, and so forth. In addition to these applications, it is also utilized in the understanding of such concepts as the mind, body, and society. Three out of Lakoff and Johnson's (1980) five examples of the MIND IS A MACHINE metaphor have to do with the functionality of the mind: "My mind just isn't *operating* today," "Boy, the *wheels are turning* now!" and "I'm *a little rusty* today" (p. 27). The same can be said of the BODY IS A MACHINE metaphor, as illustrated by "I just *can't get myself going* this morning," "You will *break down*," "My body *isn't working*," and many of the examples that Lakoff (1987, pp. 410–411) cites for the LUSTFUL PERSON IS A FUNCTIONING MACHINE metaphor. In connection with society, people talk about how societies *work or don't work*, about *smooth running* societies, about the *monkey wrench in the works*, and so on. In all of these cases, there is a prevalence of the notion of functionality in some form that seems to derive from the mapping "physical functioning is abstract functioning."

Buildings, machines, and implements all have functions. I will now discuss the aspect of function in friendship in relation to some examples that involve metaphors other than those of BUILDING and MACHINE.

Friendship as a Special Implement

Friendship may be a means of achieving life goals. This showed up in examples such as "Friendship *makes the path* of life a little bit *smoother*." Here the implement that makes it easier for people to reach their destinations (that is, the implement that makes the road smoother) is the friendship that helps them achieve life goals. The property of helping people reach their destinations is especially important in the LIFE IS JOURNEY metaphor in relation to friendship, since life is seen as a difficult journey – a special case of trial: "[A friend] is someone who *will be there* and you can depend upon. Someone *who will be there to help you through* bad times – not just someone who wants to go out and have fun." The difficult journey is often a journey by sea: "When things *get turbulent*, your friend is there *to calm* you" and "True friendship is a bond that *can weather the storms* of life." The JOURNEY and TRIAL metaphors often appear together in the interviews:

> It's easier to relate to someone who has a lifestyle and demands on their time similar to your own . . . [;] they can more understand your problems, just what you're *going through* a little better than someone who lives a different lifestyle. Someone who's *gone through* the same *trials and tribulations*.

The extent to which friends are expected to help each other achieve their life goals (that is, overcome obstacles along the journey) can be seen in the large number of examples produced by informants and the explicitness with which the idea was presented. Here are some *non-metaphorical* ones: "She definitely has a feeling of responsibility if her friends were in trouble. She is committed to caring and nurturing aspects of friendship"; "I have a pal and I would help him in the middle of the night if he needed help"; "There is no true friendship without self-sacrifice"; and the proverbial "A friend in need is a friend indeed."

Just as in the case of communication metaphors, we find that people comprehend the concept of friendship in terms of metaphors that are completely conventionalized for the understanding of other domains in the metaphorical system of English. However, here again, there is something that is specific to friendship concerning the LIFE IS A JOURNEY metaphor. It is the particular "framing" of what the journey is like in relation to friendship. As we have just seen, it is A DIFFICULT JOURNEY. The metaphors FRIENDSHIP IS A STRUCTURED OBJECT and LIFE IS A DIFFICULT JOURNEY jointly define the major function of friendship: for people who are friends to help each other. This arises from how a STRUCTURED OBJECT, an implement, helps people move along a path that is difficult.

The particular framing of LIFE'S JOURNEY as difficult is important for the understanding of friendship. It provides a specific background against which people comprehend friendship. The kind of life that underlies people's conception of friendship is a *difficult* one in which people who are friends are supposed to help each other.

Friendship as a Living Organism

The LIVING ORGANISM metaphor highlights the developmental aspects of friendship: its beginning, development, and possible ending.

FRIENDSHIP IS A LIVING ORGANISM
Friendships can *grow out of* colleague relationships.
True friendship is a *plant of slow growth*. Friendships take time *to develop*.
Our friendship *matured with time*.
The *birth* of friendship is *slow*. Our friendship *died* as suddenly as it had started. *The days* of our friendship *are numbered*.

The mappings in ontology are as follows:

- the living organism is the friendship
- the life of the organism is the existence of friendship
- the growth of the organism is the development of the friendship
- the birth (death) of the organism is the beginning (ending) of the friendship
- the health (illness) of the organism is the functionality (disfunctionality) of the friendship

The knowledge based on these mappings includes:

S: The growth of the organism is slow.
T: The development of the friendship is slow.
   True friendship is a *plant of slow growth*. Friendships take time *to develop*.

S: An organism can grow out of another organism.
T: A friendship can develop from another relationship.
   Friendships can *grow out of* colleague relationships.

S: The organism needs to be nurtured.
T: The friendship needs to be nurtured.
   Close friendships involve simple *nurturing things* such as giving one another a massage.
   Janet chose *to foster* friendship. Friendship *is not to be neglected*.

S: A strong organism may survive under extreme conditions.
T: The existence of a strong friendship may continue under extreme conditions.
   Pen pals prove that friendship can *survive* vast distance.
   No friendship can *survive* when all the giving is from one side.

In the LIVING ORGANISM (especially a PLANT) metaphor, friendship is seen as something that begins to develop at some point; that can develop out of another relationship; that develops slowly; that may be delicate at first and may have to be nurtured, but then can develop into a stable relationship that can survive adverse conditions. The same general characterization seems to be applicable to love and marriage, as indicated by the work of the authors cited above in connection with these relationships. The LIVING ORGANISM metaphor also extends to ideas/theories, society, feelings, and emotions. Consider some examples by Lakoff and Johnson (1980, p. 47): "His ideas have finally come to *fruition*," "That idea *died on the vine*," "That's a *budding* theory," "It will take years for that idea to *come to full flower*." The main theme here is the notion of abstract development and its various properties, which in turn derive metaphorically from the notion of physical growth and its characteristics. As regards the concept of society, our national economy may *grow*, there may be undesirable *growths to be gotten rid of* in the society, a society may *flourish* – all suggesting ideas having to do with stages and properties of a society's development. Similarly, my emotions may *wilt* and *whither*, may *grow* and *die*, and I may *foster* and *nourish* my feelings. It seems then that the variety of metaphors that involve a LIVING ORGANISM all center around the notion of development as based on the concept of physical growth.

To summarize, the COMPLEX SYSTEMS metaphor consists of a number of fairly general submappings. These submappings are expressed by two common conceptual metaphors: COMPLEX SYSTEMS ARE STRUCTURED OBJECTS and COMPLEX SYSTEMS ARE LIVING ORGANISMS. The special cases of these metaphors overlap to some degree in what they focus on, as we have seen especially in the discussion of epistemic correspondences. For example, maintenance work is an aspect of buildings, implements, machines, and even plants. However, the various specific-level source domains (building, machine, et cetera) tend to focus on different aspects of complex systems. Thus the BUILDING metaphor is primarily concerned with constructing a friendship and its stability, the MACHINE metaphor with the functionality of friendship, and the PLANT metaphor with the developmental aspects of friendship.

The "Positive/Negative Evaluation" System

It would be tempting to suggest that the VALUABLE COMMODITY metaphor that can also be found in the data is another instance of the COMPLEX SYSTEMS metaphor. After all, we could say, valuable commodities are complex objects in the same way that buildings, machines, and the like are. However, the VALUABLE COMMODITY metaphor does not seem to share any mappings with the COMPLEX SYSTEMS metaphor, as we will see below. Instead, the VALUABLE COMMODITY metaphor appears to be a chief metaphor for anything that is desirable. Thus, it seems more reasonable to take the metaphor FRIENDSHIP IS A VALUABLE COMMODITY to be a special case of the DESIRABLE IS VALUABLE (or DESIRABLE THINGS ARE VALUABLE COMMODITIES) metaphor.

Friendship as a Valuable Commodity

Friendship is seen as a very positive relationship. When people talk about their attitude to friendship, they do so by relying on the VALU-ABLE COMMODITY metaphor:

FRIENDSHIP IS A VALUABLE COMMODITY
Richard *valued* Rebecca's friendship more than anything else in the world. I *treasure* my friendship with Alaina.
Friendship is *like china, costly and rare.* Good friendships are *rare and worth saving.*
Friends ultimately might be *more valuable* and more enduring than love relationships.
Friendships are *more valuable than priceless jewels.* The friendship of good neighbors is *precious.*

The correspondences or mappings that reveal the precise nature of the relationship between FRIENDSHIP and VALUABLE COMMODITY are the following:

- the people who have the valuable commodity are the friends
- the valuable commodity is the friendship
- the high value of the commodity is the high desirability/worth of the friendship

The VALUABLE COMMODITY metaphor can also be found in concepts like love and marriage, that is, other positive human relationships ("I *treasure* this relationship very much," which can apply to either love or marriage). This metaphor extends to additional concepts, such as ideas and people. In IDEAS ARE (VALUABLE) COMMODITIES, we get examples like "There is always a *market* for good ideas," "That's a *worthless* idea," "He has been a source of *valuable* ideas," "Your ideas don't have a chance in the *intellectual marketplace,*" and so forth (Lakoff and Johnson, 1980). People are also assumed to have a value or worth. In *Emotion Concepts* (1990, p. 112), I provide examples including "He proved his *worth* to everyone," "She *values* him *highly,*" "She felt an *appreciation for* her parents," "The Giants *traded* Jones *for* Smith," et cetera. Furthermore, actions, states, and properties can be viewed as having value. This gives us the STATES OF AFFAIRS ARE COMMODITIES metaphor (Kövecses, 1990, pp. 96–97). Examples include "That was a *valuable* victory," "His paper *isn't worth* looking at," "The *value* of her work is tremendous," and so on. It appears then that our entire out-look on the world is embedded in the COMMODITY metaphor whose main theme is the worth and, hence, desirability of "things." This is captured by the mapping: commercial or economic value is intellec-tual/moral/emotional worth and desirability.

In the light of this use of the VALUABLE COMMODITY metaphor, I would suggest that there operates in English (and probably in other languages as well) an extremely general metaphor which factors "things" (states, events, entities, et cetera) into two opposite catego-ries: positive and negative. It is the DESIRABLE IS VALUABLE (and NON-DESIRABLE IS WORTHLESS) metaphor. Since friendship is viewed as a very desirable state, a special case of this very general metaphor, FRIENDSHIP IS A VALUABLE COMMODITY, also applies.

The "Event" System

As we have seen, friendship can be a means of achieving other life goals. It can also be a life goal itself. Long-term goals in life are com-monly captured in terms of the (PURPOSEFUL) LIFE IS A JOURNEY meta-phor (see Lakoff, 1993). When friendship is a life goal, people rely on this metaphor. For example, one subject came up with the following example: "It is worthy to *pass* all life *in the search after* friendship." In the LIFE IS A JOURNEY metaphor, life is viewed as a progression "along the path of life." The progression along the path of life corresponds to leading a life. Since any state, not just friendship, can be a life goal, this application of the LIFE IS A JOURNEY metaphor is less interesting concerning friendship.

In an earlier section, I mentioned another application of this meta-phor. This was a case where LIFE IS A (DIFFICULT) JOURNEY served as the background to the understanding of the specific function of friend-ship (i.e., to help people achieve their life goals). The use of the LIFE IS A JOURNEY metaphor for friendship (in either application) could be expected to lead to a FRIENDSHIP IS A JOURNEY metaphor, given the inheritance hierarchy of the Event Structure metaphor (see Lakoff, 1993). Indeed, some informants produced examples that suggest the existence of a JOURNEY metaphor for friendship. But the number of examples was small and to some other native speakers not always convincing. They included the following: "Their friendship *has come a long way*," "Their friendship *has traveled some rough roads*," "Our friendship is *on shaky ground*," "Our friendship *has seen many waters*,"

"Their friendship *is on the rocks.*" No matter how marginal this metaphor is in the data (in comparison with data about love and marriage, for instance), it shows that, for some people at least, friendship forms a part of another large metaphorical system – the EVENT STRUCTURE metaphor. That is, together with other target domains, friendship inherits a set of mappings (the JOURNEY metaphor) from a high-level target domain of which it is a part.

But the mappings are not complete. What is especially interesting about the examples people produced is that they do not make use of expressions like *going somewhere* (e.g., "This relationship isn't *going anywhere*") and *dead-end street* (e.g., "This relationship is a *dead-end street*") that are characteristic of, for instance, love (Lakoff and Johnson, 1980, pp. 44–45). *Going somewhere* and *dead-end street* are concerned with purposes. Friendship, unlike love, does not seem to have a clear purposive aspect (although it has a function). It makes more sense for people to talk about the purpose of love than the purpose of friendship. The property of friendship that it is not associated with a clear purpose overrides the inheritance by friendship of the PURPOSES ARE DESTINATIONS submapping in the JOURNEY metaphors.

The Metaphorical Structure of Emotions and Human Relationships

The linguistic data on which this study was based indicate that there are a large number of conceptual metaphors that apply to the American conception of friendship. The analysis of these metaphors also showed that they come from a small number of metaphorical systems: Communication, Emotion, State, Complex Systems, Event, and Positive/Negative Evaluation.

In each of these systems, we have a complex abstract concept as target domain and a simpler, nonabstract concept as a source domain. Communication is understood as the sharing of physical objects; emotions as physical phenomena (e.g., properties of physical objects); states as physical objects; complex systems as complex physical objects; events as physical motion; and the property of being positive or negative as value or lack of value.

Now we are in position to attempt to answer the question how the metaphorical conceptualization of emotion differs from that of human relationships, like friendship, love, and marriage. As regards the level of specific metaphors, we have found a rich and diverse set of source domains for both emotions and human relationships. As we have seen in this and the foregoing chapters, the specific-level metaphors that can be found in the conceptualization of most emotions and most human relationships include the following:

Emotions
Internal pressure
Opponent in a struggle
Wild animal
Social superior
Natural force (wave, wind, flood)
Trickster/Deceiver
Insanity
Fire/heat
Hunger
Physical agitation
Burden
Mechanical force
Electric force
Gravitational force
Magnetic force

Human relationships
Sharing (experience) objects
Distance (close/distant)
Warmth
Bond
Economic exchange
Building
Implement
Machine
Plant
Journey
Valuable commodity

This is not a complete set of specific source domains for either the emotions or human relationships. As I have already shown, in addition to the ones listed above, there are some source domains that apply to states in general – hence to both emotions and relationships (such as EXISTENCE IS PRESENCE, STATES ARE BOUNDED REGIONS, etc.). Furthermore, there are specific-level source domains that apply only to particular emotions or relationships (such as EMBARRASSMENT IS HAVING NO CLOTHES ON, ANGER IS TRESPASSING, LOVE IS WAR, LOVE IS A GAME, MARRIAGE IS A PRISON, etc.). Metaphorical source domains such as these are not considered in the list because they cannot be regarded as typical or characteristic of emotions and human relationships in general.

Taking the lists above as a representative set of source domains for emotions and relationships, we can make some interesting observations. There seems to be only a minimal overlap between the two sets. Human relationships share CLOSENESS and WARMTH with emotions. BURDEN from the emotion set may perhaps also apply to relationships since it has the general meaning orientation of indicating any difficulty or stress. When characteristic emotion metaphors, that is, the FORCE-related ones, apply to human relationships, they usually have to do with love only – a human relationship that is also an emotion. This is why we have found only marginal cases of FORCE metaphors for friendship, which is, as studies show, regarded as a poor case of emotion. (It may be that some of the debate concerning whether love is or is not an emotion, or whether it is a basic emotion, is also attributable to this "double-nature" of love.) In her study of love, Baxter (1992) found that FORCE metaphors form the third largest group of metaphors for love, following metaphors related to WORK and JOURNEY. In our terms, it is the COMPLEX SYSTEMS metaphor that involves all the work-related aspects of friendship and relationships in general.

But the really important point is that, as we saw in the previous chapter, the emotion metaphors are predominantly "force-related" metaphors organized into a coherent system by the underlying master metaphor EMOTION IS FORCE. What is obvious at first glance is that the typical relationship metaphors are *not* FORCE metaphors (with the exception of love, as we noted). The question is: Is there a master metaphor underlying the various specific-level nonforce metaphors for human relationships? JOURNEY seems to be a crucially important metaphor in the conceptualization of love and marriage, as the studies by Baxter and Quinn indicate. However, it appears to play only a marginal role in the comprehension of friendship. The source domains for friendship on the list above that belong to robust metaphorical systems in our conception of relationships are: INTERACTIVE RELATIONSHIPS and COMPLEX SYSTEMS. The category of INTERACTIVE RELATIONSHIPS is a conflation of what I called the "communication system" and the "state" system, respectively. The "state" system, as characterized above, includes states, relationships, and interactions. The metaphors for communication as analyzed above indicate that communication is viewed as a form of interaction, and as such it fits the INTERACTIVE RELATIONSHIP group naturally. The rest of the metaphorical source domains, such as BUILDING, IMPLEMENT, et cetera, form the COMPLEX SYSTEMS group, as has been shown in this chapter.

The evidence we have seen thus far points to the conclusion that it is these two large systems that organize most of our everyday understanding of what human relationships are. The bulk of the data presented here shows that much of the content and structure of our knowledge about relationships derives from the rich set of mappings that characterize the two systems. In this sense, we seem to have two underlying generic-level metaphors for human relationships: INTERACTIVE RELATIONSHIPS ARE ECONOMIC EXCHANGES and COMPLEX SYSTEMS ARE COMPLEX PHYSICAL OBJECTS. Of the two, the latter appears to be the more pervasive and dominant one, and thus, again in this sense, it can be regarded as the "master metaphor" for human relationships.

We can now ask how emotions are related to human relationships in the light of the two sets of metaphor that characterize the two domains. In the folk theory of the relationship between the two, human relationships are based on emotions. Emotions are regarded as the foundations on which human relationships are built. To take a real life example, let me quote from a set of interviews conducted by Daphne Guericke about marriage in America (Guericke, 1991):

> I think it's more of an affirmation that I did make the right decision, that he's just such a great person. I feel that we have a *solid foundation* and *have built on that.* There's little things on a day-to-day basis too and I say, golly, I'm so lucky, I can't believe – I didn't realize how much I really did love him. (Appendix, interview with Heather, p. 1)

In this case, the emotion is love and the human relationship of marriage is built on it. This way of thinking involves the generic-level metaphor RELATIONSHIPS IN GENERAL ARE BUILDINGS. This metaphor applies to any kind of relationship, not just human relationships. In the two sets of metaphors under consideration, the entities that participate in the relationship are EMOTIONS and HUMAN RELATIONSHIPS. The mappings are as follows: the emotions correspond to the foundations and human relationships correspond to the upper structure of the building. The foundation can be thought of as a forceful entity that supports another entity (the building). The upper structure can be thought of as a complex object with several parts (the building). This way the two sets of metaphors "meet." Since emotions are primarily forces and human relationships are primarily complex objects, the metaphor RELATIONSHIPS IN GENERAL ARE BUILDING provides a natural "meeting point" for the two master metaphors EMOTIONS ARE FORCES and HUMAN RELATIONSHIPS ARE COMPLEX OBJECTS.

This does not mean, however, that the relationship between emotions and relationships is only thought about in such passive terms. Another conceptualization of the "based-on" relationship between the two is more active. Steve Duck, a leading researcher in the field of human relationships, writes: "Aside from the *feelings* of love that drive us into relationships . . ." [italics in the original] (Duck, 1986, p. 8). Love is here viewed as an emotion that can establish a human relationship of some kind. In this case, the general metaphor for relationships is something like: A DYNAMIC RELATIONSHIP BETWEEN TWO ENTITIES IS A PHYSICAL FORCE ACTING ON ANOTHER. In the example, it is a driver that drives another living entity, but it can be almost any number of forceful entities acting on others.

Conclusion

If the analysis I have presented above concerning the two divergent sets of metaphors is correct, it reveals dramatic differences in the conceptualization of emotions versus that of human relationships. The sweeping forces of emotion stand in stark contrast to the "more rational" handling of complex physical objects, like buildings, machines, and plants, which amount to what I called the COMPLEX SYSTEMS metaphor. This conclusion concerning a potential underlying master metaphor for human relationships seems to be supported by the work of Baxter and Quinn as well.

7. Folk Versus Expert Theories of Emotion

A major goal of the approach that I have tried to develop in this book is to reveal not just how people talk but also how they think about their emotions. This means that I have a great deal of interest in the folk understandings of emotions. (These understandings are variously called folk theories/models, cultural models, or idealized cognitive models by different authors; see Holland and Quinn, 1987.) Folk understandings can be thought of as knowledge structures in our conceptual system. By a folk theory or cultural model I will mean some shared, structured knowledge that in many cases can be uncovered on the basis of ordinary language. Scientific, or expert, theories will simply be viewed here as the theories that experts, such as psychologists, philosophers, and the like, construct to account for a given area of experience (in our case, the emotions). Some well-known expert theories of emotion include Darwin's, James's, and Schacter and Singer's, to mention just a few.

What is it that people know about their emotions? This is important to uncover, but not only because so many aspects of our everyday lives depend on how we answer the question. Another reason is that if we find this out, we can begin to explore some of the complexities that exist in the relationship between folk theories and expert theories.

Most important of the issues that arise in this connection is whether and how the people who create our expert theories of emotion can free themselves from the folk theories that they obviously share with other members of their culture (in their "role" as lay people). Is this possible to do at all in the field of emotion? Or, is it something that we should do at all? As a matter of fact, there exists the view that our cultural models of emotion are quite good because they are time-tested, and so they should not be abandoned. Even more generally, some scholars claim that expert psychology is just a version of folk psychology. I will return to this issue toward the end of the chapter.

I cannot promise to provide a final and definitive answer to these questions, but I will try to isolate and outline the kinds of things that need to be considered for an informed attempt to tackle them. But before we begin to investigate this issue, we have to be clear about the nature of folk or cultural models themselves. In particular, we have to see whether the folk or cultural models for abstract concepts (such as emotions and human relationships) are conceptually literal or metaphorically constituted.

The Role of Metaphor in Cultural Models

Quinn (1991) suggests that, contrary to a claim made by Lakoff and Kövecses (1987), metaphor simply *reflects* cultural models. In contrast, Lakoff and Kövecses, using the concept of anger, claim that metaphors largely *constitute* the cultural model, or naive understanding of anger, as based on their study of American English. Implicit in Quinn's claim that metaphors simply reflect preexisting cultural models are two very important further claims: One is that abstract concepts can be understood in a literal way, and the other is that the core of culture consists of literally understood cultural models (for both concrete and abstract concepts).

The first claim arises from the fact that Quinn's generalization is based on the examination of such abstract concepts as anger and marriage. Quinn suggests that concepts such as marriage are understood literally by people. The concept of marriage is one of several other concepts indicating human relationships. Furthermore, she seems to think that anger, a prototypical emotion concept, can also be literally understood. Both concepts of human relationships and emotions are prime examples of abstract concepts. Indeed, Quinn (1991, pp. 64–65) makes a more general claim about abstract concepts: "While I certainly agree that metaphors play some role in the way we comprehend and draw inferences about abstract concepts, I take issue with the claim that they or the schemas on which they are said to be founded actually constitute the concepts." A little earlier in the paper she states: "I will be arguing that metaphors, *far from* constituting understanding, are *ordinarily* selected to fit a preexisting and culturally shared model" (p. 60; my emphasis).

This is a general claim about the nature of the human conceptual system. My discussion will focus on this particular issue. I will have nothing to say about the second assumption; namely, that the core of culture consists of literally understood cultural models. As regards this claim, I refer the reader to Bradd Shore's work (Shore, 1996), who claims, contrary to Quinn, that even the most basic notions of a culture may be metaphorically constituted. Gibbs (1994) provides additional criticism of Quinn's challenge.

In Quinn's view, the American conception of marriage can be characterized by a set of expectations: marriage is expected to be shared, mutually beneficial, and lasting (p. 67). She points out, furthermore:

> that this particular constellation of expectations derives from the mapping of our cultural conception of love onto the institution of marriage and the consequent structuring of marital expectations in terms of the motivational structure of love. Because people want to be with the person they love, they want and expect marriage to be shared; because they want to fulfill the loved person's needs and have their own needs fulfilled by that person, they want and expect marriage to be beneficial to both spouses in the sense of mutually fulfilling; and because they do not want to lose the person they love, but want that person to go on loving them forever, people want and expect their marriages to be lasting. (p. 67)

In this view, marriage takes over several properties of love, which then come to define it. The question of course becomes: Where does the abstract concept of love come from? Does it emerge literally or metaphorically? Quinn's answer is straightforward. It emerges literally from certain basic experiences, and then these experiences will structure marriage. The particular basic experiences that Quinn suggests the American conception of love and marriage derives from involve early infantile experiences between baby and the first caretaker. Here is the relevant passage:

> I speculate that the motivational constellation that is part of our understanding of love and that provides marriage with its structure itself makes sense in psychoanalytic terms. Psychoanalysts since Freud, who characterized adult love as a "re-finding" of infantile love for the first caretaker, have theorized about the relation between the two. My claim is that Americans' distinctive conception of marriage takes the particular shape it does and has the force it does for us because of the cultural model of love mapped onto marriage and, thus, indirectly because of an infantile experience that Americans have shared and that underpins our conception of adult love. (p. 67)

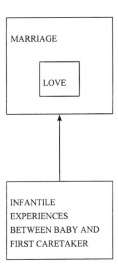

Figure 7.1. Quinn's view of the emergence of the abstract concept of marriage

The picture that Quinn paints of the emergence of the concept of marriage appears in Figure 7.1. The main point here is that no metaphor is needed for abstract concepts to emerge. The expectational structure of marriage derives from the motivational structure of love, which in turn derives from the basic infantile experience between baby and first caretaker.

Quinn, then, goes on to say that marriage has some additional aspects. In her own words again, "The remainder of the cultural model of marriage reflected in the metaphors for marital compatibility, difficulty, effort, success or failure, and risk, derives from a contradiction that arises inevitably between the expectations of mutual benefit and that of lastingness." (p. 67) She argues further that in voluntary relationships, if one's needs are not fulfilled one is free to leave the relationship. However, marriage is special in this respect: it is supposed to last. She adds, "A variety of situations can initiate a felt contradiction between the expectation of marital fulfillment and that of a lasting marriage."

If we characterize the essence of marriage, as Quinn does, as a set of expectations that can be viewed as being literal, Quinn's major claim stands: The core of the concept of marriage is literal, hence metaphors do not play a constitutive role in its understanding. More generally, abstract concepts such as marriage can exist without metaphors constituting them.

However, I believe that this analysis is incomplete and problematic. The problem is that we cannot take the expectational structure of marriage to be literal. I will claim below that in general abstract concepts can emerge from basic experiences through the mediation of metaphor only.

Let us now see what an alternative metaphor-based explanation would be like. We can begin by observing that in her discussion it remains unclear whether Quinn equates the expectational structure of marriage with the concept of marriage itself. Nowhere does she describe or define marriage itself in terms other than its "expectational structure." This leads one to believe that marriage is conceptualized by people in terms of this structure only. But is it? Don't people have an idea of what marriage is before they have an expectational structure of it? One would think that they do, yet this aspect of the concept of marriage does not show up in the paper. Marriage is presented by Quinn as an expectational structure, and all the other aspects of it that she discusses, such as compatibility, difficulty, effort, success and failure, and risk, are given as consequences of this structure. What, then, does the notion of marriage consist of before it acquires its particular expectational structure?

First and foremost, marriage is some kind of abstract union between two people. To illustrate this conception, consider some definitions of marriage in a sample of American dictionaries:

> **marriage 1** the state of being married; relation between husband and wife; married life; wedlock; matrimony **4** any close or intimate union (*Webster's New World Dictionary*, Third College Edition)
> **marry 1 a** to join as husband and wife; unite in wedlock **b** to join (a man) to a woman as her husband, or (a woman) to a man as his wife **vi. 2** to enter into a close or intimate relationship; unite (*Webster's New World Dictionary*, Third College Edition)
> **marriage 1 a:** the state of being married **b:** the mutual relationship of husband and wife; wedlock **c:** the institution whereby men and women are joined in a special kind of social and legal dependence for the purpose of founding and maintaining a family (*Webster's Ninth New Collegiate Dictionary*)
> **marry 1 a:** to join as husband and wife according to law or custom **2** to unite in close and usu. permanent relation **vi 2** to enter into a close or intimate union (these wines – well) (*Webster's Ninth New Collegiate Dictionary*)
> **marriage 1. a.** The state of being husband and wife; wedlock **b.** The legal union of man and woman as husband and wife (*The Heritage Illustrated Dictionary*)

marry 1. a. To become united with in matrimony (*The Heritage Illustrated Dictionary*)
married 1. United in matrimony *(Funk & Wagnalls Standard Dictionary)*

As these dictionary definitions show, a major component of the concept of marriage is the – legal, social, emotional, and so forth – union of two people. This seems to be a large part of the notion that is prior to the expectational structure associated with marriage. In other words, the prototypical, or stereotypical, idea of marriage must include the notion that it is an abstract union of various kinds between two people.

As Quinn suggests, the concept of marriage is structured by a mapping of the American cultural conception of love. However, she finds this only in the expectational structure of marriage. But now we can see additional structure in marriage that derives from love. This is the notion of unity involving two people. As I showed in *The Language of Love* (1988) and "A Linguist's Quest for Love" (1991), the concept of romantic love is, in large measure, understood and structured by the metaphor LOVE IS A UNITY OF TWO COMPLEMENTARY PARTS, as can be found in expressions like *"You belong to me and I belong to you," "Theirs is a perfect fit," "We're as one," "She's my better half," "They broke up," "They're inseparable,"* and *"They match each other perfectly."* It is largely the functional unity of two physical parts that may serve as the source domain for the abstract target concept of marriage. But more generally, our understanding of nonphysical – social, legal, emotional, spiritual, psychological, et cetera – unions derives from physical or biological unions. This is a perfectly regular way in which human beings conceptualize and, by conceptualizing, also build their nonphysical world. (The same regular process is at work in many other cases, as I have shown elsewhere; see Kövecses, 1998.)

In other words, in the terminology of the view of metaphor that Lakoff and Johnson (1980) initiated, we have the conceptual metaphor NONPHYSICAL UNITY IS PHYSICAL UNITY. (It is significant that the etymological root of the words *union* and *unity* is the Latin word *unus* meaning "one.") This is the metaphor that underlies our conception of various social, legal, psychological, sexual, political, emotional, and so on, unities and explains the use of such expressions as *"to join* forces," "the *merging* of bodies," "the *unification* of Europe," "to be at *one with* the world," "a *union* of minds," "a deep spiritual *union with* God," et cetera. Obviously, the metaphor also applies to marriage as a nonphysical unity between two people. Some examples from the above dictionary definitions include "*to join* in marriage," "a marriage *union*," "the legal *union* of man and woman," and "*to be united* in matrimony"; hence the metaphor MARRIAGE IS A PHYSICAL AND/OR BIOLOGICAL UNITY OF TWO PARTS. Not surprisingly, we find examples of this metaphor in the data that Quinn presents. She names what we call the MARRIAGE IS A PHYSICAL AND/OR BIOLOGICAL UNITY metaphor "two inseparable objects," as in *We knew we were going to stay together* and "an unbreakable bond," as in *That just kind of cements the bond* (p. 68).

At this point it might be objected that my analysis is largely based on dictionary data and that Americans may not conceptualize marriage according to the unity metaphor. We have some evidence that they do. However, the evidence is only indirect and comes from a set of interviews that a student of mine, Ted Sablay, conducted concerning romantic love in the summer of 1996 at the University of Nevada, Las Vegas. The interview subjects were seven male and seven female students from roughly the same white middle-class background. What the interviews reveal about romantic love should be taken seriously in dealing with marriage because, as Quinn herself claims, marriage is in many ways structured by our understanding of love. In his report on the project, Ted Sablay found that the most frequent metaphor for love is the unity metaphor for his interview subjects. This gives us some reason to believe that, at least for some Americans, the conception of marriage is still built on the idea of forming a unity with another and that this notion is not just an antiquated dictionary definition.

What is the relationship between the idea of marriage-as-a-nonphysical-unity and the expectational structure of marriage that Quinn describes? We can suggest that the conception of marriage as a unity between two people is the basis, or the foundation, of its expectational structure; namely, that marriage is expected to be shared, beneficial, and lasting. The reason that marriage is expected to be all these things is that it is conceptualized as a unity of a particular kind: the physical unity of two complementary parts, which yields the metaphor MARRIAGE IS THE PHYSICAL AND/OR BIOLOGICAL UNITY OF TWO COMPLEMENTARY PARTS. The details of the UNITY metaphor for marriage can be given as a set of mappings:

1. the two physical parts   → the married people
2. the physical joining of the   → the union of the two people in
   parts   marriage

3. the physical/biological unity	→	the marriage union
4. the physical fit between the parts	→	the compatibility between the married people
5. the physical functions of the parts in the unity	→	the roles the married people play in the relationship
6. the complementariness of the functions of the parts	→	the complementariness of the roles of the married people
7. the whole physical object consisting of the parts	→	the marriage relationship
8. the function of the whole object	→	the role or purpose of the marriage relationship

What we have here is a source domain in which there are two parts that fit each other and form a whole, where the particular functions of the parts complement each other and the parts make up a larger unity that has a function (or functions). It is this structure that appears in the way we think about marriage. The relationship between two people in marriage can only be conceived as a metaphorical unity. This way of conceptualizing marriage is simply a special case of the larger process whereby nonphysical unities in general are constituted on the analogy of more physical ones.

This metaphorically structured understanding of marriage forms a definition of marriage and provides its expectational structure. The definition could be given as follows: "Marriage is a union of two people who are compatible with each other. The two people perform different but complementary roles in the relationship. Their union serves a purpose (or purposes) in life." This is, of course, a generic-level definition that can be filled out with specific details in individual cases.

The expectational structure arises from the definition in the following way: Because a part by itself is not functional, people want to share their lives with others in marriage. Because only one or some parts fit another part, people want compatible partners in marriage. Because (to get a functioning whole) a part must perform its designated function, people want to fulfill their designated roles in a marriage relationship. Because wholes have a designated function to perform, marriage relationships must be lasting.

As can be seen, this is similar to Quinn's expectational structure. One difference, though, is that in our characterization compatibility is a mapping in the UNITY metaphor, while in hers it is a consequence that follows from the expectational structure. Another difference is more substantial. It is that we have given the expectational structure of marriage as a consequence of a certain metaphorical understanding of marriage, one that is based on the metaphor NONPHYSICAL UNITY IS PHYSICAL UNITY. It is in this sense that I claim that the concept of marriage is metaphorically constituted.

In sum, what Quinn calls the expectational structure results from a certain metaphorical understanding of marriage. Thus, marriage is not a literally conceived abstract concept, although the metaphor that yields the expectational structure is based on certain bodily experiences.

The Language of Love and Scientific Theories

What is love? Can we give it a "scientific" definition? Can we define it at all? Shouldn't we best view it as a mystic experience that defies attempts at definitions?

In an attempt to answer these questions, I suggested that emotion concepts such as love are best viewed as being constituted by a large number of cognitive models centered around a small number of (or just one) prototypical model(s). The conceptual content of the various cognitive models, especially that of the prototypic ones, arises, in the main, from three sources: metaphors, metonymies, and what I call "related concepts." The metaphors, metonymies, and related concepts can be identified by an examination of the everyday words and phrases that native speakers of a language commonly use to talk about particular emotional experiences (like anger, fear, happiness, love, and so forth).

Metaphors of Love

As was noted in chapter 2 and the previous section, a linguistic examination of the language of love reveals that the central metaphor for love is UNITY OF TWO COMPLEMENTARY PARTS. The metaphorical implications of this way of conceptualizing love are numerous (see Kövecses, 1988, 1991a), and, consequently, we find many UNITY-related linguistic expressions of love. An examination of the literature on love also shows that this way of conceptualizing love abounds in scholarly writings as well (see, e.g., Hatfield, 1988; Solomon, 1981).

As we saw in chapter 5, the NATURAL FORCE and PHYSICAL FORCE metaphors give rise to perhaps the most common belief about love: namely, that it is a force (either external or internal) that affects us and that we are passive in relation to it. The importance of our essential passivity in love according to our language-based model is reflected in the fact that several scientific theories define love in contradistinction to this property. In these views, love is not a force acting on us, but, at least in part, a rational judgment, a cognitive decision (see, e.g., Solomon, 1981; Fromm, 1956; Sternberg, 1986). More generally, one could say that if there is a folk theory with a salient feature (such as passivity for love), experts will tend to create scientific theories in contradistinction to that feature.

Other force metaphors are also commonly used to conceptualize love. They include MAGIC, INSANITY, and RAPTURE (e.g., intoxication). When we are *spellbound, crazy,* or *drunk,* we are not under control. The implication for love is that, when we are in love, we lose our common sense and become a "different person." What the RAPTURE, or HIGH, metaphor adds to this is that love is also a pleasant state. The HIGH metaphor may be regarded as the nonexpert (i.e., language-based) counterpart of Peele's theory of certain forms of love as addiction (see Peele, 1975).

Metonymies of Love

Love also abounds in metonymies and they can be related to expert theories as well. (The notion of metonymy, as opposed to metaphor, was introduced in chapter 1.) Linguistic expressions that describe physiological, expressive, and behavioral responses of love can be regarded as metonymies, in that there is a "stand-for" relationship between these and the concept of love as a whole (i.e., the part can stand for the whole). If somebody is described by these expressions, we can legitimately infer that the person is in love. Given the following metonymies of love, mention of linguistic expressions that describe physiological, expressive, and behavioral responses of love may enable us to infer that the person of whom the statements are made is in love. This need not be a strong inference. The point is that it is possible to draw it.

INCREASE IN BODY HEAT STANDS FOR LOVE: I *felt hot all over* when I saw her.

INCREASE IN HEART RATE STANDS FOR LOVE: He's a *heart-throb*.

BLUSHING STANDS FOR LOVE: She *blushed* when she saw him.

DIZZINESS STANDS FOR LOVE: She's in a *daze* over him. I *feel dizzy* every time I see her.

PHYSICAL WEAKNESS STANDS FOR LOVE: She makes me *weak in the knees*.

SWEATY PALMS STAND FOR LOVE: *His palms became sweaty* when he looked at her.

INABILITY TO BREATHE STANDS FOR LOVE: You *take my breath away*.

INTERFERENCE WITH ACCURATE PERCEPTION STANDS FOR LOVE: He *saw nothing but her*.

INABILITY TO THINK STANDS FOR LOVE: He *can't think straight* when around her.

PREOCCUPATION WITH ANOTHER STANDS FOR LOVE: He spent hours *mooning* over her.

PHYSICAL CLOSENESS STANDS FOR LOVE: They *are always together*.

INTIMATE SEXUAL BEHAVIOR STANDS FOR LOVE: She *showered* him *with kisses*. He *caressed* her gently.

SEX STANDS FOR LOVE: They *made love*.

LOVING VISUAL BEHAVIOR STANDS FOR LOVE: He *can't take his eyes off of* her. She's *starry-eyed*.

JOYFUL (VISUAL) BEHAVIOR STANDS FOR LOVE: *Her eyes light up* when she sees him. He *smiled* at her and the world stood still.

When I list these metonymies, no claim is made that they all exclusively characterize romantic love alone. Some of them can occur in other emotions or states in general. For example, the phrase *"her eyes light up"* may characterize happiness (as a matter of fact, the phrase is more common and natural with it). The point is that this and other phrases on the list can occur in love situations because they encode various responses typical of love (such as looking and behaving in a way suggesting happiness).

Researchers have often based their theories of love on physiological, expressive, and behavioral responses. Some focused on physiological arousal. For example, Walster (1971), following Schachter and Singer (1962), proposed that under the appropriate circumstances (as in the presence of an attractive confederate) people often interpret their intense physiological arousal (which may have nothing to do with those circumstances) as passionate love. The forms of physiological arousal they interpret include many of the responses given above: body heat, increase in heart rate, blushing, dizziness, and so forth.

Some other researchers concentrate on expressive and behavioral responses. For example, Rubin (1970) places emphasis on what has been called here "loving visual behavior." Of course, sex and sex-related behaviors are often regarded as criterial aspects of love by scholars.

Finally, many of the responses given above, like loving visual behavior, sexual intercourse, intimate sexual behavior, and physical closeness, would be considered by Buss (1988) as love acts. In Buss's theory, the key aspect of love is that it "involves overt manifestations or actions that have tangible consequences" (Buss, 1988, p. 100). In other words, this view of love is in large measure based on metonymy, that is, on what have here been called expressive and behavioral responses (although the theory is not exhausted by these).

Related Concepts

There is a large range of emotion concepts that are related to love. The concepts I have in mind express, and also define, the range of attitudes we have toward the beloved. I call them "related concepts." These concepts comprise literal general knowledge based on our idealized conception(s) of love (see Kövecses, 1988). Some of the most important related concepts for love include: liking, sexual desire, intimacy, longing, affection, caring, respect, friendship, and the like. Another claim concerning related concepts is that they can be placed along a gradient of their centrality to love; some of them are inherent parts of the conception of !ove (such as liking and affection), some of them are only loosely associated with it (such as friendship or respect), and some fall in between (such as caring). (For the linguistic justification of these claims, see Kövecses, 1988, 1990, 1991a.)

What I call related concepts also show up in some expert theories of love. For example, related concepts seem to form the basis of Rubin's Love Scale (Rubin, 1970). The scale consists of items that have to do with three (in my terminology) related concepts and one response (eye contact). The three related concepts are care, need, and trust, two of which (care and need, or longing) have been identified above.

Philosophers have also striven to define love in terms of inherent concepts. Taylor (1979), for example, views love as being constituted by (mutual) sacrifice, affection, longing, and interest. Another philosopher, Newton-Smith (1973), suggests that the concept of love consists primarily of care, liking, respect, attraction, affection, and self-sacrifice. As we have seen, most of these concepts have been identified above as part of the language-based folk understanding of love.

Folk and Expert Theories of Love

We are now in a position to ask: What is the relationship between the language-based folk or naive theory and scientific theories of love? This is a large and extremely complex issue. However, there are some simple observations that we can make in the light of the study of love-related language.

First, it seems that many scientific theories enhance and elaborate on just one or two aspects of the folk model. We have seen this, for instance, in the case of physiological arousal (e.g., Walster, 1971), behavioral responses (e.g., Buss, 1988), and attitudes (e.g., Rubin, 1970). A question arises in this connection: Is the folk theory overinclusive, or are these (and similar) scientific theories incomplete?

Second, there seems to be a positive correlation between the acceptance of scientific theories and the amount of overlap they have with the folk model(s). That is, my impression is that the more a scientific theory overlaps with a folk theory, the more popular or accepted it is within the scientific community. Thus, for example, the expert theories offered by Sternberg (1986), Hatfield (1988), and Shaver, Hazan, and Bradshaw (1988) appear to be more often referred to and used as a standard or reference point than theories that emphasize just one or two aspects of the language-based folk theory of love.

Third, scientific theories that attempt to provide explanations for love in terms of concepts largely or entirely missing from the folk theory appear to look more scientific but are less intuitively appealing. Thus, for example, Buss's (1988) evolutionary explanation (which is, of course, absent from the folk theory) "looks very good" as a scientific account, but it is not as intuitively appealing as, say, Sternberg's (1986) (which "caters" more to the folk conception).

These observations naturally lead to the question: What is a scientific theory of love or what should it look like? Should it be one that provides a systematic but not obviously related explanation of an assumed folk theory or a part of it? One that provides a systematic description of all facets of an assumed folk theory? Or, one that provides an account in terms of a single (or some) aspect(s) of an assumed folk theory? It should be noticed that all of these possibilities assume the correctness of the entire folk theory or at least a part of it. However, it could be suggested that a scientific theory of love is one that negates the entire folk theory. This possibility takes us to my fourth observation.

Fourth, it could be argued that a scientific theory is scientific because it rejects what ordinary people "merely believe" concerning a domain such as love. We know that many of our language-based beliefs about the physical world are mistaken. For example, we know that the sun does not really *come up* or *go down*. Does the language of love, or that of the emotions in general, work like this example? Is there a larger scientific explanation behind our language-based beliefs about love and other emotions? If there is, what is its relationship to the folk model? We have seen some of the possibilities above.

Emotion Concepts as Cognitive Models

The particular metaphors, metonymies, and related concepts that we discussed in connection with love do not represent the concept of love in its entirety. More generally, the metaphors, metonymies, and related concepts taken individually do not amount to what we would normally take emotion concepts to be like (e.g., the metaphor ANGER IS FIRE does not exhaust our idea of what we mean by anger). However, it can be claimed that they jointly produce them. They produce them in the sense that the ingredients of emotion concepts (i.e., the metaphors, metonymies, etc.) converge on a certain prototypical scenario or cognitive model. What this means is that the metaphors, metonymies, and related concepts either map a great deal of conceptual content and structure onto previously existing parts of these models or they, in large measure, create or bring about the existence of these parts. This process of mapping conceptual material from one domain of experience onto another will give us the fourth ingredient of emotion concepts: prototypical cognitive models.

Emotion is largely conceptualized in terms of a variety of metaphors (see chapter 5). It is mostly the conceptual material mapped from the various source domains of the metaphors to the target domain of emotion that constitutes our commonsense understanding of what we mean by the concept of emotion. We have seen many exam-

ples of the process of mapping in chapter 5. As a result of these mappings, we have a rich and complex understanding of emotion:

Self (S) is emotionally calm, but then an external event happens
suddenly that involves S as a patient and that disturbs S. The event
exerts a sudden and strong impact on S. Emotion (E) comes into
existence, and S is passive with regard to this. E is a separate entity
from S and it exists independently of S. S becomes agitated, his
heart rate increases, there is an increase in body temperature, the
skin color on the face changes, and respiration becomes more intense. E is intense. S's experiences of E are primarily of physical
sensations inside the body. S shows his emotion through a variety
of expressive acts, such as crying or visual behavior, and S may also
be in an energized state. Involved in E is a desire (D), and D forces
S to perform an action (A) that can satisfy this desire. S knows that
A is dangerous and/or unacceptable to do. It can cause physical or
psychological harm to himself and/or others. S knows that he is
under obligation not to perform A required by E's D. He applies
some counterforce to prevent A from happening. It requires a great
deal of effort for S to counteract the force of the emotion. However,
S is now (i.e., in the emotional state) nonrational, and the strength
of the force quickly increases beyond the point that S can counteract. The force becomes much greater than the counterforce. As a
result, S cannot perceive the world as it is, is unable to breathe
normally, and engages in extremely agitated behavior. S is now
irrational. S ceases to resist the force affecting him. S performs A,
but he is not responsible for A, since he only obeys a force larger
than himself. E's D is now appeased and S no longer feels emotional. E ceases to exist and S is calm.

Needless to say, this is just one of the many commonsense models of
emotion that people have. What gives it privileged status is the fact
that it is a central one from which all kinds of deviations are possible.
These "deviations" represent further, less prototypical cases. Less prototypical cases include situations in which, in "weaker" emotions, the
issue of control does not even arise and situations in which at the end
of an intense emotional episode, the self does not calm down but
remains "emotional." There are many such additional nonprototypical
cases.

What emerges from this description of emotion is that the prototype of the concept has at least the following aspects: it has a cause,
the cause produces the emotion, the emotion forces us to respond, we

try to control the emotion but usually fail to do so, there is a response. This characterization suggests a sequentially arranged five-stage model for the concept. Thus there is a temporal sequence in which the events above unfold: the cause of the emotion precedes the existence of the emotion, which in turn precedes the attempt at control, which in turn precedes the loss of control, and which in turn precedes the action. This is the skeletal schema that was discussed in chapter 5, where I pointed out that the stages are not simply temporally but also causally connected:

(1) cause of emotion ⟹ (2) emotion ⟹ (3) attempt at control ⟹ (4) loss of control ⟹ (5) response

The causality is due to the variety of EMOTION IS FORCE specific-level metaphors that produce this conceptually richer prototypical cognitive model for the concept. The description of the generic-level concept of emotion given above can thus be taken as an elaboration on the skeletal schema.

Thus I take the concept of emotion and other emotion concepts to be defined and represented by prototypical cognitive models of this kind. An obvious question that arises is whether this is indeed how the concept is conceived by speakers of English. Parrott's sociopsychological studies indicate that this is pretty much what people have in mind in connection with the term *emotion* (Parrott, 1995). The prototypical models of intense individual emotions are also expected to bear a great deal of resemblance to the model of emotion above. Rippere's (1994; in Siegfried, 1994) study of depression shows that the prototypical schema of depression shares many of the components of the model outlined above.

Emotion Concepts and Expert Theories of Emotion

Let us now cast our net wider and see whether and how the diverse expert emotion theories are related to the everyday notion of emotion, as characterized by the major parts of the concept: prototypical cognitive models, metaphors, metonymies, and related concepts.

Prototypical Cognitive Models and Expert Theories

Let us begin with a brief look at the relationship between the prototypical cognitive model of emotion and the corresponding expert theories. (Note that when I am talking about "cognitive models of emotion," I do not have in mind *cognitive theories* of emotion. "Cognitive model," as I use the term here, is intended to be synonymous with "folk theory" or "folk understanding.") In this connection, we find a valuable source of information in Alston (1967). Alston provides the following as typical features of emotion:

1. A cognition of something as in some way desirable or undesirable.
2. Feelings of certain kinds.
3. Marked bodily sensations of certain kinds.
4. Involuntary bodily processes and overt expressions of certain kinds.
5. Tendencies to act in certain ways.
6. An upset or disturbed condition of mind or body. (p. 480)

Alston arrived at these typical features of emotion through an examination of the scholarly literature on emotion. He writes, "There are a number of typical features of emotional states which most thinkers agree are connected with emotion in one way or another" (p. 480). What is most remarkable about these features in the present context is that each of them finds its counterpart in the prototypical folk model as outlined above. (1) corresponds to the cause of emotion; (2) corresponds to the general experience of some emotions as given in stage two above; (3) corresponds to the physical sensations in stage two; (4) corresponds to the physiological and behavioral responses in stage two; (5) corresponds to certain actions associated with emotion, given as stage five; and (6) corresponds to the emotional disturbance and bodily agitation in stage two. Thus the typical features of emotion as provided by expert theories can be accommodated in three stages of the folk model: stage one, stage two, and stage five. It seems then that the folk model recoverable from English is a fairly rich and comprehensive model of emotion, which contains most, if not all, of the features found important for the characterization of emotion by experts.

It is also remarkable what the expert theories typically leave out of consideration. It seems that the aspect of "control," so clearly present in the folk theory, does not find its natural place in most expert theories of emotion (see the next section). I will not attempt to speculate about the possible reasons for this here.

Finally, expert theories may define themselves in opposition to the prototypical folk theory above. As has been pointed out, the commonsense folk model of emotion involves the basic schema "cause $\Rightarrow$ emotion $\Rightarrow$ (control) $\Rightarrow$ response." (This schema may also be universal. See

Heider, 1991, pp. 6ff.) There is one well-known expert theory of emotion that suggests the reverse of this flow of emotion: "perception of cause ⇒ bodily changes (response) ⇒ emotion" (James-Lange view). In the section on love, I have already mentioned the possible influence of such a change in an expert theory on either its lay or scientific acceptability; it is not well tolerated. Interestingly, James was fully aware of this potential negative influence on his own views. He remarked that such a "hypothesis is pretty sure to meet with disbelief" (James, 1890/1950, p. 450). The reason is that there is no folk theory corresponding to the Jamesian view of emotion. As Radden (1998) observed in his study of English prepositions related to the emotions, while many scientific theories of emotion have counterparts in folk models of emotion (as expressed by various prepositions such as *in*, *with*, and *for*), the theory espoused by James does not have such a counterpart. I will discuss this interplay between folk and expert theories further in the next section and the last.

I will show in the next three sections that various emotion theories bring into focus different aspects or parts of the prototypical cognitive model inherent in everyday language. (I will rely heavily on joint work with Jim Averill, as reported in Kövecses, 1990, chap. 10, which in turn is partly based on Averill, 1990.)

Metaphors and Expert Theories

In the accounts of "theory-types" below, I will not provide a complete characterization of the theories, only those aspects of them that define and distinguish them from other theories.

First, there is a group of theories that view emotion as a form of agitation, that is, as a form of physical agitation, or bodily disturbance. The emotion theories that belong to this group include psychoanalytic theories of emotion and many behaviorist ones (see, e.g., Young, 1943). Correspondingly, there is a group of conceptual metaphors (implicit in ordinary language) whose main theme is "emotion as agitation." We have seen above how the CONTAINER metaphor suggests, among other things, that lack of agitation corresponds to lack of emotion and that intense emotion may lead to an explosion. The EMOTIONS ARE NATURAL FORCES metaphor also indicates that emotion characteristically is a state of agitation (e.g. "Emotions *swept over* her," "There was a *groundswell* of emotion," "Emotions were *running high*"). But the metaphor that most clearly presents emotion as agitation is EMO-

TIONAL DISTURBANCE IS PHYSICAL AGITATION. Consider linguistic examples of the metaphor like the following: "Why are you so *upset?*" "I am all *shook up,*" "The speech *stirred* everybody's feelings." They all seem to indicate that, according to one of our language-based commonsense models, emotion is a state of disturbance. In other words, the part that the emotion theories in this group bring into focus in the model given above is "S is disturbed" and "S experiences the physiological effect of agitation."

Second, some other theories of emotion, unlike the previous one, emphasize the organizing and functional properties of emotion. According to one version of these theories, emotion is a kind of force or drive that impels the person to respond (see, e.g., Plutchik, 1980). The conceptual metaphors that depict emotion as a driving force include EMOTIONAL EFFECT IS PHYSICAL MOVEMENT (as in "I was *moved* by the speech," "She was *swept away*") and EMOTION IS AN ELECTRIC FORCE (as in "I was *shocked,*" "She was *electrified,*" "I feel *energized*"). The focus of the former is on the motion-producing (i.e., motivating) effects of emotion, while that of the latter is on how emotion provides one with the energy needed to respond to a situation. A second variety of motivational theories takes a more dispositional view (see, e.g., Leeper, 1970). Here, emotion is perceived as a state of readiness to respond in characteristic ways to a certain class of environmental stimuli. This conception of "emotion as motivation" is best captured by the EMOTIONS ARE SOCIAL SUPERIORS metaphor (as in "His emotions *dominate* his actions," "She is *ruled* by her emotions"). It seems then that the part that is highlighted in the folk model is the proposition "Emotion involves a desire which forces S to perform an action."

Third, some emotion theorists reduce the experience of emotion to subjective physical sensations. "Emotion as physical sensation" is the central idea of such well-known theories of emotion as James's (1890) and Schachter's (1971). This idea also shows up in at least two conceptual metaphors that are commonly used. Take EMOTIONAL EFFECT IS PHYSICAL CONTACT first (as in "His mother's death *hit* him *hard,*" "The idea *bowled* me *over,*" "I was *staggered* by what I saw," "I was *touched*"). This metaphor implies a physical sensation. In the metaphor, a physical object or force (corresponding to the cause of emotion) comes into contact with a physical body (corresponding to the subject of emotion). The second metaphor places the sensation inside the body. Examples for the EMOTION IS AN INTERNAL SENSATION metaphor include "I *felt* it *in my heart,*" and "There was a *feeling in my guts.*" Indeed, the use of the word *feeling* for emotion is based on the broader metaphor EMOTION IS A PHYSICAL SENSATION, because the primary application of the word involves its use to denote the various physical impacts (like heat, smell, etc.) that can affect us through our senses. Taken together, this view of emotion then is primarily concerned with the proposition that is given in our model as "Emotion manifests itself for S primarily in terms of physical sensations (inside the body)."

Fourth, another theoretical tradition holds that emotions are remnants of biological evolution (see, especially, Darwin, 1872/1965). This view takes emotions to be instinctive reactions that are common to "lower" animals and humans. The notion of "emotion as animal" finds expression in the metaphor EMOTION IS (WILD/CAPTIVE) ANIMAL. Examples include "He *unleashed* his emotions," "He is *violently* emotional," "She acted with *unbridled* passion." The main implication of this metaphor is that acting in accordance with emotion is a dangerous thing. Thus, the proposition in the folk model that receives special emphasis in this view of emotion is "S knows that A is dangerous and/or unacceptable to do."

Finally, there is a group of views that are often called "cognitive" theories of emotion. The common thread in these theories is that emotion is considered a form of nonrational judgment. "Nonrational" can take a variety of forms, including intuitive judgments (Arnold, 1960), magical transformations of the world (Sartre, 1948), and evaluative judgments (Solomon, 1976). Corresponding to the notion that emotion is a nonrational judgment is a set of conceptual metaphors in our everyday conceptual system. Thus we have the metaphors EMOTION IS INSANITY (as in "She *drove* him *berserk*," "She was *crazed* with emotion"), EMOTION IS A HIGH, or RAPTURE (as in "He was *drunk* with emotion," "They were *high on* emotion," "It was a *delirious* feeling"), and EMOTION IS A TRICKSTER or DECEIVER (as in "He was *misled* by his emotions," "Her emotion *tricked* her"). The propositions in the folk model that are highlighted by cognitive theories seem to be "S is nonrational" and "S is irrational."

Metonymies and Expert Theories

Several emotion theories place a great deal of emphasis on the physiological changes that occur in people when in an emotional state (e.g., Schachter, 1971; Wenger, 1950). Other researchers, those who believe that visceral changes are insufficient to account for the experience of emotion, often emphasize feedback from facial expressions (e.g., Ekman and Friesen, 1975; Izard, 1977). The proponents of these theories conceive of emotion as being primarily constituted by physiological processes and expressive reactions.

In everyday English, there are a large number of linguistic expressions that people use to talk about these physiological and expressive responses. The expressions so used are metonymies, not metaphors. This is because there exists in our conceptual system a very general metonymic principle: THE PHYSIOLOGICAL AND EXPRESSIVE RESPONSES OF AN EMOTION STAND FOR THE EMOTION. (And even more generally, we have EFFECTS OF A STATE STAND FOR THE STATE.) Here are examples for some of the conceptual metonymies that describe the physiological and expressive responses that are most commonly associated with emotion: BODY HEAT (as in "He did it in the *heat* of passion), CHANGE IN HEART RATE (as in "He entered the room *with his heart in his mouth*"), CHANGE IN RESPIRATION (as in "She was *heaving* with emotion"), CHANGE IN THE COLOR OF THE FACE (as in "She *colored* with emotion"), FACIAL EXPRESSIONS (as in "His emotions were *written all over his face*"). These responses appear in the model as physiological and behavioral responses.

Related Concepts and Expert Theories

There is a long-standing tradition in the literature of emotion that operates with a distinction between primary, or basic, and secondary, or nonbasic, emotions. The claim is that there are a small number of basic emotions (the number of which typically ranges between five and nine) from which all the nonbasic emotions are compounded (see, e.g., McDougall, 1908/1961). This view of emotion is similar to the commonsense idea that inherent in some emotion concepts are other (though not necessarily in any sense more basic) emotion concepts. What I call "inherent concepts" here is a subcategory of the more general category of related concepts as discussed above. In the brief discussion of concepts related to love, it was mentioned that, for example, the concept of romantic love assumes the concept affection. According to our folk understanding of romantic love, affection is a necessary condition, or component, of this type of love. The definitions of romantic love in most dictionaries employ the concept of affection. In addition, most people find a sentence like "I am in love with her, but I do not feel any affection for her" bizarre and even unacceptable. The contradictory character of loving someone romantically and at the same time not feeling affection for the person is an indication that affection is an inherent conceptual element of romantic love.

What comes closest to the status of inherent(ly related) concepts in the folk model of emotion above is the concept of DESIRE. Associated with most specific-level emotion concepts, hence with the generic concept of emotion as well, is a goal that the person having the emotion wants to achieve. It is this built-in goal that I tried to capture in the proposition "Emotion involves a desire" as given in the prototypical cognitive model above. Note that this inherent concept also has its linguistic manifestations in ordinary language, as when we say things like "His emotions were *insatiable*," "His emotions could not be *appeased*," or "Nothing was enough to *satisfy* her passion."

In sum, emotion theories that view emotions as being composed of other, more basic ones bring into focus that aspect of the folk model of emotion that has to do with inherent concepts as a subcategory of related concepts.

The Nature of the Relationship

It is common knowledge that lay theories conflict with lay theories, expert theories with expert theories, and lay theories with expert theories (see, e.g., Smith, 1995). But exactly what is the relationship between any two theories?

In the last three sections, I have dealt with the relationship between the prototypical cognitive model of emotion (as it is produced by metaphors, metonymies, and related concepts) and expert theories of emotion. It has been pointed out that the relationship between the two is such that the various emotion theories bring into focus one or more particular aspects, or parts, of the folk model. What remains to be done is to examine the *nature* of the relationship between metaphors, metonymies, and related concepts, on the one hand, and expert theories, on the other. This is the same issue that I discussed in connection with love in a previous section. That is, now I will not be concerned with the complete and comprehensive folk model; instead, the focus of attention will be on the metaphors, metonymies, and related concepts, independent of the complete picture.

In talking about the nature of the relationship so far, I have used the neutral term *correspond*. For example, I said that there is a group of theories that view emotion as nonrational judgment, and that there is a group of metaphors (INSANITY, TRICKSTER) that *corresponds* to this group of theories. What needs to be done is to attempt to specify the precise nature of the *corresponds* relation. I believe that one can think of the nature of this relationship in several ways.

First, in my discussion of the CONTAINER metaphor and its relationship to the Freudian views of emotion (see Kövecses, 1990), I suggested that the Freudian notion of emotion *derives directly from* the commonsense hydraulic model, or that the hydraulic model *gives rise to* the Freudian notion. This may overestimate the relationship. Secondly, Averill and I (in Kövecses, 1990, chap. 10) put the connection between the metaphors and expert theories in milder terms. We claimed that the existence of particular metaphors *lends intuitive appeal to* or, in this sense, *motivates* the corresponding scientific theories. That is, the metaphors can make theories more or less natural and hence more or less acceptable for laymen and experts alike. For example, if we have in our ordinary conceptual system the metaphor EMOTIONAL EFFECT IS PHYSICAL CONTACT, we (either as laymen or experts) will find those emotion theories appealing that present emotion as a form of sensation.

Third, a further possibility for the relationship is the opposite of the first. It may also be the case that it is the expert theory that gives rise to a pervasive metaphor in the ordinary conceptual system. As an example, we can take one of the most common metaphors for love: LOVE IS A UNITY OF TWO COMPLEMENTARY PARTS (see chapter 2). This metaphor derives from an expert theory that was proposed by Plato. Today it pervades both ordinary language and thought, and we do not think of it as an expert theory anymore. To complicate matters further, we have seen in this chapter that, among the many theories for love, there also exist some modern expert versions of this ancient expert theory. Another example is the "humoral theory" of anger in early European thought. (I will discuss this metaphor in the next two chapters.) This has become part and parcel of our conception of anger today (see Geeraerts and Grondelaers, 1995).

It should be noted that what has been said about the nature of the relationship concerning metaphor also applies to metonymy and inherent concepts.

Conclusions

To attempt to answer the question whether metaphors constitute or simply reflect cultural models requires an answer to the question how abstract concepts emerge. I argued against the view that maintains that abstract concepts emerge directly – without the mediation of metaphor – from basic human experience. In particular, I pointed out that Quinn's analysis of American marriage leaves out of consideration a large and significant portion of this concept – the part which is metaphorically conceived and from which the expectational structure of marriage derives. The notion of marriage, in our analysis, is partially based on and constituted by the generic metaphor NONPHYSICAL UNITY IS PHYSICAL UNITY. Given this metaphor, we can naturally account for why marriage has the expectational structure that it has, as well as for the fact that the same metaphor applies to many domains that are seemingly unrelated to marriage or love.

Furthermore, it can be suggested that a variety of relationships exist between metaphor, metonymy, and inherent concepts, on the one hand, and expert theories, on the other. It may well be that several other such relationships could be isolated. Maybe the task of determining the exact number and the precise types of these relationships awaits historians of culture and science. Clearly, this is an extremely important task if we wish to understand more thoroughly the nature and history of either our scientific or commonsense views of emotion. I think a major attraction of the approach that I present here is that it enables us to identify in a precise and systematic way the constructs that play a decisive role in this process, namely, prototypical cognitive models, conceptual metaphors, conceptual metonymies, related concepts, and their linguistic manifestations.

These points lead to a further issue – the issue whether the expert or scientific psychology of emotions is merely a more structured version of the folk understandings of emotion. I have shown in this chapter that many expert theories of emotion can be regarded as extensions of folk theories of emotion based on language. It would follow from this conclusion that I view expert emotion theories in general as merely "dressed up" variants of folk or cultural models. Clearly, this would be a radical step, and I am hesitant to take it for two reasons. First, as I repeatedly point out in this work, not all expert psychological theories of emotion can be regarded as variants of folk models. For example, several scientific theories mentioned in the preface cannot be viewed as extensions of folk models of emotion. Second, as briefly indicated in the previous passage, historical studies of the emotions are needed with this particular question in mind to track the precise development and recycling of both expert and folk models of emotion. This work is only beginning. (See, e.g., Geeraerts and Grondelaers, 1995; Burnyeat, 1997; Padel, 1992, the latter two with a critical edge of the metaphor approach.)

8. Universality in the Conceptualization of Emotions

Are the emotions conceptualized in the same way or differently across different cultures? No one would be surprised to hear that there are major differences in the way members of different cultures think about and interpret their emotional experiences. No one would be surprised either, however, to hear that there are certain similarities across cultures; after all, we talk about particular emotion concepts as (at least roughly) corresponding to each other or being each other's counterparts in different cultures. So instead of our initial question, the more important and revealing question seems to be: What exactly is universal and what is not in the conceptualization of the emotions? Basically, I will suggest that there are certain conceptual metaphors that are at least near-universals and that their near-universality comes from universal aspects of bodily functioning in emotional states. At the same time, I will also claim that this way of thinking about the issue also leaves room for cultural variation. I will take up this aspect of the question in the next chapter.

How can we show that the conceptualization of the emotions has certain near-universal aspects? The answer is simple: We have to look at how people in different cultures talk about their emotions in a detailed way. We cannot stop with examining the uses of a single emotion term (corresponding to anger, fear, love, shame, or whatever) in a culture. We have to check all the available linguistic evidence for the many figurative ways of talking about the emotions, including metaphors and metonymies, that characterize talk in presumably all cultures. There is no reason to believe that people in cultures other than English do not use heavily figurative language in their talk about their emotions. If the study of figurative emotion language matters in English, it should also matter in other languages. We should study not just a handful of literal words but the widest possible variety of figurative linguistic expressions relating to the emotions in several languages. To me, this seems to be the only reasonable basis for the linguistic study of emotions cross-culturally.

Emotion Language in English and Hungarian

English and Hungarian are two genetically unrelated languages. English is an Indo-European language and Hungarian belongs to the Finnish-Ugrian language family. Given this, one would expect that most of the figurative language that applies to the emotions in English does not apply to the same emotions in Hungarian. On the other hand, however, it is obvious that the two languages have been in (direct or indirect) contact with each other to some extent due to their relative geographical proximity in Europe. Given this, one would expect some degree of similarity between the two, when figurative language is used in connection with the same emotions. These are clearly hypotheses that simplify, yet they can serve as a useful way to begin to determine the relative differences and similarities between two languages in the domain of figurative emotion language.

Several students of mine and I have looked at two Hungarian women's magazines (*Nők Lapja* and *Kiskegyed*) and some corresponding English ones (*McCall's, Hello,* and *Best*). We wanted to see the extent to which Hungarian magazines are similar to or dissimilar from the English ones in describing emotions. The use of figurative language in the English magazines conformed to what has been reported in previous chapters (especially in chapter 2). All the major conceptual metaphors and metonymies that we have seen in this book were found in the magazines. What is more surprising is that my students and I found the same metaphoric and metonymic patterns in the Hungarian magazines as well. Below let me offer a small selection of these major figurative patterns in Hungarian illustrated by some examples translated into English (not necessarily into idiomatic English).

First, let us take some conceptual metaphors related to romantic love:

LOVE IS FIRE

Idővel majd elválik, hogy mi volt ez, *fellángolás,* vagy olyan érzelem, amire tartós kapcsolatot építhetnek.

With time we will see what this was; a *flare-up,* or a feeling on which a lasting relationship can be built.

De ne *játsszon a tűzzel*, a férfiak nem tudják megbocsátani, ha hite-
getik őket.
But do not *play with the fire*, men cannot forgive if they are fed with
promises.

LOVE IS MAGIC
Találkoztunk. És valami megfoghatatlan *varázslat kerített hatalmába*.
We met. And an inconceivable *magic overpowered* me.

LOVE IS A PHYSICAL FORCE (MAGNETIC)
A lány *mágnesként vonz*.
The girl *attracts me as a magnet*.

LOVE IS AN OPPONENT
Szerelem vagy birodalom? Antonius életét felőrli a dilemma. Nem
a józan ész, a vak szerelem *győz*.
Love or the empire? The dilemma is taking its toll on Antonius's
life. Not good sense, but blind love *wins*.

LOVE IS AN ECONOMIC EXCHANGE BASED ON MUTUALITY
Engedje szabadon érzelmeit, merjen őszintén örülni, és legyen hálás
annak, aki ez örömöt szerzi. A szeretetért szeretet *jár cserébe*.
Let your feelings (go) free, dare to be sincerely joyous, and be grateful to the person who brings that joy. Love *should be returned* with
love.

Some more metaphors relating to the emotions in general:

EMOTIONS/HAPPINESS ARE CAPTIVE ANIMALS
Engedje szabadon érzelmeit, merjen őszintén örülni, és legyen hálás
annak, aki ez örömöt szerzi. A szeretetért szeretet jár cserébe.
Let your feelings *(go) free*, dare to be sincerely joyous, and be grateful to the person who brings that joy. Love should be given in
exchange for (returned with) love.

EMOTIONS ARE SUBSTANCES INSIDE A PERSON/CONTAINER
EMOTIONAL TENSION IS PRESSURE INSIDE THE CONTAINER
Az édesanyám tényleg türelmes, érzékeny asszony volt, de *bennem
rengeteg az indulat*. ... *Bennem gyűlik, egyre gyűlik* a feszültség ...
nyolcvanszor meggondolom, mielőtt valakit kiosztok, inkább so-
káig tűrök, tűrök, azután egyszer *kitörök,*
My mother was a truly patient, sensitive woman, but there is much
temper *within me*. ... Tension *gathers and gathers inside me* ...
eighty times I think over before I give somebody a piece of my
mind, I rather take it and take it, and then I *burst out* all at once.

Finally, here is an example that contains both a metonymy and metaphor of anger:

REDNESS IN THE FACE STANDS FOR ANGER
ANGER IS A HOT FLUID IN A CONTAINER
Arca piros volt az indulattól, dac és düh *fortyogott benne,* . . . halálos méreg.
Her *face was red* from emotion/temper, spite and anger *were seething inside him,* . . . deadly poison.

All of these metaphors and metonymies can be found in English. How is it possible that two unrelated languages, such as English and Hungarian, share figurative ways of talking and thinking about the emotions to such a great degree? Can it be that contacts alone have produced such a high degree of similarity in conceptualizing the domain of emotion? It is unlikely, as we will see below when we examine languages that are not likely to have influenced each other to a considerable degree. Nevertheless, final conclusions concerning this issue can only be drawn in the light of detailed historical studies of emotion language in the English-speaking and Hungarian-speaking communities before extensive contacts between the two cultures were established. These studies pending, let me try to offer a hypothesis of how this remarkable degree of similarity in conceptualization can come about. The emotion concept that I will use for the purpose of demonstrating my hypothesis will be anger.

Folk Understandings of Anger and Its Counterparts in Different Languages and Cultures

Lakoff and Kövecses (1987) showed that conceptual metaphors and metonymies play an important role in the conceptualization of anger in English. More specifically, in regard to metaphors, we uncovered a number of conceptual metaphors such as anger as a HOT FLUID IN A CONTAINER, as FIRE, as DANGEROUS ANIMAL, as OPPONENT, as BURDEN, and so forth, and suggested that the concept is largely constituted by them. Furthermore, we pointed out that the "heat" metaphors, especially the HOT FLUID IN A CONTAINER metaphor, are central in the metaphorical system of anger in English.

In recent years, several studies have been conducted to investigate the concept that roughly corresponds to anger in languages belonging to non-Indo-European language families by using the linguistic methodology Lakoff and I employed in our study of anger. In particular, King (1989) and Yu (1995) studied the counterpart of the concept of anger in Chinese (the Chinese term is *nu*); Matsuki (1995) analyzed *ikari* in the Japanese language; and my students and I have done a study of the closest Hungarian concept, *düh* (Bokor, 1997). Furthermore, Munro (1991) studied the language that the Wolof use for the description of the concept corresponding to anger. Finally, descriptions by anthropologists and philosophers also often make mention of particular conceptual metaphors that are employed by members of different cultures. I will also make use of Solomon's (1984) comments on Levy's (1973) study of the Tahitian description of anger.

Lakoff and Kövecses (1987) characterized the naive, or folk, understanding of anger in English as a prototypical cognitive model. The following cognitive model was suggested:

1. Offending event
    Wrongdoer offends self.
    Wrongdoer is at fault.
    The offending event displeases self.
    The intensity of the offense outweighs the intensity of the retribution (which equals zero at this point), thus creating an imbalance.
    The offense causes anger to come into existence.
2. Anger
    Anger exists.
    Self experiences physiological effects (heat, pressure, agitation).
    Anger exerts force on the self to attempt an act of retribution.
3. Attempt to control anger
    Self exerts a counterforce in an attempt to control anger.
4. Loss of control
    The intensity of anger goes above the limit.
    Anger takes control of self.
    S exhibits angry behavior (loss of judgment, aggressive actions).
    There is damage to self.
    There is danger to the target of anger, in this case, the wrongdoer.

5. Retribution

Self performs retributive act against wrongdoer (this is usually angry behavior).

The intensity of retribution balances the intensity of offense.

The intensity of anger drops to zero.

Anger ceases to exist.

The main idea here was that the metaphors and metonymies associated with anger converge on and constitute the model, with the different metaphors and metonymies mapping onto different parts of the model.

Native speakers of Hungarian seem to have the same cultural model of anger (*düh*). The *but*-test that Lakoff and Kövecses (1987) used to ascertain the validity of the model for English yields the same results for speakers of Hungarian as it does for speakers of English. (On using the *but*-test in psycholinguistic experiments concerning "anger," see Gibbs, 1990.)

King (1989) suggests that there are two prototypical cognitive models operating in Chinese:

1. Offending Event

Wrongdoer offends self.

The offending event displeases self.

The offense causes an imbalance in the body.

2. Anger

Anger exists.

Self experiences physiological effects (heat, pressure, agitation).

3. Attempt to control anger

Self exerts a counterforce in an attempt to control anger.

4. Release of anger.

Self releases anger by exhibiting angry behavior.

5. Restoration of equilibrium

The amount of discharged anger balances the excess in the body.

The imbalance disappears and equilibrium is restored.

The other model differs from the one above in stages 4 and 5:

4. Diversion

The force of anger is diverted to various parts of the body.

Self exhibits somatic effects (headaches, stomachaches, etc.)

5. Compensating event

The compensating event pleases the self (this is usually sympathetic behavior directed at self).

The intensity of compensation balances the intensity of the offense.

The somatic effects of anger disappear.

Anger ceases to exist.

In the characterization of Japanese *ikari* (and, less typically, also *hara*), Matsuki (1995) notes in connection with the model found in American English: "The scenario applies to Japanese anger, although Stage 3 is more elaborate than in English" (p. 145). In the Japanese conception, the control aspect of *ikari* is more elaborate because anger first appears in *hara*, then it goes up to *mune*, and finally to *atama*. As Matsuki points out, *hara* is a container (the stomach/bowels area) and, metonymically ("container for content"), can also be the emotion itself. *Mune* is the chest and *atama* is the head. If anger reaches *atama*, the angry person is unable to control anger.

These models have several things in common. Each seems to be composed of several successive stages and each seems to have an ontological, a causal, and an expressive aspect. Based on the characterizations given above, the following general structure of the respective emotion concepts (*anger, düh, ikari*, and *nu*) can be identified. The prototypical cognitive models have an *ontological* part that gives us an idea of the ontological status and nature of anger, that is, what kind of thing/event it is: in all four languages anger, or its counterpart, is a force inside the person that can exert pressure on him or her. The ontological part also includes some physiological processes associated with the respective emotion. It is the ontological part of the model that constitutes the second stage of the cognitive model or scenario as a whole. The first stage in the model is the *causal* part. This presents anger and its counterparts as an emotion that is caused, or produced, by a certain situation. Still another part of the model is concerned with the *expressive* component; that is, the ways in which anger, or its counterpart, is expressed in the different cultures. The cognitive models tell us that all four cultures conceive of anger as something that is somehow expressed. Finally, the expressive component is preceded by a *control* component that is manifested as two separate stages of the model: attempt at controlling expression and loss of control over expression. Thus, the resulting five-stage model for the four cultures seems to be the following: cause → existence of anger, or its counterpart (in the form of a force) → attempt at control → loss of control → expression. Since expression and control are closely linked with each other (at issue is the control of expression), it is possible to conceive of the two as a single aspect and refer to them as the expression part of the model, yielding simply: cause → existence (force) → expression. This then seems to be the *basic structure* that all four cultures share in their folk understanding.

Given these observations, we can conclude that the four emotion concepts in four very different languages and cultures are remarkably similar in regard to *their basic structure*. (It is arguable whether or to what extent Chinese and Japanese are two "very different" languages and cultures or just variants of a single one.) This should not happen if emotion concepts like anger were only determined by the broader culture of which they form a part. Several possible explanations for this similarity present themselves. One is that the similarity is completely accidental. We could suggest that by some incredible coincidence, the four cultures happen to have very similar folk understandings of anger and its counterparts. Another way of accounting for the situation is to suggest that once the basic structure as a folk understanding emerged (it does not matter where), it was transmitted to the other cultures. Finally, a third explanation could be to say that the basic structure is the product of human conceptualization that is profoundly influenced by certain universal properties of the human body. It is this third option that I will try to develop here.

Why the Similarities?

The short answer to the question of why emotion concepts in diverse cultures share a *basic structure* is that the cultures also share a central metaphor that informs and structures the concepts (i.e., the folk understandings). This is the CONTAINER metaphor. The details are as follows.

As linguistic usage indicates, all four cultures seem to conceptualize human beings as containers and anger (or its counterparts) as some kind of substance (a fluid or gas) inside the container. This conceptualization can be captured in terms of the metaphors THE BODY IS THE CONTAINER FOR THE EMOTIONS and ANGER IS A SUBSTANCE (FLUID/GAS) IN THE CONTAINER. Let us refer jointly to these two submetaphors as the CONTAINER metaphor. Here are some examples of this from the four languages:

English
He was filled with anger.
Try to get your anger out of your system.

Chinese
man qiang fen nu [full cavity anger]
to have one's body cavities full of anger

Japanese
Ikari ga karadajyu ni jyuman shita [anger in my body to be filled was].
My body was filled with anger.
Ikari o uchi ni himeta [anger inside to lock in].
I contained my anger.

Hungarian
Tele van dühvel [full is düh-with].
He is full of anger.
Nem tudta magában tartani dühét [not could himself-in to keep anger-his].
He could not keep his anger inside.

A major attraction of the CONTAINER metaphor for the purposes of conceptualizing anger (and other, according to Hume, "violent passions") is that it captures a great number of aspects and properties of anger. It allows us to conceptualize intensity (*filled with*), control (*contain*), loss of control (*could not keep inside*), dangerousness (*brim with*), expression (*express/show*), and so forth. Indeed, it appears that no other conceptual metaphor associated with anger can provide us with an understanding of all these facets of anger. This feature of the CONTAINER metaphor may in part be responsible for the singular popularity of the metaphor both historically in a given civilization (Geeraerts and Grondelaers, 1995) and cross-culturally (Solomon, 1984). It is also the metaphor that appears to be the most popular both as a folk theory and also as a scientific theory of emotion (Solomon, 1984; Lutz, 1988; Kövecses, 1990).

As we have just seen, the same general CONTAINER metaphor exists in the four cultures, meaning that anger and its counterparts are viewed in all of the cases as some kind of substance (fluid or gas) inside a closed container that is the human body. However, the general metaphor seems to be elaborated in more or less different ways at a more specific level of metaphorical understanding.

English

The metaphor that characterizes English at this specific level is ANGER IS A HOT FLUID IN A CONTAINER. Consider the following examples from Lakoff and Kövecses (1987):

> You make my blood boil.
> Simmer down!
> Let him stew.

All of these examples assume a container (corresponding to the human body), a fluid inside the container, as well as the element of heat as a property of the fluid. It is the hot fluid or, more precisely, the heat of the fluid that corresponds to anger. That this is so is shown by the fact that lack of heat indicates lack of anger (as in "Keep *cool*").

The HOT FLUID metaphor in English gives rise to a series of metaphorical entailments. This means that we carry over knowledge about the behavior of hot fluids in a closed container onto the concept of anger. Thus we get:

> When the intensity of anger increases, the fluid rises:
>
> > His pent-up anger welled up inside him.
> > She could feel her gorge rising.
> > We got a rise out of him.
>
> Intense anger produces steam:
> > Billy's just blowing off steam.
> > Smoke was coming out of his ears.
>
> Intense anger produces pressure on the container:
> > He was bursting with anger.
> > I could barely contain my rage.

And a variant of this that emphasizes control:
> > I suppressed my anger.

> When anger becomes too intense, the person explodes:
> > When I told him, he just exploded.

She blew up at me.
We won't tolerate any more of your outbursts.

When a person explodes, parts of him go up in the air:
I blew my stack.
She flipped her lid.
He hit the ceiling.

When a person explodes, what was inside him comes out:
His anger finally came out.

Hungarian

The Hungarian version of the CONTAINER metaphor also emphasizes a hot fluid in a container. The Hungarian metaphor ANGER IS A HOT FLUID IN A CONTAINER differs from the English one in only minor ways.

Forrt benne a düh [boiled in-him the anger].
Anger was boiling inside him.

Fortyog a dühtől [seethed the anger-with].
He is seething with anger.

The only difference in relation to English seems to be that in Hungarian, in addition to the body as a whole, the head is a container that can hold the hot fluid.

As can be seen from the examples below, most of the entailments of the HOT FLUID IN A CONTAINER metaphor also apply in Hungarian.

When the intensity of anger increases, the fluid rises:

Felgyülemlett benne a harag [up-piled in-him the wrath].
Wrath built/piled up in him.
Feltört benne a harag [up-welled in-him the wrath/anger].
Anger welled up inside him.

Intense anger produces steam:

Teljesen begőzölt [completely in-steamed-he].
He was all steam.
Füstölgött magában [smoked in-himself].
He was fuming alone/by himself.

Intense anger produces pressure on the container:

Majd szétvetette a harag [almost apart-burst-him the anger].
His anger almost burst him.
Majd eldurrant a feje [almost burst the head-his].
His head almost burst.
Majd szétrobbant dühében [almost apart-exploded-he anger-in].
He almost exploded with anger.
Alig birta magában tartani dühét [hardly could-he himself-in to hold anger].
He could hardly hold his anger inside.

When anger becomes too intense, the person explodes:

Megpukkadt mérgében [burst-he anger-in].
He burst with anger.
Szétrobbant dühében [apart-exploded-he anger-in].
He exploded with anger.
Nem tűröm kitöréseidet [not tolerate-I out-bursts-your].
I do not tolerate your outbursts.

When a person explodes, parts of him go up in the air:

A plafonon van már megint [the ceiling-on is already again].
He is on the ceiling again.

When a person explodes, what was inside him comes out:

Kitört belőle a düh [out-burst from-inside-him the anger].
Anger burst out of him.
Kifakadt [out-burst-he].
He burst out.

Chinese

Chinese offers yet another version of the CONTAINER metaphor for the Chinese counterpart of anger (*nu* in Chinese). The Chinese version makes use of and is based on the culturally significant notion of *qi* (see King, 1989, and Yu, 1995). *Qi* is energy that is conceptualized as a fluid or gas that flows through the body. It is also a fluid or gas that can increase and then produce an excess. This is the case when we have the emotion of anger. King (1989) isolated the "excess *qi*" metaphor for anger on the basis of the following examples:

ANGER IS EXCESS *QI* IN THE BODY:

xin zhong de nuqi shizhong wei neng pingxi [heart in POSS anger
    qi]
the anger qi in one's heart

chen zhu qi [deep hold qi]
to hold one's qi down

qi yong ru shan [qi well up like mountain]
one's qi wells up like a mountain

bie yi duzi qi [hold back one stomach qi]
to hold back a stomach full of qi

yuji zai xiong de nuqi zhongyu baofa le [pent up at breast POSS
    anger qi finally explode LE]
the pent up anger qi in one's breast finally explodes

bu shi pi qi fa zuo [NEG make spleen qi start make]
to keep in one's spleen qi

First, it may be observed that in Chinese anger *qi* may be present in a
variety of places in the body, including the breast, heart, stomach, and
spleen. Second, anger *qi* seems to be a fluid that, unlike in English,
Hungarian, and Japanese, is not hot. Its temperature is not specified.
As a result, Chinese does not have the entailment involving the idea
of steam being produced. Third, anger *qi* is a fluid whose buildup
produces pressure in the body or in a specific body organ. This pressure typically leads to an explosion that corresponds to loss of control
over anger.

Another metaphor, ANGER IS THE MOVEMENT OF QI, gives us a sense
of what happens after the explosion. Consider the following examples:

dong nu [move anger]
to move one's anger

yi zhi ziji de fen nu [restrain self POSS anger]
to restrain one's anger

ta nu qi shao ping le [he anger qi a little level LE]
His anger qi calmed down.

ping xin jing qi [level heart quiet qi]
to have a level heart and quiet qi

The excess *qi* is now gone and *qi* flows through the body harmoniously once again.

Japanese

Matsuki (1995) observed that the ANGER IS A HOT FLUID IN A CONTAINER metaphor also exists in the Japanese language. One property that distinguishes the Japanese metaphor from both the English and the Hungarian metaphors is that, in addition to the body as a whole, the stomach/bowels area (called *hara* in Japanese) is seen as the principal container for the hot fluid that corresponds to anger. Consider the following Japanese examples (taken from Matsuki, 1995, and my two Japanese informants Noriko Ikegami and Kyoko Okabe) and Takashi Kusumi (personal communication, July 1997):

> harawata ga niekurikaeru
> one's intestines are boiled

> Ikari ga karada no naka de tagiru.
> Anger seethes inside the body.

> Ikari ga hara no soko wo guragura saseru
> Anger boils the bottom of stomach.

Some of the metaphorical entailments are also the same as in English, Hungarian, and Chinese:

> When the intensity of anger increases, the fluid rises:
> > Ikari ga kokoro-no naka-de mashita-itta.
> > Anger in my mind was getting bigger.

> Intense anger produces steam:
> > Atama kara yuge ga tatsu.
> > Steam rises up from the head.
> > Kanojo-wa yugeotatete okotte-ita [she with steam/steaming up was angry].
> > She got all steamed up.

> Intense anger produces pressure on the container:
> > Ikari no kimochi wo osaekirenai.
> > Cannot suppress the feeling of anger.
> > Watashi-wa ikari-o osaeta [I anger suppressed].
> > I suppressed my anger.
> > Atama ni chi ga noboru.
> > Blood rises up to the head.

When anger becomes too intense, the person explodes:
Haha wa toutou bakuhatsu shita.
My mother finally exploded.
Kannin-bukuro-no o-ga kireta ["patience bag" tip/end was cut/broken/burst].
His patience bag burst.
Ikari-ga bakuhatsu-shita [anger exploded].
My anger exploded.

The entailments that do not carry over in the case of Japanese are "when the person explodes, parts of him go up in the air" and "when a person explodes, what was inside him comes out." This finding may be due to insufficient linguistic evidence. What is clear, however, is that all my sources unanimously indicated that Japanese does have the first four of the entailments, the fourth being the explosion corresponding to loss of control over anger. Indeed, the others that follow this in the sequence may be regarded as mere embellishments on the notion of loss of control.

It was noted above that anger is conceptualized in Japanese as a hot fluid that is primarily in the stomach/bowels area (*hara*) that functions as a container. But there appears to be another metaphor in Japanese that portrays anger as being in *hara* without it being simultaneously conceptualized as a hot fluid. (In regard to this metaphor, I depart somewhat from Matsuki's analysis, reanalyze some of her examples, and rely on additional linguistic information provided for me by two Japanese informants.) Thus we also have "the *hara* is a container for anger" metaphor. The main difference between the "*hara* as container" and the HOT FLUID IN A CONTAINER metaphors seems to be that while the HOT FLUID metaphor clearly implies a pressurized container, the "hara" metaphor does so only marginally, if at all. Let us now see the examples:

hara ga tatsu [stomach to stand up]
get angry

hara no mushi ga osamaranai [stomach bug no calm down]
I can't calm down.

Kimochi wa wakaru keredo hara ni osamete kudasai
I understand how you feel, but save it inside stomach

Hara ni suekaneru
cannot lay it in stomach

Anmari hara ga tatta node hon wo nagetsuketa
I threw a book because stomach rose up so much.

Haradatatashisa ni mune wo shimetsukerareru
feel strangled with mune (= chest) because of the rise of stomach

Toutou atama ni kita
Finally it (anger, blood) came to atama (head).

As Matsuki (1995) points out, a particularly interesting feature of the "hara" metaphor is that it has an elaborate control aspect. An increase in the intensity of anger is indicated by *hara rising*, the chest (*mune*) getting filled with anger, and eventually anger reaching the head (*atama*). These three successive and increasing degrees in the intensity of anger are associated with different possibilities for controlling anger. It is only when anger reaches the head that the angry person cannot control his anger. (This may have to do with the folk theory that extreme anger can interfere with one's normal mental functioning, thus making it impossible for the angry person to control his anger.) However, when the anger is in *hara* or *mune*, one is still in a position to overcome, and thus hide (for instance, often by smiling), one's anger. In regard to the conceptualization of anger in Japanese, the significance of all this is that it shows the Japanese concern with and emphasis on trying to hide and control one's anger (see Averill, 1982).

Other Languages

We also have some evidence from other cultures for the existence of a CONTAINER metaphor for counterparts of anger. Tahitian can serve as an additional illustration of a culture where anger is conceptualized as a force inside a container. For example, Levy (1973) quotes a Tahitian informant as saying: "The Tahitians say that an angry man is like a bottle. When he gets filled up he will begin to spill over" (quoted in Solomon, 1984, p. 238).

In Wolof, an African language spoken in Senegal and Gambia, the word *bax* means "to boil" in a literal sense. It is also used metaphorically in the sense of "to be really angry" (Munro, 1991). The existence of this metaphor indicates that Wolof has something like the CONTAINER metaphor as a possible conceptualization of the counterpart of anger.

The Structure of the "Container" Metaphors

Notice that what is common to these CONTAINER metaphors is that, in anger, the container is a pressurized container, either with or without heat. The basic correspondences, or mappings of the metaphor include:

the container with the fluid is the person who is angry
the fluid in the container is the anger
the pressure of the fluid on the container is the force of the anger on the angry person
the cause of the pressure is the cause of the anger force
trying to keep the fluid inside the container is trying to control the anger
the fluid going out of the container is the expression of the anger
the physical dysfunctionality of the container is the social dysfunctionality of the angry person

I believe that these are the mappings that play a constitutive role in the construction of the basic structure of the folk understandings of anger and its counterparts in different cultures. Without these mappings (i.e., imposing the schematic structure of how the force of a fluid or gas behaves in a container onto anger), it is difficult to see how anger and its counterparts could have acquired the structure they seem to possess: a situation producing a force inside a person and then the force causing the person to act in certain ways that should be suppressed. The "cause, force, forced expression" structure remains a mystery and a completely random occurrence without evoking the PRESSURIZED CONTAINER metaphor. Through its detailed mappings, the metaphor provides a coherent structure for the concepts.

In other words, we now find that anger and its counterparts in four (and, as we saw, possibly more) very different cultures are conceptualized in terms of roughly the same PRESSURIZED CONTAINER metaphor. If the four cultural models given in the previous section differed from each other fundamentally, this should not be possible. Because, in the Quinn view, it is cultural models that produce or select the metaphors, fundamentally different models should have produced considerably different metaphors. Because this is not the case, we can conclude that Quinn's view is too strong to be a general account of the relationship between cultural models and their corresponding metaphors. It is not an adequate general explanation of the culture-metaphor relationship because it does not seem to be applicable to the emotion concept of anger.

To conclude this section, we can now perhaps see how the PRESSURIZED CONTAINER metaphor can be viewed as accounting for a large portion of the similarity in the four concepts, similarities involving basic structure. But now a new question arises: How does the PRESSURIZED CONTAINER metaphor come into the picture in the four cultures in the first place?

How Do Roughly the Same Metaphors Emerge for Anger and Its Counterparts?

How did languages and cultures as different as English, Hungarian, Japanese, Chinese, and probably Wolof and Tahitian produce a remarkably similar shared metaphor – the PRESSURIZED CONTAINER metaphor? The answer I would propose is that, as linguistic usage suggests, English-speaking, Hungarian, Japanese, Chinese, et cetera, people appear to have very similar ideas about their bodies and seem to see themselves as undergoing the same physiological processes when in the state of *anger, düh, ikari,* and *nu.* They all view their bodies and body organs as containers. And as linguistic evidence also suggests, they respond physiologically to certain situations (causes) in the same ways. They seem to share certain physiological processes including body heat, internal pressure, and redness in the neck and face area (as a possible combination of pressure and heat). It is important to bear in mind that at this point in the argument I am not making a biological and/or physiological claim (although I will do exactly that later on). The claim here is a linguistic one and is based on the linguistic examples to follow:

Body heat:
  English:
  Don't get hot under the collar.
  Billy's a hothead.
  They were having a heated argument.

  Chinese [example from Yu, 1995]:
  Wo qide lianshang huolalade.
  My face was pepperily hot with anger.

Japanese [data obtained from Noriko Ikegami and Kyoko Okabe]:
(Watashi-no) atama-ga katto atsuku-natta [my head get hot].
My head got hot.
atama o hiyashita hoo ga ii [head cool should]
You should cool down.

Hungarian:
forrófejű
hotheaded
felhevült vita
heated argument

Tahitian [Solomon (1984) does not contain data for heat]:

Wolof [data obtained from Munro (1991)]:
tang [to be hot]
to be bad-tempered
Tangal na sama xol [he heated my heart].
He upset me, made me angry.

Internal pressure:

English:
Don't get a hernia!
When I found out, I almost burst a blood vessel.

Chinese [data obtained from King, 1989]:
qi de naomen chong xue [qi DE brain full blood]
to have so much qi that one's brain is full of blood
qi po du pi [break stomach skin]
to break the stomach skin from qi
fei dou qi zha le [lungs all explode LE]
one's lungs explode from too much qi

Japanese [data obtained from Noriko Ikegami and Kyoko Okabe]:
kare no okage de ketsuatsu ga agarippanashi da [he due to blood pressure to keep going up]
My blood pressure keeps going up because of him.
sonna ni ikiri tattcha ketsuatsu ga agaru yo [like that get angry blood pressure to go up]
Don't get so angry; your blood pressure will go up.

Hungarian:
agyvérzést kap [cerebral-hemorrhage gets]
will have a hemorrhage
felmegy benne a pumpa [up-goes in-him the pump]
pressure rises in him
felment a vérnyomása [up-went the blood pressure-his]
His blood pressure went up.

Tahitian: [no data]

Wolof: [no data]

Redness in face and neck area:

English:
She was scarlet with rage.
He got red with anger.

Chinese [data obtained from King, 1989]:
ta lian quan hong le yanjing mao huo lai [he face all red LE
   eyes emit fire come]
His face turned red and his eyes blazed.

Japanese [data obtained from Noriko Ikegami and Kyoko
   Okabe]:
kare wa makka ni natte okotta [he red to be get angry]
He turned red with anger.

Hungarian:
Vörös lett a feje [red became the head-his].
His head turned red.

Tahitian: [no data]

Wolof: [no data]

English, Hungarian, Japanese, Wolof, and, to some degree, Chinese
seem to share the notion of body heat. This notion, perhaps together
with the idea of the felt warmth of blood, seems to be the cognitive
basis for the heat component of the English, Hungarian, Japanese, and
Wolof CONTAINER metaphors. The fact that Chinese does not have a
large number of metonymies associated with body heat may be responsible for the Chinese CONTAINER metaphor *not* involving a hot
fluid. Internal pressure is present in English, Chinese, Japanese, and
Hungarian. We do not have data for internal pressure in Tahitian and
Wolof. The physiological response "redness in the face and neck area"
can be taken to be the result of both body heat and internal pressure.

This response seems to characterize English, Chinese, Japanese, and Hungarian. There is no data for Tahitian and Wolof, although the word *boy* that means "to be red hot (of charcoal)" also means "to be really angry" (Munro, 1991).

Since human blood is present in many of the linguistic examples we have seen, it is reasonable to assume that it is mainly blood (but perhaps some other body fluids as well) that accounts for the fluid component in the CONTAINER metaphors. Many of the examples suggest that blood is often seen as producing an increase in blood pressure when a person is angry, and this, together with muscular pressure, may be responsible for the pressure element in the CONTAINER metaphors. All four languages seem to have the image of a pressurized container, with or without heat.

I propose then that conceptualized physiology (i.e., the conceptual metonymies) provides cognitive motivation for people for the metaphorical conceptualization of the angry person as a PRESSURIZED CONTAINER. Specifically, conceptual metonymies make this particular conceptualization natural for people. If conceptualized physiological responses include an increase in internal pressure as a major response in a given culture, people in this culture will find the use of the PRESSURIZED CONTAINER metaphor natural. In the case of anger, naturalness arises out of embodiment (see Lakoff, 1987, and Johnson, 1987). Embodiment occurs when it is really the case that people's temperature and blood pressure rise in anger. This is what makes studies of human physiology during emotional states crucially relevant for cognitive approaches to the study of the language and conceptual system of emotion. As a result of these studies, we have evidence that anger does indeed go together with objectively measurable bodily changes such as increases in skin temperature, blood pressure, and pulse rate and more intense respiration; we have also seen that other emotions, like fear and sadness, go together with a different set of physiological activities (see, e.g., Ekman, Levenson, and Friesen, 1983; Levenson, Ekman, and Friesen, 1990; Levenson, Carstensen, Friesen, and Ekman, 1991). These studies were conducted with American subjects only. Levenson, Ekman, Heider, and Friesen (1992) extended their research cross-culturally, however, and found that emotion-specific Autonomic Nervous System (ANS) activity is the same in Americans and the Minangkabau of West Sumatra. For example, skin temperature rises in anger in both Americans and the Minangkabau. These findings give us reason to believe that the actual physiology might be universal. The universality of actual physiology might be seen as leading to the similarities (though not equivalence) in conceptualized physiology (i.e., the conceptual metonymies), which might then lead to the similarity (though again not equivalence) in the metaphorical conceptualization of anger and its counterparts (i.e., the CONTAINER metaphor).

That is, in addition to giving rise to motivation (i.e., naturalness), embodiment may be seen as having another function in the conceptualization of anger. It puts certain limitations (either directly or through naturalness) on the possible ways in which anger is conceptualized (including conceptualizations expressed in expert theories – many of which are "hydraulic," i.e., CONTAINER metaphors, in nature; see Solomon, 1984). It is not suggested, however, that embodiment actually produces the PRESSURIZED CONTAINER metaphor but that it makes a large number of other possible metaphorical conceptualizations either incompatible or unnatural. It would be odd to conceptualize anger as, say, softly falling snow, an image completely incompatible with what our bodies are like and what our physiology does in anger. It is in this sense that the particular embodiment of anger is seen as limiting the choice of available metaphors for anger.

A major implication of this state of affairs is that the embodiment of anger appears to constrain, in the sense above, the kinds of metaphors that can emerge as viable conceptualizations of anger. This seems to be the reason why very similar metaphors have emerged for the concept in a variety of different cultures. It is on the basis of this similarity that the metaphors in different cultures can be viewed as forming a category of metaphors, a category that we have called the CONTAINER metaphor. Without the constraining effect of embodiment, it is difficult to see how such a surprisingly uniform category (of metaphors) could have emerged for the conceptualization of anger. The widely different cultures we have examined should have produced a great deal more diversity in (metaphorical) conceptualization than what appears to be the case on the basis of the data available to me in this study.

It is important to understand what is not claimed in this discussion. It is not claimed that wherever physiological responses that have to do with anger are perceived and named, a version of the CONTAINER metaphor for anger will necessarily exist. That is, physiological responses do not automatically produce the metaphor. For example, we know of cultures where anger is talked about in terms of body heat. In Chickasaw (a language in the Muskogean family), the expression *sa-palli* means "I am hot" and it can also mean "I am angry" (Munro, 1991). As Munro observes, however, Chickasaw does not seem to have a HOT FLUID IN A CONTAINER metaphor for anger. What is claimed then is that languages in which, say, body heat is richly elaborated will be more likely to have the HOT FLUID version of the CONTAINER metaphor than languages in which it is not. Since Chickasaw (as well as Chinese, as we saw above) does not have a linguistically productive elaboration of heat in relation to anger (though it may have one or two expressions for it), it is not likely to have and will not have the HOT FLUID metaphor for anger.

Furthermore, there are cultures in the world where the CONTAINER metaphor for anger and its counterparts plays an insignificant role in comparison with folk conceptions that are very different from them; for example, on Ifaluk, a Micronesian atoll, the folk conception of anger emphasizes the *prosocial, moral, ideological* aspects of anger (Lutz, 1988) – as opposed to the antisocial, individualistic, and physical aspects that the PRESSURIZED CONTAINER metaphor emphasizes in Western cultures. That is, although the Ifaluk may well have a very similar physiology in anger to the Chinese, this fact does not necessarily lead them to conceptualize *song* as pressure in a container (although the word for the concept of *feel* appears to be *niferash* meaning also "insides" in Ifaluk, suggesting at least some CONTAINER image at work in that culture as well).

In summing up this section, the view of the body as a container, the presence of blood (and other fluids) in that container, and the physiological responses of internal pressure and body heat together make it very natural for human beings to conceptualize *anger* and its counterparts in other cultures as a (hot) fluid or gas in a pressurized container.

Conclusions

We have seen linguistic evidence in several very different languages and cultures that suggests that the concept of anger and its counterparts are largely understood as having a "cause-force-expression" basic structure. It was argued that this structure emerges from a PRESSURIZED CONTAINER metaphor. Further, it was proposed that this cross-cultural similarity in the conceptualization of anger is in all probability attributable to similarities in the human body and its functioning in anger. These similarities can be clearly observed in the metonymies used in connection with anger. Most (though, as we saw, not all) metonymies of anger – expressions that indicate physiological processes that are assumed to accompany anger – seem to be shared in the four cultures. In general, embodiment appears to be a key component in cross-culturally similar conceptualizations of the same domain. Further evidence for this notion is provided by Michelle Emanatian's study of lust in Chaga, in which she found that most of the English metaphors for lust also exist in Chaga (see Emanatian, 1995).

I have shown that the cultural models of anger and its counterparts share a basic structure. It was suggested that this shared basic structure can be seen as emerging in widely different cultures in only a limited number of ways: (1) It may be the result of sheer coincidence; (2) it may have been transmitted from one culture to the others; or (3) it may have come about as a result of shared human biology. I believe that the first two are unattractive choices, although they cannot be completely excluded as possible explanations. (E.g., Takashi Kusumi informed me, in personal communication, that many concepts, including *qi*, were transmitted from Chinese to Japanese over the centuries.) The third option is my favorite candidate for an explanation. I have tried to show how systematic links can take us from (possibly universal) actual human physiology in anger through metonymy and metaphor to corresponding cultural models. However, in the next chapter I will also argue that another part of the "metaphor-cultural model" relationship is the broader cultural context that fills out the details left open in the schematic basic structure.

Thus, the view of the relationship I have arrived at in this chapter involves five elements: (possibly universal) actual human physiology, conceptualized physiology (metonymy), metaphor, cultural model (with its schematic basic structure), and the broader cultural context (to be discussed in the next chapter). I have suggested that the cultural models of anger and its counterparts are the joint products of metaphor, metonymy, (possibly universal) actual physiology, and cultural context. I do not think that this account of the emergence of the cultural model of anger necessarily commits me to saying that the cultural model came *after* the metonymies and the metaphor. Instead, we can say, giving in somewhat – but not completely – to a suggestion made by Dorothy Holland (personal communication), that the metonymies, the CONTAINER metaphor, the cultural model, and the broader cultural context all evolved simultaneously on the substratum of actual human physiology. (Holland does not seem to accept the notion that a potentially universal physiology can play a determining role in the emergence of a cultural model.) In the course of this joint evolution, the conceptualized physiology and the emerging metaphor contributed to the basic schematic structure of the cultural model, while (as we will see) the simultaneously emerging cultural context filled out the details of this schema.

9. Cultural Variation in the Conceptualization of Emotion

My main interest in this chapter is to attempt to offer a coherent framework for the study of cultural variation in the conceptualization of emotion from the perspective of cognitive linguistics. Cultural variation subsumes two large issues: (1) How does the conceptualization of emotion vary cross-culturally? (2) How does it vary intraculturally, that is, within a single culture? A great deal, of course, has been said about these issues, especially in the anthropology, psychology, sociology, and social history of emotion (for overviews, see Besnier, 1990, and Russell, 1991). My main goal, however, is to argue and demonstrate that the cognitive linguistic approach can contribute significantly to our understanding of how emotion concepts vary cross-culturally and within a culture. I will begin with cross-cultural variation.

Cross-Cultural Variation

In the previous chapter, I discussed certain universal aspects of the conceptualization of emotion concepts. One aspect is the presumably universal nature of the human body and its physiology (e.g., real physiology in anger, as studied by Ekman and his colleagues). Another is the potentially universal *metonymic conceptualization* and verbalization of the body's physiological functioning in intense emotional states (e.g., the metonymies for physiological functioning, like blood pressure and body heat in anger). A third is the potentially universal *metaphorical conceptualization* and verbalization of intense emotions based on the metonymic conceptualization (e.g., the PRESSURIZED CONTAINER metaphor for anger). A fourth is the potentially universal *schematic conception* of intense emotions largely based on the conceptual metaphors (e.g., the image-schematic structure of the cultural model of anger). I use the phrase "potentially universal" because with the exception of "real physiology" it does not have to be the case that all cultures will, or do, verbalize and conceptualize their emotions in the same way. My view is that, given the universal real physiology, members of different cultures cannot conceptualize their emotions in a way that *contradicts* universal physiology (or maybe even their conceptualization of universal physiology); but nevertheless they can choose to conceptualize their emotions in many different ways *within the constraints* imposed on them by universal physiology. These limits leave a lot of room for speakers of very different languages to conceptualize their intense emotions in sometimes very different ways, as we will see in this chapter.

Taylor and Mbense's (1998) study of the way the Zulu talk about and conceptualize anger provides further evidence for the view of universality proposed above. Speakers of Zulu, like speakers of English (see Lakoff and Kövecses, 1987), use the conceptual metaphors of internal pressure, fire, dangerous animal, et cetera. They also conceptualize their anger as producing an increase in body heat, agitation, and interference with normal perception and functioning. Interestingly, they even have the same metonymy "darkening/reddening of the skin." And they also seem to have the same basic anger scenario. However, as we will see below, Taylor and Mbense, like the scholars working on Chinese, Japanese, and so on, also draw our attention to some important differences in language and conceptualization.

Cultural variation is something to be expected. But the really interesting question is: In precisely what ways do cultures vary? How does my model of the conceptualization of the emotions handle culture-specificity? In other words, given the model that I tried to outline in this work, where exactly do we find or can we expect to find cultural differences?

I propose that the following areas are all potential sources for cross-cultural variation:

1. the content of prototypical cultural models of emotions
2. the general content and specific key concepts of the broader cultural context
3. the range of conceptual metaphors and conceptual metonymies
4. the special elaborations of conceptual metaphors and metonymies
5. emphasis on metaphor versus metonymy, or the other way around

As we will see in the discussion below, all these areas can affect each other, as predicted by the hypothesis of potential universality presented above and the notion of the cultural embeddedness of folk models of emotion to be explained below.

To see how cross-cultural variation works, first let us return to some of the ideas that were introduced in the previous chapter. I begin the survey of cross-cultural variation in emotion concepts with possible differences in the content of prototypical cultural models.

Variation in the Content of Prototypical Cultural Models

To say that the concepts of anger in English, Chinese, Japanese, and Hungarian all share a basic image-schematic structure is not to say that there are no differences in the folk understanding of anger and its counterparts at a more detailed or specific level (see Averill, 1982). Clearly, there are. In chapter 8, we saw some noteworthy cultural differences in conceptualization.

In the discussion of Japanese *ikari/hara*, it was suggested that the (possibly more traditional) Japanese model gives the angry person more chance to exercise control over anger than the Western model does. This seems to be in line with traditional Japanese values governing behavior and is often regarded as the main distinguishing characteristic of Japanese culture (see, e.g., Reischauer, 1964, and Doi, 1973, as cited in Averill, 1982).

Another example of cultural differences in prototypes can be found in the expressive part of the model. As has been seen above, King (1989) suggests that according to the Chinese conception of *nu*, instead of the angry person losing control, he or she can and will choose not to express his or her anger and will instead divert it to various parts of the body. This is one of the prototypical courses anger takes in a clearly definable set of situations in Chinese culture and would seem to stand in sharp contrast with the Western conception in which anger is prototypically expressed as a form of retaliation against another person. Even the other common form of expressing anger in China that King reports is less directed at another person than at the release of excess *qi*; that is, the main desire associated with anger (*nu*) seems to be to get rid of anger *by* possibly directing it at another and thus regaining equilibrium in the body, rather than harming another *as a result* of having a large amount of the emotion.

In the view presented here, the conceptual metaphors and metonymies contribute actively to the content of the prototypical cultural models. Thus it does matter, in regard to the content of the respective emotion concepts (i.e., cultural models), which conceptual metaphors or conceptual metonymies are emphasized or elaborated. For instance, at least in my reading of Taylor and Mbense's (1998) examples, speakers of Zulu elaborate on two metaphors that speakers of English do not or do to a much smaller degree: ANGER (DESIRE) IS HUNGER and ANGER IS A NATURAL FORCE. If you elaborate on DESIRE IS HUNGER as voracious appetite that devours everything indiscriminately (see below) and on NATURAL FORCE as a force that destroys everything (see also below), then this will probably influence the cultural model of anger, as is indeed the case according to Taylor and Mbense (1998). Instead of venting their anger on a specific target (in English the person who offended you), Zulu people appear to respond in a less clearly directed way and behave aggressively toward everyone indiscriminately. This is not to say that English cannot have this response or that Zulu cannot have a directed response; rather, the two languages seem to differ in what they consider the prototypical cultural model.

Broader Cultural Context

We are now in a position to discuss the issue that despite the similarities in body and physiological functioning, there are considerable differences in the conceptualization of anger across the four cultures, as discussed in chapter 8. If we are so much alike physically and our physical makeup matters as much in conceptualization as has been suggested, why don't speakers of English, Hungarian, Japanese, Chinese, and other languages perceive anger in exactly the same ways? The answer may be simple. I suggest that, on the one hand, each of the four cultures has developed its own distinctive concepts that dominate explanations in the given culture and through which members of the culture interpret their (emotional) experiences and, on the other, subtle differences in the conceptualization of physiology may also lead to differences in folk understandings.

In the Euro-American tradition (including Hungary), it is the classical-medieval notion of the *four humors* from which the Euro-American conceptualization of anger (and that of emotion in general) derived (Geeraerts and Grondelaers, 1995). However, the use of the humoral view as a form of cultural explanation extended far beyond anger and the emotions. In addition to being an account of emotional phenomena, it was also used to explain a variety of issues in physiology and medicine (Geeraerts and Grondelaers, 1995).

In Japan, as Matsuki (1995) tells us, there seems to exist a culturally distinct set of concepts that is built around the concept of *hara*. Truth, real intentions, and the real self (called *honne*) constitute the content of *hara*. The term *honne* is contrasted with *tatemae*, or one's social face. Thus when a Japanese person keeps his anger under control, he is hiding his private, truthful, innermost self and displaying a social face that is called for in the situation by accepted standards of behavior.

King (1989) and Yu (1995) suggest that the Chinese concept of *nu* is bound up with the notion of *qi*, that is, the energy that flows through the body. *Qi* in turn is embedded not only in the psychological (i.e., emotional) but also the philosophical and medical discourse of Chinese culture and civilization. The notion and the workings of *qi* are predicated on the belief that the human body is a homeostatic organism, the belief on which traditional Chinese medicine is based. And the conception of the body as a homeostatic organism seems to derive from the more general philosophical view that the universe operates with two complementary forces, *yin* and *yang*, which must be in balance to maintain the harmony of the universe. Similarly, when *qi* rises in the body, there is anger (*nu*), and when it subsides and there is balance again, there is harmony and emotional calm.

Thus the four emotion concepts – *anger* in English, *düh* in Hungarian, *ikari* in Japanese, and *nu* in Chinese – are in part explained in the respective cultures by the culture-specific concepts of the *four humors, hara*, and *qi*. What accounts for the distinctiveness of the culture-specific concepts is the fact that, as we have just seen, the culture-specific concepts that are evoked to explain the emotion concepts are embedded in very different systems of cultural concepts and propositions (as pointed out, e.g., by Lutz, 1987). It appears then that the broader cultural contexts account for many of the differences among the four emotion concepts under investigation.

Ning Yu (1995) observed that Chinese abounds in anger- and happiness-related expressions that employ a variety of internal organs, like the heart, liver, spleen, and gall. According to Yu, this is so because of the influence of Chinese medicine on the conceptualization and hence verbalization of emotion.

The influence of the particular "content" of cultures can be seen in more trivial examples as well. A Zulu expression translates into English as "to grind rotten mealies." The expression refers to the pointlessness of anger (Taylor and Mbense, 1998). It derives its meaning from the staple food of the Zulu people (mealies, or maize corn) and the idea that one shouldn't expend energy on a useless activity (i.e., to grind mealies that are rotten). To the degree that mealies are limited to the Zulu (or Bantu) people, it will uniquely characterize their language about anger.

The broader cultural context also influences how emotion concepts are evaluated. In American culture, anger, for example, has a very negative evaluation for a variety of historical reasons (see Stearns, 1994). This is probably shared by many cultures. However, for speakers of Zulu it may also have a very positive side, due possibly to its association with intense activity. In Zulu culture an active person is more highly valued than a person who is inert or phlegmatic. This gives the angry person a more positive evaluation as well, something that he does not have, or has to a smaller degree, in English-speaking countries (Taylor and Mbense, 1998).

Range of Conceptual Metaphors

There can also be differences in the range of conceptual metaphors that languages and cultures have available for the conceptualization of emotion.

Matsuki (1995) observes that all the metaphors for anger in English as analyzed by Lakoff and Kövecses (1987) can also be found in Japanese. At the same time, she also points out that there are a large number of anger-related expressions that group around the Japanese concept of *hara* (literally, "belly"). As we saw, this is a culturally significant and unique concept, and so the conceptual metaphor ANGER IS HARA is limited to Japanese.

As was noted at the beginning of the chapter, Zulu shares many of the conceptual metaphors that English has. This doesn't mean, however, that it cannot have metaphors other than the ones English has. One case in point is the Zulu metaphor that involves the heart: ANGER IS (UNDERSTOOD AS BEING) IN THE HEART (Taylor and Mbense, 1998). When the heart metaphor applies to English, it is primarily associated with love, affection, and the like. In Zulu it applies to anger and patience – impatience, tolerance – intolerance. The heart metaphor conceptualizes anger in Zulu as leading to internal pressure since too much "emotion substance" is crammed into a container of limited capacity. The things that fill it up will be other emotions that happen to a person in the wake of daily events.

Chinese shares with English all the basic metaphors of happiness: UP, LIGHT, FLUID IN A CONTAINER. A metaphor that Chinese has, but English doesn't, is HAPPINESS IS FLOWERS IN THE HEART (Yu, 1995). According to Ning Yu, the application of this metaphor reflects "the more introverted character of Chinese" (p. 75). He sees this conceptual metaphor as a contrast to the (American) English metaphor BEING HAPPY IS BEING OFF THE GROUND, which does not exist in Chinese at all. Hungarian appears to be halfway between English and Chinese in regards to the BEING OFF THE GROUND metaphor: There are some expressions in Hungarian that could be seen as instances of it but that do not indicate a well-delineated and full-fledged HAPPINESS IS BEING OFF THE GROUND metaphor.

Elaborations of Conceptual Metaphors

In other cases, two languages may share the same conceptual metaphor, but the metaphor will be elaborated differently in the two languages. For example, English has the ANGER IS A HOT FLUID IN A CONTAINER. One metaphorical elaboration of this metaphor in English is that the hot fluid produces steam in the container (cf. "He's just *blowing off steam*"). Now this particular elaboration is absent in, for instance, Zulu (Taylor and Mbense, 1998).

Hungarian shares with English the conceptual metaphors THE BODY IS A CONTAINER FOR THE EMOTIONS and ANGER IS FIRE. The body and the fire inside it are commonly elaborated in Hungarian as a pipe, where anger is a burning substance inside a container (Bokor, 1997). This conceptual elaboration seems to be unique to Hungarian.

Hungarians also tend to use the more specific container of the head (with the brain inside) for the general body container in talking about anger, and a number of Hungarian expressions mention how anger can affect the head and the brain. Linguistic expressions in English do not seem to emphasize the head (or brain) to the same degree (except for the expression "to lose one's head").

Both English and Zulu have FIRE as a source domain for anger, but Zulu elaborates the metaphor in a way in which English does not (Taylor and Mbense, 1998). In Zulu you can *extinguish* somebody's anger by pouring water on them. This possible metaphorical entailment is not picked up by the English FIRE metaphor in the form of conventionalized linguistic expressions. Notice, however, that the metaphorical entailment is perfectly applicable to enthusiasm in English, as when you can be a *wet blanket* at a party.

As noted above, the DESIRE IS HUNGER metaphor in anger works both in English (see chapter 5) and in Zulu. The latter, however, elaborates it in unique ways. In Zulu an angry person's appetite can be so voracious that he eats food that is not even prepared or he does not even separate edible from inedible food (Taylor and Mbense, 1998).

In both English and Zulu, anger can be comprehended as A NATURAL FORCE (for English, see chapter 2). But speakers of Zulu go much further in making use of the metaphor than speakers of English. In Zulu you can say of an angry person that "the sky became dark with thunderclouds," "the sky (=lightning) almost singed us," or "why did he blow a gale?" These elaborations do not exist in English in conventionalized form, but speakers of English may well understand them given the shared conceptual metaphor.

The Range of Metonymies

Not only conceptual metaphors but also conceptual metonymies can participate in producing cross-cultural variation. One language-culture may have metonymies that the other does not have in a conventional linguistic form. Conceptual metonymies, as defined here, are physiological and expressive responses associated with an emotion. The major conventionally verbalized conceptual metonymies for anger in English include body heat, internal pressure, agitation, and interference with accurate perception (see chapter 8). Now these certainly exist in Zulu, but in addition Zulu uses nausea, interference with breathing, illness, perspiration, crying (tears), and inability to speak, as reported by Taylor and Mbense (1998). Most of these can also be found in English, but not in association with anger.

Elaborations of Metonymies

A further source of variation is in the conceptualization of physiology. It was noted above that the physiological responses that are perceived and recognized in language seem to vary. But even the same conceptual metonymies vary cross-culturally in terms of their elaboration and the importance given to them. As we have seen, Chinese culture appears to place a great deal more emphasis on the increase in internal pressure in anger than on body heat. King's (1989) and Yu's (1995) data suggest that Chinese abounds in metonymies relating to pressure but not to heat. The conceptual metonymy of heat is recognized, but it is not emphasized and elaborated. This seems to result in a particular kind of CONTAINER metaphor, one in which the component of pressure is emphasized to the exclusion of heat.

While the eyes are commonly viewed as the "window to the soul" in many cultures, languages vary in the ways in which they make use of the eyes in the conceptualization of emotion. English, for example, employs primarily the intensity of the "light" of the eyes as a metonymic indicator of happiness: the verbs *gleam, glint, shine, sparkle* can all be used to describe a happy person (Kövecses, 1991b). Chinese, however, elaborates primarily on the eyebrows to talk about happiness. Eyebrows in Chinese "are regarded as one of the most obvious indicators of internal feelings" (Yu, 1995, p. 79).

Metonymy Versus Metaphor

Cultural linguistic variation may arise from whether a language emphasizes metaphors or metonymies in its conceptualization of emotion. For example, Taylor and Mbense (1998) note that English primarily uses metaphors to understand the concept of anger, whereas Zulu predominantly uses metonymies. In addition, metonymic processes appear to play a bigger role in the understanding of emotions in Chinese than in English, as the work of King (1989) and Ning Yu (1995) indicates.

Within-Culture Variation

In this section, I will be concerned with variation in the conceptualization of emotion that occurs within a culture. This is a much more difficult task than handling cross-cultural variation because there has been practically no work done on this aspect of emotion from a cognitive linguistic point of view.

In what follows, I will rely on studies of emotion that have been done outside the discipline of linguistics but are detailed enough and contain enough linguistic information to make them amenable to interpretation along the lines of the methodology that I have proposed.

We know from the research outside linguistics that the conceptualization of emotion is not the same, not homogeneous within a culture or society. Individuals vary, and there is variation according to social factors and through time. My question is: How can this within-culture variation be captured with the same conceptual machinery that was used to make generalizations about cross-cultural differences?

Alternative Cultural Models

Cognitive linguistic research has shown that most linguistic categories are polysemous by nature. Some members, or cases, of categories stand out; they are more representative of a category than others. The other members of the category are seen as deviations from the central representative members. The natural polysemy of linguistic categories can be thought of as a large set of cultural models, with one or some models in the center that serve as "cognitive reference points" for all the other models that deviate from them in some way. The reference points are the prototypes, while the others that are seen as deviating from them in some way are nonprototypical cases.

This characterization of linguistic categories also holds for emotion categories, like anger, fear, love, et cetera. There is not just one kind of anger, fear, or love, but literally dozens (see Kövecses, 1986, 1988, 1990). The implication for the study of emotion categories is that at any given time there are a large number of alternative cultural models of emotion available to speakers to interpret and use in talk about their emotional experience. There are at least two interesting issues here that bear on within-culture variation: (1) prototypes of emotion may change through time within the culture, and (2) there can exist several competing or complementary prototypes of emotion at the same time. Let us look at an example of each in American culture.

Prototypes Changing Through Time

Anger. Based on our study of American English, Lakoff and Kövecses (1987) proposed that Americans operate with something like a five-stage prototypical cultural model of anger when they think about this emotion: cause of anger, existence of anger, attempt at control, loss of control, and retribution (see also Gibbs, 1990, for psycholinguistic confirmation of this model). One of the alternative nonprototypical models for anger we suggested is given in the phrase: *channel your anger into something constructive.* This presents anger as something useful in that it provides energy for action and is directed toward a constructive use in that it allows the angry person to achieve positive goals instead of retaliating. What is probably a nonprototypical form of anger today was quite possibly the ideal form of anger in the Victorian period (Stearns, 1994). Stearns observes that "[a]dherence to the ideal of channeled anger showed in at least two settings," one being its use by male politicians and the other by reformers and businessmen (p. 84). A major goal of Victorian emotionology "was to teach controlled use, so that properly socialized adults would be masters of a fund of anger, with the experience to target it appropriately" (p. 31). Anger had to be controlled, just like today, but there was a major prototypical alternative to control: "channeled anger." In other words, what was one of the prototypes of anger in the Victorian period in America became clearly a nonprototypical one in more recent times.

Friendship. Friendship provides another example where there has been a change in the cultural prototype. As Stearns (1994) observes, friendship between two males in the Victorian period was characterized by something that we would probably identify today as romantic love. He writes (Stearns, 1994, pp. 81–82):

> Like the women, they commented on their physical contacts with each other and dreamed of a life of mutual intimacy. When the time came to separate, usually when one friend married, the emotionality of friendship came to the surface again: "[O]ur hearts were full of that true friendship which could not find utterance by words, we laid our heads upon each other's bosom and wept, it may be unmanly to weep, but I care not, the spirit was touched."

This way of talking about friendship does not sound like the language we saw in the analysis of the interviews in chapter 6. This does not, however, mean that love is not a part of the concept of friendship for many people. Indeed, Americans often do talk about love in connection with friendship, but it is not the intense kind of passionate love that is present in the quotation above (see Kövecses, 1993b). This example shows that what was probably the prototype in an earlier period in American culture became less prototypical and was replaced by a new prototype.

Simultaneous Multiple Models

Love. Given that emotion categories consist of a large number of models, we can expect within-culture variation in another sense: There will be competing models, or views, of any given emotion at any point of time. That is, people will contest what, for example, love "really is." What is especially relevant to this is the notion that there can simultaneously be several prototypical models at work in a culture. In *The Language of Love* I suggested that there are at least two prototypes for the concept of love: an ideal and a typical one. One of the main differences between the two is in the intensity of love. While the ideal version is highly passionate and intense, the version represented in "typical love" is much less so. There will be people who favor the ideal model and people who favor the typical one. Who and how many favor which and why is an open empirical question.

However, scholars of American culture do observe that both types of love are present, although probably not believed in or lived by equal numbers of people. Peter Stearns writes (1994, p. 242):

> Love-struck couples wandered around high school corridors less often than in the 1950s. Many observers found the same emotional loosening among adults. As Alan Bloom put it, even the replacement of the phrase "in love" with the word "relationship" suggested greater tentativeness.

Friendship. The concept of friendship reflects the same situation. There seem to be two main alternative, but in this case complementary rather than rival, views of friendship in American culture today. In chapter 6, we saw that friendship, for at least some Americans, is a concept that involves two people who communicate their "real selves" to each other and who help each other when in trouble. Another prototypical model of friendship that is often called "friendliness" exists simultaneously with this model (e.g., Moffatt, 1989). Moffatt (n.d., p. 24, in D'Andrade, 1995, p. 132) explains:

> American friendliness thus bridges or mediates the opposition which contemporary American culture itself posits between the real inner self and more problematic social identities. It is a small, routine daily ritual, and involves assertion of the self and of the values of the self in even the most hostile and anti-individualistic of settings. It is the way Americans remember, and periodically "express," what they are *really* like, even when functioning with their unfortunately necessary social masks on: authentic, individualistic persons who are open, given the right conditions and free choice, to egalitarian friendships with *anyone*."

Thus we can see here two prototypical models of friendship: "true friendship" and "friendliness." Why is it that when we interviewed Americans about friendship they did not talk about this latter kind of friendship? It is possible that of the two it is "true friendship" that most people think of when asked to talk about friendship. It seems to be the "best example," that is, the ideal prototype, whereas "friendliness" is a sociologically common and very visible kind of friendship that people exercise every day (that is, its centrality derives from its typicality). The point is that Americans appear to have two major and complementary conceptions of friendship, not just one, and they use the one that fits their purposes best in a given social situation.

In other words, what is true of love as regards multiple prototypes seems also to be true of other emotions and relationships.

Metonymy Versus Metaphor

As was pointed out above, the language of emotion may emphasize metaphoric or metonymic understanding of a given emotion, and different cultures may prefer one way of understanding rather than the other. The same can apply to a single culture through time. There can be a shift from one to the other, probably typically from metonymic to metaphoric understanding. It is worth quoting in full what Stearns (1994, pp. 66–67) has to say about such a process in connection with the United States:

> Prior to the nineteenth century, dominant beliefs, medical and popular alike, attached anger, joy, and sadness to bodily functions. Hearts, for example, could shake, tremble, expand, grow cold. Because emotions were embodied, they had clear somatic qualities: people were gripped by rage (which could, it was held, stop menstruation), hot blood was the essence of anger, fear had cold sweats. Emotions, in other words, had physical stuff. But during the eighteenth century, historians increasingly realize, the humoral conception of the body, in which fluids and emotions alike, could pulse, gave way to a more mechanistic picture. And in the body-machine emotions were harder to pin down, the symptoms harder to convey. Of course physical symptoms could still be invoked, but now only metaphorically.

And so Victorian Americans used the PRESSURIZED CONTAINER metaphor for anger, which emphasized less the bodily basis of anger (although it was obviously motivated by it), but allowed the Victorians to conceptualize their anger as something in a container that could be channeled for constructive purposes. This was still not the metaphor that is in common use today: the PRESSURE COOKER metaphor. In order for this more recent CONTAINER metaphor for anger to emerge, certain changes had to occur in the general social and cultural setting.

Conceptual Metonymy

If it is true that conceptual metonymies of emotions reflect, at least for the most part, real universal physiology, then it should not be the case that they vary a whole lot either cross-culturally or within a culture (either through time or at the same time). Indeed, we saw some evidence for this in the previous chapter in regards to cross-cultural variation. The metonymies appear to remain roughly the same through time in a given culture, as Stearns's study shows. Analyzing descriptions of Victorian anger, he writes: "Another angry wife almost dies herself: her face reddens with rage, every vein swells and stands out, every nerve quivers, foam covers her lips, and finally she falls as blood gushes from her nose and mouth" (Stearns, 1994, p. 24). Despite the exaggerated character of the description, we can easily identify aspects of the folk theory of the physiological effects of anger that is prevalent today: REDNESS IN THE FACE, INTERNAL PRESSURE, PHYSICAL AGITATION, and INSANE BEHAVIOR. As we would expect, physiological responses associated with anger in the 19th century must have coincided largely with the ones that characterize the folk model today. Moreover, in their experimental studies of the emotions, Ekman and Levenson and their colleagues found consistently that American men and women, young and old, exhibit the same responses when in intense emotional states (Ekman et al., 1983; Levenson et al., 1990).

Alternative Conceptual Metaphors

Friendship. The conceptual metaphors for a given emotion can change through time within a given culture. For example, it was mentioned in the section on alternative cultural models that in Victorian times what we would identify today as romantic love was part of the concept of friendship between males. This came through clearly in the contemporary letters and journals that Peter Stearns studied (1994, pp. 81–82): "In letters and journals they described themselves as 'fervent lovers' and wrote of their 'deep and burning affection.'" As we have seen (in chapters 2 and 5), the FIRE metaphor characterizes passions, like romantic love, while affection today is more commonly thought of in terms of WARMTH rather than (the heat of) FIRE. Indeed, in the interview materials when people talked about love in relation to friendship, friendship was always a more subdued, less intense form of love (affection) conceptualized as warmth. This shows that a metaphor that was conventionally associated with male friendship (through love) for the Victorians was dropped and replaced by a metaphorical source domain indicating less intensity.

Love. Alternative conceptual metaphors may also be available for a given emotion simultaneously in a culture. This seems to be the case with two very prevalent metaphors of love today: LOVE IS A UNITY and LOVE IS AN ECONOMIC EXCHANGE. Importantly, these are the two metaphors that play a central role in the constitution of the two cultural models of love mentioned in a previous section: "ideal love" and "typical love." The ideal version of love is mainly characterized by the UNITY metaphor, whereas the typical version mainly by ECONOMIC EXCHANGE (Kövecses, 1988). The ideal version reflects more traditional ideas about love, the typical case more recent ones. Stearns (1994, p. 173) notes in this connection that after the Victorian period "the sexual emphasis also tended, if only implicitly, to highlight the rewards an individual should get from a relationship rather than the higher unity of the relationship itself." Obviously, talk about "higher unity" and "the rewards the individual should get from a relationship" correspond to the UNITY and EXCHANGE metaphors, respectively. In her study of American love in the 1970s, Ann Swidler (1980, in Bellah, Sullivan, Swidler, and Tipton, 1985, p. 119) reaches a similar conclusion:

> In a *successful exchange* each person is enhanced so that each is more complete, more autonomous, and more self-aware than before. Rather than becoming *part of a whole, a couple, whose meaning is complete only when both are together,* each person becomes stronger; each *gains* the skills he was without and, thus strengthened, is *more "whole."* If we enter love relationships to complete the missing sides of ourselves, then in some sense when the *exchange* is successful we have learned to get along without the capacities the other person had *supplied.* (My italics)

In the passage, as in the two metaphors, love is viewed in two possible ways: In one, there are two parts and only the unity of the two makes them a whole. This is the essence of the traditional conception of love (see also Fuller, 1843). The more recent metaphor takes two wholes that are each not as complete as they could be, but in the process of the exchange they both become stronger, complete wholes. In Swidler's words: "The emerging cultural view of love . . . emphasizes exchange. What is valuable about a relationship is 'what one gets out of it' " (p. 119). Apparently, the EXCHANGE metaphor has become a prevalent metaphor in American culture. This does not mean, however, that the UNITY metaphor is completely forgotten. On the contrary, there are many people in the United States (as briefly discussed in chapter 7) who still use the UNITY metaphor as well.

Broader Cultural Context

But why did all these changes occur in the conceptualization of anger, friendship, and love in American culture? The explanation comes from nonlinguistic studies of the broader cultural context.

Anger. As Stearns (1994, p. 32) notes in connection with Victorian emotionology, anger was not a permissible emotion in the homes, but, for men, it was actually encouraged at the workplace and in the world of politics. Women were supposed to be "anger-free," and men, while calm at home, were expected to make good use of their anger for purposes of competition with others and for the sake of certain moral ends. But why did this "channeled anger" give way to the ideal of "anger-free" people or to the ideal of suppressing anger under all circumstances? Why did anger become a completely negative emotion? There were a variety of specific reasons, as Stearns argues, including the following:

> New levels of concern about anger and aggression followed in part from perceptions of heightened crime, including juvenile delinquency, and the results of untrammeled aggression in Nazism and then renewed world war. It was difficult, in this context, to view channeled anger as a safe or even useful emotional motivation. (p. 195)

As a result, the attacks on any form of anger, which started around the 1920s, continued throughout the Depression period and World War II, leading to a global rejection of the emotion by the 1960s in mainstream culture. The new metaphoric image that became prevalent was that of the "pressure cooker waiting to explode." This was a fully mechanical metaphor that depicted anger as something completely independent of the rational self, the angry person as incapable of any rational judgment, and the resulting angry behavior as extremely dangerous. The process (that started in the 18th century) of the separation of the emotion from the self and the body, that is, the "mechanization" of anger, was now completed.

Friendship. To turn to friendship, we can ask why, in addition to the view of friendship in the Victorian period as almost lovelike, did there emerge a very different, less intense form of friendship called "friendliness" in American culture? Again, the causes are numerous and I can't go into all of them here (but see Stearns, 1994). One of them, however, is that there were demands for a "new emotionology" from outside the "private sphere," especially the world of business and large corporations (see Hochschild, 1983). Again, Stearns (1994, pp. 292–293) explains:

> American language continued to reflect incorporation of a pleasant but nonintense emotionality. "Niceness" became a watchword for sales clerks and others in casual contact. "Have a nice day" struck many foreigners – even neighboring Canadians – as a remarkably insincere phrase. At the same time though, they noted that Americans did seem "nice," an attribute that includes unusual discomfort with emotional outbursts on the part of those raised in different cultures where displays of temper might be more readily accepted. In American culture, "nice" did have a meaning – it connoted a genuine effort to be agreeably disposed but not deeply emotionally involved while expecting pleasant predictability from others.

Furthermore the new emotionology considerably "reduced tolerance to other people's intensity" (p. 244). Although, as we saw, friendship for many Americans is an opportunity to talk out their problems, "intense emotion was also a sign of immaturity, and it could be shunned on that basis" (p. 245).

Love. Finally, why did the conception of love change? But even before that happened, why was romantic love so intense in the Victorian period to begin with? According to Stearns (1994, p. 66): "Hypertrophied maternal love increased the need for strong adult passion to aid products of emotionally intense upbringing in freeing themselves from maternal ties." In addition, "in intense, spiritualized passion, couples hoped to find some of the same balm to the soul that religion had once, as they dimly perceived, provided. . . . More concluded that true love was itself a religious experience" (p. 69). Now, in the wake of increasingly looser family ties and the ever-weakening importance of religion, the intensity of romantic love also declined. Romantic love ceased to be regarded "as the spiritual merger of two souls into one" (p. 172). Rationality was emphasized in all walks of life, possibly due to the influence of business and the rational organization of large corporations. By 1936, marriage manuals stressed the idea of "rational, cooperative arrangements between men and women. Soaring ideals and spirituality were largely absent. . . . Companionship, not emotional intensity, was the goal" (pp. 175–176). And after the 1960s, relationships were regarded as "exchange arrangements in which sensible partners would make sure that no great self-sacrifice was involved" (p. 180).

The overall result was that "twentieth-century culture . . . called for management across the board; no emotion should gain control over one's thought processes" (Stearns, 1994, p. 184). The rational culture of the computer was in place, together with the new and highly valued emotional attitude of staying "cool."

Conclusion

In sum, the conceptual tools of prototypical and nonprototypical cultural models, conceptual metaphors and metonymies, and cultural context can all be put to useful work in the study of cultural variation of emotion concepts. They enable us to see with considerable clarity precisely where and how cultural variation occurs both cross-culturally and within a culture. Moreover, given the cultural context and its influence on conceptualization, we can see why the changes take place in the cultural models and the conceptual metaphors.

10. Emotion Language
A New Synthesis

I believe that the several detailed analyses in this work of various issues concerning the emotions make possible certain generalizations, and possibly not only about emotion language. As a matter of fact, one of the generalizations is that most emotion language, and hence thought about emotion, is a "shared property" of several aspects of our folk theory of the mind and not an exclusive property of our conception of the emotions. Another generalization that naturally emerges from what has been done is that we should not forever be imprisoned in the mutually exclusive camps of "universalists" versus "relativists" or "essentialists" versus "social constructionists" in regard to our views about the conceptualization of emotion. Finally, a general picture of emotion language also emerges, a picture that, hopefully, sheds some light on important aspects of emotional meaning.

These then are the topics of this last chapter. I will begin with a proposed new synthesis between the social constructionist and the cognitive linguistic views of emotion concepts.

The New Synthesis with Social Constructionism

In his *Andaman Islanders*, published in 1922, Radcliffe-Brown defined a *sentiment* as "an organized system of emotional tendencies centered about some object" (p. 234). He asserted that "a society depends for its existence on the presence in the minds of its members of a certain system of sentiments by which the conduct of the individual is regulated in conformity with the needs of the society" (pp. 233–234). In his view, these emotional dispositions permeated the social system. The major function of ceremonials was to serve as collective expressions that transmitted social sentiments from one generation to the next. Significantly, he asserted that "in human society the sentiments in question are not innate but are developed in the individual by the action of the society upon him" (p. 234).

This view provides a useful historical point of reference as we examine contemporary theories of emotion and emotion language. For example, we find in Radcliffe-Brown significant points in common with the contemporary social constructionist approach to emotion language, a position that is currently gaining popularity. Lutz (1988) argues that it is wrong to "essentialize" human emotions by holding the view that there are a few basic innate or universal emotions. But, nevertheless, on the basis of the evidence presented in this book, it seems that a position denying the universality of a few basic emotions cannot be sustained.

At the same time, it seems possible to propose a synthesis that merges the social constructionist (SC) and universalist approaches into a unified view of emotions and emotion language. It seems appropriate to call this unified approach "body-based constructionism" (BBC) and the prototypical cultural models that the approach aims to uncover the "embodied cultural prototype." I can of course only suggest this as a hypothesis; much further research will be required to prove it. Many additional languages will have to be analyzed by the methodology described in this book, focusing on emotions other than just the few emotion concepts we have looked at here. It will be important that the languages examined in this light include the ones that provided the evidence for the social-constructionist thesis in the first place.

Essentially, the synthesis involves acknowledging that some aspects of emotion language and emotion concepts are universal and clearly related to the physiological functioning of the body. Once the universal aspects of emotion language are parsed out, the very significant remaining differences in emotion language and concepts can be explained by reference to differences in cultural knowledge and pragmatic discourse functions that work according to divergent culturally defined rules or scenarios (see Palmer, 1996). This approach also allows us to see points of tension where cultural interests might contradict, suppress, or distort innate tendencies of expression. Thus, we need not be forever aligned in opposing camps, the innatists pitted against the social constructionists. The two approaches should be regarded as complementary (as also suggested by Stearns, 1994).

Even the methodological differences are not as big as they seem to be at first. Unlike the BBC approach, which has been amply demonstrated in the previous chapters, the SC approach is typically to work with a small set of emotion concepts, like anger fear, sadness, et cetera, and to try to see how these are used in a given culture for certain social, ideological, and pragmatic purposes. This need not be the case, however. There is nothing in the theory or fundamental principles of SC that prevents it from looking at the richness of linguistic data that has been offered in this work. Indeed, the basic ideas of SC would require that researchers working in SC pay just as much attention to the richness of the linguistic data as those in cognitive linguistics do. One of originators of the SC movement, Rom Harré, says: "Instead of asking the question, 'What is anger?' we would do well to begin by asking, 'How is the word *anger*, and other expressions that cluster around it, actually used in this or that cultural milieu and type of episode?' " (Harré, 1986 p. 5). In other words, Harre is interested in not just how the word *anger* is used but also in the "other expressions that cluster around it." This is because one of the basic ideas of SC is to see the entire range of "language games" that are played in a culture. This requirement is hardly ever met, however, in actual case studies done along the SC lines.

The same seems to apply to the role that researchers attribute to metaphor and figurative language in general in SC. Figurative language is regarded as merely an epiphenomenon, something that can be ignored. But this need not be the case either. Again, Harré is aware of the need for research on and the potential significance of figurative language in the conceptualization of emotions:

> We do say that someone is *puffed up or swollen with pride*, too. These metaphors may perhaps be traced to an element of the ridiculous in an exaggerated or excessive display. The matter deserves further research. The same could be said for hope, which also benefits from a cluster of characteristic metaphors, such as *surging, springing*, and the like. (Harré, 1986, p. 9)

The present work can be seen as a demonstration of precisely how metaphor and figurative language "benefit" emotion concepts in general. In this sense, it could even be claimed that the "best constructivists," that is, the researchers who most completely realize the SC program, are the cognitive linguists. It is another matter that, obviously, the social constructionists have paid a lot more attention to the social aspects of emotion concepts than cognitive linguists do or should.

To some degree, the difference between the BBC and SC approaches may be simply a matter of emphasis. In chapters 8 and 9, I made a distinction between general image–schematic and potentially universal aspects of emotion concepts, on the one hand, and more specific cultural aspects, on the other. It is the general schemas that are filled out in diverse ways with specific cultural material. One can put the emphasis on both sides. I did not mean, however, to place more stress on the general image–schematic aspects than on the cultural ones. As a matter of fact, my descriptions of, for instance, romantic love in 1986 and 1988 included such explicitly social "propositions" as "I view myself and the other as forming a unity," "I experience the relationship as a state of perfect harmony," "I see love as something that guarantees the stability of the relationship," and "Love is mutual." Moreover, Lakoff and my description of even anger involved similarly explicit social propositions concerning control, responsibility, wrongdoer, victim, and the like (Lakoff and Kövecses, 1987). While the SC approach does not deny the presence of bodily "stuff" in our cultural models, it places a lot more emphasis on social, ideological, and pragmatic functions (see, e.g., Harré, 1986).

But it is precisely when it comes to this bodily "stuff" that the SC and BBC approaches differ from each other. For proponents of SC, the bodily, physiological aspects of emotion concepts simply cooccur with or merely augment more important social, ideological, and so forth functions. They talk about "embodiment" and "embodied emotion concepts," in the sense that emotions are taken to be associated with bodily and physiological processes, but they do not attribute a major role to this embodiment. With the BBC approach, however, this plays a crucial role. As I suggested in chapter 8, embodiment appears to place some constraints on the kinds of emotion concepts that can emerge. Lutz's scenario of *song* looks like a conceptualization of Ifaluk anger that contradicts this claim. This is why it is all-important to reexamine the language of Ifaluk with the same methodology that was used in the study of anger in several fundamentally different cultures in this work.

It is not necessary that we brand either approach as entirely right or entirely wrong. Both have strengths and weaknesses. However, to be complete, as one would aim to be in writing a grammar, it is necessary, where emotional complexes exist as stable sociocultural/psychobiological entities, to describe them in all their detail, both linguistic and social. The merger may obviously benefit both approaches.

At this point interesting questions arise: How far can the BBC approach take us in accounting for emotions that are less clearly bodily based than anger? And, conversely, could the SC approach tell us the whole story about emotion concepts like anger as conceptualized in diverse cultures? If the results of the last two chapters in this book are sound, the answer to the latter question, I suspect, is that it could not. It could not account for the striking similarities in conceptualization that we found in several unrelated languages.

It is more difficult to answer the first question. We do not have detailed linguistic evidence for less obviously bodily based emotion concepts, like hope and pride, in fundamentally different languages. Until this evidence is "in," it is impossible to say whether the BBC approach can be extended to such concepts in different languages. My study of the English concepts of pride and respect indicates that the understanding of these concepts is motivated by certain kinds of bodily behavior, such as "chest out" for pride and "more powerful is up: less powerful is down" for respect (Kövecses, 1990). Consideration of this type of behavior would of course mean that when in the BBC approach I talk about "body based constructions," I also include bodily behavior in a wider sense and not just physiological processes of the body.

The General Picture of Emotional Meaning

In this section, I will go through the main ideas that have emerged in the work point by point.

Content of Emotional Experience

An emotion concept typically evokes content pertaining to all aspects of experience: social, cognitive, and physical. This complex content is organized as a more or less stable configuration. The richness of content makes it difficult to accumulate comparable data on diverse languages and cultures because different researchers tend to select different kinds of data as representative. The scenario of ideal love described in Kövecses (1988) includes knowledge pertaining to social action, cognition, and physiology. The account of *song* in Ifaluk (Lutz, 1988) is concerned entirely with social events in stages 1–3 and 5. Only stage 4 mentions the emotion "fear," hinting at the possible inclusion of cognitive and physiological information in the Ifaluk conceptualization of *song*.

Scenario Structure

The content of emotion concepts can best be described as scenarios. These vary widely on the dimensions of abstraction and complexity of phasing. The scenario of ideal love in *The Language of Love* (Kövecses, 1988) is relatively abstract. It covers the whole process of falling and being in love, but it has only three stages or phases. The account of *song* in Ifaluk lies at the middle level of abstraction and deals with what appears to be a relatively short-term process with five stages.

Culture-Specificity

The social action content of emotion language can best be described as culturally specific social scenarios. In folk knowledge, these scenarios are probably represented simultaneously at several levels of abstraction. Choosing the right descriptive level may depend upon one's intended audience or readership.

Universal Psychobiological Basis

Feeling states have an irreducible and probably universal psychobiological basis that accounts for many similarities in the conceptualization of emotions. Taking anger as an example, we find that both English and Zulu figurative language characterizes anger as pressure in a container, as heat, as bile, and so forth (Taylor and Mbense, 1998). Chinese shares with English all the basic metaphors of happiness: It is up, it is light, and it is fluid in a container (Yu, 1995).

Feeling States as Culturally Determined

Feeling states are also, in part, culturally determined. This is because events that evoke parallel emotions in different cultures are unlikely to induce them in precisely the same way. Perhaps it is only Zulus who experience the onset of anger as a "squashing in the heart" (Taylor and Mbense, 1998). Perhaps it is only the Japanese who experience extreme anger as coming to the head (*atama*) with a "click" (Matsuki,

1995). Perhaps it is only the Chinese who conceptually distribute their anger to various parts of the body rather than directing it toward offenders (King, 1989). Perhaps it is only Hungarians who conceptualize the angry body as a pipe containing a burning substance.

Prototypes

Emotion concepts occur as prototypes and even multiple prototypes (see, e.g., Kövecses, 1991a, 1991b), with variants on them, providing a basis for polysemy in emotion language. Emotion concepts are not monolithic but come in a variety of cultural models for each emotion.

Language Focus

Languages vary in respect to whether their vocabularies of emotion terms are chiefly metaphoric or chiefly metonymic, or more or less elaborate and focused in one domain or another, that is, in the domains of physiological experience, cognition, or social action. Thus, Tahitians apparently lack a general term for sadness and they lack the concept that it has external, social causes. In Tahiti, sadness may be "hypocognized" (Levy, 1984).

Figurative Language

Figurative language, including metaphor and metonymy, contributes a great deal to the conceptualization of emotion concepts. Some metaphors reflect (potentially) universal notions, such as the idea that anger is conceptualized as pressure in a container. Metonymies may also denote universal aspects of emotions, such as the idea that anger is internal pressure, loss of muscular control, redness, a rise in body temperature, and loss of rationality. Other metaphors and metonymies may be specific to a culture, perhaps in part because their particular physical experience of anger is not shared by all cultures. For example, Zulus become wet with anger, but Americans do not (Taylor and Mbense, 1998).

Emotion Language and Meaning

Emotion language thus consists in much more than the names of emotions. The wide range of emotional experience requires us to describe these experiences by means of an equally wide range of linguistic expressions. It follows that the study of emotional meaning is also more than the explication of the meaning of words naming emotions (as conceived, e.g., by Wierzbicka, 1995).

Universality of Emotional Meaning

Emotional meaning consists of two complementary parts: a basic image-schema of force and cultural content. The cultural content is culture-specific, while the force-schema that structures this content appears to be a (potential) universal. The cultural content is much richer and more specific than Wierzbicka's schematic configurations of assumed universal semantic primitives.

Folk Theory Versus Expert Theory

There seem to be systematic correspondences between folk and expert theories of emotion. The precise nature of these correspondences is not clear at this point and further investigation is needed by cultural historians and historians of science. The contribution of the present approach to this issue is that it can lay bare the folk theory of emotions and can thus offer explicit and detailed folk models to the historians for their investigations.

Returning to Some Issues

The synthesis of body, culture, and language above enables us to return to some of the major issues raised at the beginning of this work. First, the synthesis allows us to see why LeDoux's (1996) suggestion concerning the role of conscious feelings in human emotions is not acceptable. According to LeDoux, conscious feelings "are the frills that have added icing to the emotional cake." What we saw instead in this book is that conscious feelings as encoded in language are constituted by a rich diversity of humanly relevant factors that are crucial aspects of the experience of human emotions; they include social, cognitive, and bodily factors, without which no truly human emotions are imaginable. And we might also add various discourse-pragmatic factors (not treated in the present book) as shown in the work of a number of authors (e.g., Rosaldo, 1980; Abu-Lughod, 1986; Lutz, 1988; Lutz and Abu-Lughod, 1990; Irvine, 1995; Palmer and Brown, 1998). The social, cognitive, pragmatic, and bodily factors together provide the key constituents of the experience of emotion in human society for beings working under certain biological pressures, with a particular brain and cognitive system for handling these pressures, communicating in language or otherwise under certain pragmatic conditions, and having a particular kind of body. It is not really possible to take any one of these factors out from a comprehensive view of human emotions. They jointly define and constitute what we as human beings experience as emotion.

This said, we can agree with LeDoux in a limited but very important sense. It is the functioning of the body in emotion, especially our physiology, that appears to constrain the language we use to talk about the emotions and the emotional experiences (the conscious feelings of emotion) that we can have. Based on the study of anger in chapter 8, I argued that the functioning of the human body in emotion that all human beings share influences the conceptualization and experience of anger across a range of genetically unrelated cultures. In this specific and limited sense, the body does indeed play an important role in emotion.

What is the relationship between folk, or cultural, models of emotion and scientific theories of emotion? As was described above, the conceptualization and experience of emotional feelings is structured by cultural models. The cultural or folk models are both generic and specific-level structures. At least in the case of the basic emotions, the generic-level schema involves "cause-force-response." In the light of the evidence we have so far, this schema seems to be universal. Most of the richness of human emotional experience is, however, given by the specific-level cultural models. As we just saw, these appear to encapsulate a rich variety of culturally determined experiences and vary cross-culturally. My argument in chapter 7 was that many expert or scientific theories of emotion can be viewed as extensions of folk, or cultural, models or parts of these, such as particular metaphors, metonymies, or related concepts. This idea and the issue from which it arises gains additional significance in the light of the controversy in the philosophy of mind concerning the relationship between folk psychology and scientific psychology. The debate centers around the issue of whether all scientific psychology is merely an organized and structured form of folk psychology. Some neuroscientists, such as the Churchlands (see e.g., Patricia S. Churchland, 1986), argue that by finding in the brain all the material processes that underlie the phenomena that are of interest to both folk and scientific psychology (such as the emotions), it will be possible to explain the "really important" aspects of these phenomena. If this can be done, the argument goes, they will prove wrong not only folk psychology but also scientific psychology. Thus, scientific psychology together with folk psychology, can be eliminated.

How does this kind of neural and bodily reductionism fit into the spirit of this book? On the one hand, it would seem that the kind of work that I have been engaged in here would support the views of the eliminativists. After all, it could be argued, if the body plays such an important role as I attribute to it in shaping folk models of emotion and if expert theories of emotion are mere extensions of the folk models, then my findings support these reductionist views. The most important "things" happen in the physical brain and body. This is true to some extent. But the crucial question is exactly how much role I attribute to the body in shaping the conceptualization and experience of human emotion. As I indicated above, I view it as playing an important but limited role in this. Moreover, the bulk of our emotional experience is constituted by conscious feelings that derive from social, cognitive, bodily, and discourse-pragmatic factors. In this sense, then, I disagree with this reductionist tendency.

Why Metaphor Matters

The most conspicuous feature of emotion language in English is its metaphoric and metonymic nature. The metonymies are unique to the emotions, but they contribute relatively little to the conceptualization of emotions (i.e., to conceptual content). However, a surprising finding of this study appears to be that there does not seem to exist a metaphorical language that "belongs" only to the emotions. Most of emotion language is not specific to the emotions. (We discussed two possible cases of exceptions to this: the metaphorical language that refers to the "inside" of the person, i.e., aspects of the CONTAINER metaphor, and some metaphors that have to do with specific causes and effects of emotions. See chapter 3.) This feature of emotion language does not make metaphor any less significant in our comprehension of emotion and emotional experience. In fact it makes the role of metaphor even more intriguing, as I hope to show below on the basis of the results of this book. Emotion language is largely metaphorical in English (and in all probability in other languages as well) in order to capture the variety of diverse and intangible emotional experiences. Methodologically, then, this language is important in finding out about these experiences. The language, however, is not only a reflection of the experiences but it also creates them. Simply put, we say what we feel and we feel what we say. These experiences are unique to human beings. Only human beings have the kind of consciousness and language that can work figuratively.

This metaphorical language has been shown to be shared by three large systems: the force dynamic system (chapter 5), the event structure metaphor (chapter 4), and the larger conceptual system (chapter 3). One can think of the three as hierarchically related, such that the force dynamic system is part of the event structure metaphor, which is part of the conceptual system as a whole.

The Force Dynamic System

Force is the "master" metaphor for emotion. The specific-level metaphors that characteristically apply to the emotions are all instantiations of this metaphor. In force dynamics, two forces interact according to our naive understanding of how physical forces interact and this is mapped onto our conception of emotion in a systematic fashion. It is in this sense that we can talk about "the force of emotion."

This finding becomes especially interesting in the light of one of LeDoux's (1996) suggestions. LeDoux argues that emotions come in separate systems. Different parts and aspects of the brain and body participate in each such system. There is a distinct system for fear, for anger, for joy, for sadness, and so on. There may be some connections and overlaps among them, but they basically function as separate systems. Now one of the key findings of this book suggests a very different picture. We found an overarching master metaphor for emotions in which emotions are conceptualized as forces, yielding the generic metaphor EMOTIONS ARE FORCES. In other words, in the domain of "conscious feelings" there seems to exist a unitary system that organizes the distinct emotions into a coherent whole. I find this a remarkable feature of the conceptualization of emotions, as it contrasts markedly with what LeDoux suggests on the basis of his experiments. Obviously, I cannot and do not want to compare "apples with oranges," that is, a property of conscious feelings (their unitary organization) with a property of brain systems (their separateness). Nevertheless, it seems to me that this incongruence in results calls for some explanation. Assuming that both claims are correct, I find it strange that the emotions as brain states and bodily responses appear to form distinct and separate systems, while the (conceptualization of) conscious feelings in the various emotions appear to form a single unitary and overarching system. Although I cannot reconcile the discrepancy, I believe that it is legitimate at least to raise the issue.

The Event Structure Metaphor

Force is a part or aspect of the EVENT STRUCTURE metaphor. Forces cause events, and as a result of this (metonymic) relationship we have in Event Structure the metaphor CAUSES ARE FORCES. Emotions are related to events in a variety of ways, as we saw. The overlap of emotion with Event Structure accounts for the several ways in which emotions can be subcategorized.

The General Conceptual System

But the EVENT STRUCTURE metaphor, and hence the FORCE metaphor, has a scope of application much wider than the emotions. It pervades our entire conceptual system. In chapter 3, I showed that most of the emotion metaphors are employed wherever we have the need to conceptualize such extremely general dimensions or aspects of experience as "existence," "control," "passivity," "difficulty," "harm," "intensity," "desire," and the like. (There are some exceptions to this noted in chapter 3, but, on the whole, the exceptions are marginal.)

In this sense, most of the language about, and the conceptualization of, the emotions is not an exclusive property of the emotions.

Emotions and How They Differ from Other Domains

If this is the case, then how does the domain of emotion differ from other abstract domains in our conceptual system? Let us begin by first looking at a domain that was discussed earlier: human relationships. After this, I will contrast the language of emotion with that of morality and rational thought.

Human Relationships and Emotions. Human relationships are one of the closest conceptual "neighbors" of emotions by virtue of the fact that they commonly incorporate emotions or are half emotions and half relationships themselves (like love). In their "pure" capacity of human relations, the conceptualization of relationships, like love, marriage, and friendship, differs from that of emotions in that they are characterized by what I called the COMPLEX SYSTEMS and INTERACTIVE RELATIONSHIPS metaphors. The former enables people to view complex abstract systems metaphorically as complex physical objects, while the latter enables them to view interactive relationships of any kind, including communication, as economic exchanges. This is why relationships are "built," "maintained," or "strengthened," and this is why they can "function," "break down," or "need repair" (the COMPLEX SYSTEMS metaphor). In addition, people in a relationship are engaged in a "give and take," "invest" in the relationship, and can "benefit" from it (the INTERACTIVE RELATIONSHIP metaphor). By contrast, the force metaphor for the emotions provides a diametrically opposed way of comprehending the emotions, one in which people in an emotional state can *explode, go crazy, be burdened, be swept off their feet,* and *be ruled* by an emotion.

Morality and Emotion. But there may be other abstract domains besides the emotions that also have physical forces in their conceptualization. One of these is the domain of morality. We are moral if we can *"resist* temptations," if we have "moral *strength,"* and if we can *"stand up to"* evil. All these cases assume two different physical forces: the *force* of people to *withstand* something and the *force* to which people can *stand* up and which they can *resist.* But this gives us a problem: How is EMOTION-AS-FORCE distinguished from MORALITY-AS-RESISTING A PHYSICAL FORCE? In order to see this, we have to go into some of the details of the metaphorical conceptualization of morality in English.

The MORALITY-AS-RESISTING-A-PHYSICAL FORCE metaphor was analyzed by Lakoff in his recent book entitled *Moral Politics.* Lakoff (1996, p. 72) points out that the dominant metaphor for morality in America is a complex metaphor:

BEING GOOD IS BEING UPRIGHT
BEING BAD IS BEING LOW
DOING EVIL IS FALLING
EVIL IS A FORCE
MORALITY IS STRENGTH

(Other metaphors for morality are provided and analyzed by both Lakoff, 1996, and Johnson, 1993.) In this metaphor complex, a physical force can cause objects to fall from high to low, that is, evil can make people commit immoral acts, as a result of which they move from a moral ("high") to an immoral ("low") position. The best example of this is, of course, the biblical *fall*. If, however, people have enough moral *strength*, they can *resist* the force of evil.

Now we can see more clearly how the EMOTION-AS-FORCE metaphor differs from the MORALITY IS STRENGTH TO RESIST A FORCE metaphor. In the discussion of the application of force dynamics to the emotions, intense emotions were shown to be understood as a situation involving the interaction of two forces: self and emotion (Agonist and Antagonist). The typical situation is such that the emotion (Antagonist) overcomes the self (Agonist), who thus loses control over the emotion. This is represented diagrammatically in Table 10.1 and contrasts with the conceptualization of morality as shown in Table 10.2. Thus, while in emotion the self typically loses control over strong emotion, the moral self maintains its control over evil. In other words, the emotional person is "weak," whereas the moral person is "strong."

In this metaphorical conception, morality is the "strength" of the self to maintain control over the "forces" of evil; hence the notion of "moral strength." In the same way as emotion cannot be understood without the underlying metaphor of physical forces in interaction, mo-

Table 10.1. *Emotion and Force*

Metaphorical Mapping	Agonist's Force Tendency	Antagonist's Force Tendency	Resultant Action
Source	*Physical object* to withstand damage	*Physical force* to cause damage to object	damage is done
Target	*Self* to maintain self-control over emotion	*Emotion* to make self lose control over emotion	self loses control over emotion

Source: Two physical forces.
Target: Emotion.

Table 10.2. *Morality and Force*

Metaphorical Mapping	Agonist's Force Tendency	Antagonist's Force Tendency	Resultant Action
Source	*Physical object* to withstand damage	*Physical force* to cause damage to object	no damage
Target	*Self* to maintain control over evil (i.e., to maintain morality)	*Evil* to make self lose control over evil (i.e., to make him immoral)	self maintains control over evil (i.e., maintains morality)

Source: Two physical forces.
Target: Morality.

rality cannot either. However, the force metaphor applies to the two abstract domains differentially. The details of these differences are necessary to see exactly how the conceptualization of emotion is at the same time similar to and different from that of morality.

Rational Thought and Emotion. How is our comprehension of rational thought different from that of emotion? We would expect that it should be exactly opposite the way the emotions are understood. Indeed, as Jäkel (1995) shows, the workings of the mind and rational thought are conceptualized through the notion of direct physical manipulation. In this master metaphor, the mind is a workshop where a variety of "activities" take place: we *work* on a problem, *store* ideas in memory, *look at* questions *from all sides, hammer out* a solution, *put things on the back burner* for a while, and so forth. This is a large and intricate metaphorical system that helps us understand various aspects of the mind and rational thought, such as problem solving, memory, attention, and the like. According to Jäkel, what informs and unifies all these aspects of the mind is the underlying master metaphor: MENTAL ACTIVITY IS MANIPULATION. This direct manipulation of physical objects takes place in the "workshop" of the mind. The metaphor is based on the main mappings below:

workman → rational self
physical objects → objects of thought

Table 10.3. MENTAL ACTIVITY IS MANIPULATION

Metaphorical Mapping	Agonist's Force Tendency	Antagonist's Force Tendency	Resultant Action
Source	*Physical objects* to resist change by the workman	*Workman* to change the physical objects	the physical objects undergo change
Target	*Objects of thought* to resist change by the self	*Rational self* to change the objects of thought	the objects of thought undergo change

Source: Manipulation (of physical objects).
Target: Mental activity.

physical manipulations → mental activities
tools → intellect
workshop → mind

Here the entity that tries to change another entity (the objects of thought) is the workman corresponding to the rational self, whereas in emotion and morality it was the rational self that was the "target" of change by another forceful entity (the emotion and temptation, respectively). We can restate these mappings in the terminology of force dynamics. If we continue to use the term Antagonist for a stronger entity whose tendency is to change another (weaker) entity that resists this change (at least initially), we get the representation in Table 10.3. That is to say, in thought the self is the Antagonist (whose force tendency is to change an entity), not the Agonist (the entity whose force tendency is to remain unchanged), as was the case in the other two domains. In thought, the entity that is in control is the rational self, just as the workman is in the workshop.

Some Implications

If this analysis of the three domains is correct, it has some important implications – both practical and theoretical. On the practical side, the analysis helps us understand why many practicing psychologists and counselors, as well as many self-help books, are preoccupied with the notion of control. A large part of therapeutic practice is devoted to issues of control. The concept of control is important in this field because therapy often involves questions about the emotions and morality. In particular, counselors often encourage people to be less inhibited emotionally, that is, "to give in to the forces" of emotion. In addition, in many cases psychologists and counselors offer the opposite advice; that is, they encourage people to exercise tighter control in their lives. These are the standard cases. However, it can also happen that people exercise more control then they should. Some people who consider themselves especially moral often control their emotions very tightly. They connect the emotion and morality domains in such a way that they conceive of their emotions as forces of temptations, thus seeing their emotions as dangerous or even evil forces that they should resist. These people are often talked about as being *uptight* and *control freaks*. (I owe these observations to Bonnie Howe.) Based on this case, it seems to me possible that in domains where the emotions are somehow present, we will find the same metaphorical themes and perhaps the same or similar issues.

On the theoretical side, the analysis has an important implication for the cognitivist theory of metaphor. Several authors (e.g., Lakoff and Johnson, 1980) have suggested that source domains (such as CONTAINER, JOURNEY, BUILDING, HOT FLUID IN A CONTAINER, FIRE, BURDEN, INSANITY, SUPERIOR, and many others) simply cluster around particular target domains and map onto different aspects of the target. The idea has been demonstrated for a large number of target domains, including ARGUMENT (Lakoff and Johnson, 1980), ANGER (Lakoff and Kövecses, 1987), and HAPPINESS (Kövecses, 1991b). Now we can see that this view is only part of the story of metaphorical understanding. Another part is that the metaphorical source domains characterizing targets that are related to a common superordinate concept appear to form a large and intricate system. In the case of the emotions, we called this system the FORCE system and presented it as the metaphor EMOTION IS FORCE, where emotion is a superordinate concept to a number of basic-level emotion categories, such as anger, fear, sadness, and joy. Now most of the source domains that characterize these and other basic-level emotion concepts form a part of the FORCE SYSTEM. In other words, individual conceptual metaphors cohere into a system at the superordinate level. It remains to be seen whether this finding applies to other domains with the same kind of superordinate–subordinate structure.

Another theoretical implication involves the general metaphorical structure of our conceptual system. The domains of emotion, morality, and thought are the major faculties of the mind in traditional philosophy and psychology. This division of the mind is also our folk theory of the mind. What is at the center of the three domains is a particular kind of self – the self that faces the issue of losing or maintaining control. In emotion the self turns out to lose control, in morality it turns out to maintain control, while in rational thought the self is "its own master," that is, the Antagonist in control, at least in the normal, everyday "operations" of the mind (which is not to say that we can't have a hard time remembering, deciding, solving, etc., things, i.e., face a powerful "counterforce"). This discourse is based entirely on the notion of two interacting physical forces. This is a metaphorical way of thinking about three essential and abstract aspects of the human mind. The three aspects are related by the metaphorical source domain of PHYSICAL FORCE. They cohere into a large metaphorical system: the FORCE SYSTEM. The various applications of this system provide much of our understanding of the human mind. In this light, emotion can be seen as being coherently integrated into the conceptualization that structures the human mind as a whole at an extremely general level. This conceptualization is inescapably metaphorical, as I tried to show for the concept of emotion in some detail in this book and for the others sketchily in this chapter. And it is metaphorical in a nontrivial way; it creates a large interlocking and coherent system into which various domains, or faculties, of the folk theory of the mind neatly fit.

References

Abu-Lughod, Lila. (1986). *Veiled sentiments: Honor and poetry in a Bedouin society.* Berkeley and Los Angeles: University of California Press.

Alston, W. P. (1967). Emotion and feeling. In P. Edwards (Ed.), *The Encyclopedia of philosophy* (Vol. 2.). New York: Macmillan and the Free Press.

Arnold, M. B. (1960). *Emotion and personality.* (2 vols.). New York: Columbia University Press.

Averill, J. R. (1974). An analysis of psychophysiological symbolism and its influence on theories of emotion. *Journal of the Theory of Social Behavior, 4,* 147–190.

Averill, J. R. (1982). *Anger and aggression: An essay on emotion.* NY: Springer-Verlag.

Averill, J. R. (1990). Inner feelings, works of the flesh, the beast within, diseases of the mind, driving force, and putting on a show: Six metaphors of emotion and their theoretical extensions. In D. Leary (Ed.), *Metaphors in the history of psychology,* (pp. 104–132). Cambridge: Cambridge University Press.

Averill, J. R., & Kövecses, Z. (1990). The concept of emotion: Further metaphors. In Z. Kövecses, *Emotion concepts* (pp. 160–181). New York: Springer-Verlag.

Barcelona, Antonio. (1986). On the concept of depression in American English: A cognitive approach. *Revista Canaria de Estudios Ingleses, 12,* 7–33.

Baxter, L. A. (1992). Root metaphors in accounts of developing romantic relationships. *Journal of Social and Personal Relationships, 9,* 253–275.

Bellah, R. N., Sullivan, W. M., Swidler, A., & Tipton, Steven M. (1985). *Habits of the heart: Individualism and commitment in American life.* Berkeley and Los Angeles: University of California Press.

Berlin, Brent, & Kay, Paul. (1969). *Basic color terms: Their universality and evolution,* Berkeley: University of California Press.

Besnier, Nico. (1990). Language and affect. *Annual Review of Anthropology, 19,* 419–451.

Bokor, Zsuzsanna. (1997). Body-based constructionism in the conceptualization of anger. Paper 17 in the *C.L.E.A.R. series (Cognitive Linguistics: Explorations, Applications, Research).* Working papers of the Department of English, Hamburg University, and Department of American Studies, Eötvös Loránd University, Budapest.

Burnyeat, M. F. (1997). Anger and revenge. Paper presented at the conference *La Rabbia e il furore*, December, Città di Castello.

Buss, D. M. (1988). Love acts. In R. J. Sternberg & M. L. Barnes (Eds.), *The psychology of love*. New Haven, CT: Yale University Press.

Churchland, Patricia Smith. (1986). *Neurophilosophy: Toward a unified science of the mind/brain*. Cambridge, MA: The MIT Press.

Csábi, Szilvia. (1998). The conceptualization of lust in English. Paper presented at the meeting of the *Viennese Semiotic Society*. March 26–29.

D'Andrade, Ray G. (1995). *The development of cognitive anthropology*. New York: Cambridge University Press.

Darwin, Charles. (1872/1965). *The expression of the emotions in man and animals*. Chicago: The University Press of Chicago.

Davitz, J. (1969). *The language of emotion*. New York: Academic Press.

De Rivera, Joseph. (1977). *A structural theory of the emotions*. New York: International Universities Press.

Duck, Steve. (1986). *Human relationships: An introduction to social psychology*. Beverly Hills, CA: Sage Publications.

Duck, Steve. (1994). *Meaningful relationships*. Newbury Park, CA: Sage Publications.

Ekman, Paul, & Friesen, W. V. (1975). *Unmasking the face*. Englewood Cliffs, NJ: Prentice Hall.

Ekman, P., Levenson, R. W., & Friesen, W. V. (1983). Autonomic nervous system activity distinguishes among emotions. *Science, 221*, 1208–1210.

Emanatian, Michele. (1995). Metaphor and the expression of emotion: The value of cross-cultural perspectives. *Metaphor and Symbolic Activity, 10*(3), 163–182.

Fauconnier, Gilles. (1997). *Mappings in language and thought*. Cambridge: Cambridge University Press.

Fehr, B., & Russell, J. A. (1984). Concept of emotion viewed from a prototype perspective. *Journal of Experimental Psychology: General, 113*, 464–486.

Fónagy, Iván. (1981). Emotions, voice, and music. *Research aspects on singing, autoperception, computer synthesis, emotion, health, voice source*. Publications issued by the Royal Swedish Academy of Music, No. 33, 51–79.

Frijda, Nico H. (1986). *The emotions*. Cambridge: Cambridge University Press.

Frijda, Nico H., Markam, Suprapti, Sato, Kaori, & Wiers, Reinout. (1995). Emotions and emotion words. In J. A. Russell et al. (Eds.), *Everyday conceptions of emotion* (pp. 121–143). Dordrecht: Kluwer.

Fromm, Eric. (1956). *The art of loving*. New York: Harper and Row.

Fuller, Margaret. (1843). The great lawsuit. MAN versus MEN. WOMAN versus WOMEN. *Dial, 4* (July), 1–47.

Geeraerts, Dirk, & Grondelaers, Stefan. (1995). Looking back at anger: Cultural traditions and metaphorical patterns. In J. Taylor and R. MacLaury (Eds.), *Language and the cognitive construal of the world* (pp. 153–179). Berlin: Mouton de Gruyter.

Gibbs, Raymond W. (1990). Psycholinguistic studies on the conceptual basis of idiomaticity. *Cognitive Linguistics*, 1–4, 417–451.

Gibbs, Raymond W. (1994). *The poetics of mind: Figurative thought, language, and understanding.* New York: Cambridge University Press.

Guericke, Daphne. (1991). *Die Alltagstheorie der Ehe: Eine empirische Untersuchung zur konzeptuellen Metaphorik im amerikanischen Englisch.* Unpublished master's thesis, Hamburg University.

Harré, Rom. (1986). An outline of the social constructionist viewpoint. In R. Harré (Ed.), *The social construction of emotion* (pp. 2–14). Oxford: Oxford University Press.

Hatfield, E. (1988). Passionate and companionate love. In R. J. Sternberg and M. L. Barnes (Eds.), *The psychology of love.* New Haven, CT: Yale University Press.

Heider, Karl. (1991). *Landscapes of emotion: Mapping three cultures of emotion in Indonesia.* Cambridge: Cambridge University Press.

Hochschild, Arlie R. (1983). *The managed heart: Commercialization of human feeling.* Berkeley and Los Angeles: University of California Press.

Holland, D. (1982). All is metaphor: Conventional metaphors in human thought and language. *Reviews in Anthropology, 9*(3), 287–297.

Holland, D., & Kipnis, Andrew. (1995). "The not-so-egotistic aspects of American self." In J. A. Russell et al. (Eds.), *Everyday conceptions of emotion* (pp. 181–202). Dordrecht: Kluwer.

Holland, D., & Quinn, N. (1987). *Cultural models in language and thought.* Cambridge: Cambridge University Press.

Irvine, J. (1995). A sociolinguistic approach to emotion concepts in a Senegalese community. In J. A. Russell et al. (Eds.), *Everyday conceptions of emotion* (pp. 251–265). Dordrecht: Kluwer.

Izard, C. E. (1977). *Human emotions.* New York: Plenum Press.

Jäkel, Olaf. (1995). The metaphorical concept of mind: "Mental activity is manipulation." In J. Taylor and R. MacLaury (Eds.), *Language and the Cognitive construal of the world* (pp. 197–229). Berlin: Mouton de Gruyter.

James, William. (1890/1950). *The principles of psychology* (2 vols.). New York: Henry Holt.

Johnson, Mark. (1987). *The body in the mind: The bodily basis of meaning, imagination, and reason.* Chicago: The University of Chicago Press.

Johnson, Mark. (1992). Philosophical implications of cognitive semantics. *Cognitive Linguistics, 3–4,* 345–366.

Johnson, Mark. (1993). *Moral Imagination.* Chicago: The University of Chicago Press.

Kendrick-Murdock, Debra L. (1994). The emotion concepts: Shock and surprise. Unpublished manuscript, Department of Anthropology, University of Nevada, Las Vegas.

King, B. (1989). *The conceptual structure of emotional experience in Chinese.* Unpublished doctoral dissertation, The Ohio State University.

Kövecses, Zoltán. (1986). *Metaphors of anger, pride, and love: A lexical approach to the structure of concepts.* Amsterdam: John Benjamins.

Kövecses, Zoltán. (1988). *The language of love: The semantics of passion in conversational English.* Lewisburg, PA: Bucknell University Press.

Kövecses, Zoltán. (1990). *Emotion concepts.* New York: Springer-Verlag.

Kövecses, Zoltán. (1991a). A linguist's quest for love. *Journal of Social and Personal Relationships, 8,* 77–97.

Kövecses, Zoltán. (1991b). Happiness: A definitional effort. *Metaphor and Symbolic Activity, 6,* 29–46.

Kövecses, Zoltán. (1993a). Minimal and full definitions of meaning. In R. A. Geiger and B. Rudzka-Ostyn (Eds.), *Conceptualizations and mental processing in language* (pp. 247–266). Berlin: Mouton de Gruyter.

Kövecses, Zoltán. (1993b). Friendship. In Z. Kövecses (Ed.), *Voices of friendship: Linguistic essays in honor of László T. Andras* (pp. 131–176). Budapest: Eötvös Loránd University Press.

Kövecses, Zoltán. (1994a). Ordinary language, common sense, and expert theories in the domain of emotion. In J. Siegfried (Ed.), *The status of common sense in psychology.* Norwood, NJ: Ablex.

Kövecses, Zoltán. (1994b). Tocqueville's passionate "beast": A linguistic analysis of the concept of American democracy. *Metaphor and Symbolic Activity, 9*(2), 113–133.

Kövecses, Zoltán. (1995a). Metaphor and the folk understanding of anger. In J. A. Russell et al. (Eds.), *Everyday conceptions of emotion* (pp. 49–71). Dordrecht: Kluwer.

Kövecses, Zoltán. (1995b). Anger: Its language, conceptualization, and physiology in the light of cross-cultural evidence. In J. Taylor and R. E. MacLaury (Eds.), *Language and the cognitive construal of the world* (pp. 181–196). Berlin: Mouton de Gruyter.

Kövecses, Zoltán. (1995c). American friendship and the scope of metaphor. *Cognitive Linguistics, 6* (4), 315–346.

Kövecses, Zoltán. (1998). *A student's guide to metaphor.* Unpublished manuscript.

Kövecses, Zoltán. (n.d.). The scope of metaphor. In A. Barcelona (Ed.), *Metaphor and metonymy at the crossroads.* Berlin: Mouton de Gruyter.

Kövecses, Zoltán, & Radden, Günter. (1988). Metonymy: Developing a cognitive linguistic view. *Cognitive Linguistics, 9–7,* 37–77.

Lakoff, George. (1987). *Women, fire, and dangerous things: What categories reveal about the mind.* Chicago: The University of Chicago Press.

Lakoff, George. (1990). The invariance hypothesis: Is abstract reason based on image schemas? *Cognitive Linguistics, 1–1,* 39–74.

Lakoff, George. (1993). The contemporary theory of metaphor. In A. Ortony (Ed.), *Metaphor and thought* (2nd ed., pp. 202–251). Cambridge: Cambridge University Press.

Lakoff, George. (1996). *Moral politics.* Chicago: The University of Chicago Press.

Lakoff, George, Espernson, Jane, & Goldberg, Adele. (1989). *Master metaphor list.* Berkeley: University of California at Berkeley, Cognitive Linguistics Group.

Lakoff, George, & Johnson, Mark. (1980). *Metaphors we live by.* Chicago: The University of Chicago Press.

Lakoff, George, & Kövecses, Zoltán. (1987). The cognitive model of anger inherent in American English. In D. Holland and N. Quinn (Eds.), *Cultural models in language and thought* (pp. 195–221). New York: Cambridge University Press.

Lakoff, George, & Turner, Mark. (1989). *More than cool reason: A field guide to poetic metaphor*. Chicago: The University of Chicago Press.

Langacker, Ronald. (1987). *Foundations of cognitive grammar: Theoretical prerequisites* (Vol. 1). Stanford: Stanford University Press.

Langacker, Ronald. (1991). *Foundations of cognitive grammar: Practical applications* (Vol. 2). Stanford: Stanford University Press.

LeDoux, Joseph. (1996). *The emotional brain*. New York: Simon and Schuster.

Leeper, R. W. (1970). The motivational and perceptual properties of emotions as indicating their fundamental character and role. In M. B. Arnold (Ed.), *Feelings and emotions: The Loyola symposium*. New York: Academic Press.

Levenson, R. W., Carstensen, L. L., Friesen, W. V., & Ekman, P. (1991). Emotion, physiology, and expression in old age. *Psychology and Aging, 6*, 28–35.

Levenson, R. W., Ekman, P., & Friesen, W. V. (1990). Voluntary facial action generates emotion-specific autonomic nervous system activity. *Psychophysiology, 27*, 363–384.

Levenson, R. W., Ekman, P., Heider, K., & Friesen, W. V. (1992). Emotion and autonomic nervous system activity in the Minangkabau of West Sumatra, *Journal of Personality and Social Psychology, 62*, 972–988.

Leventhal, Howard, & Scherer, Klaus. (1987). The relationship of emotion to cognition: A functional approach to a semantic controversy. *Cognition and Emotion, 1* (1) 3–28.

Levy, R. I. (1973). *Tahitians: Mind and experience in Society Islands*. Chicago: The University of Chicago Press.

Levy, R. I. (1984). Emotion, knowing, and culture. In R. A. Shweder and R. A. LeVine (Eds.), *Culture theory: Essays on mind, self, and emotion* (pp. 214–237). Cambridge: Cambridge University Press.

Lutz, Catherine A. (1987). Goals, events, and understanding in Ifaluk emotion theory. In D. Holland and N. Quinn (Eds.), *Cultural models in language and thought* (pp. 290–312). Cambridge: Cambridge University Press.

Lutz, Catherine A. (1988). *Unnatural emotions: Everyday sentiments on a Micronesian atoll and their challenge to Western theory*. Chicago: The University of Chicago Press.

Lutz, Catherine A., & Abu-Lughod, Lila. (1990). *Language and the politics of emotion*. Cambridge: Cambridge University Press.

Lyons, J. (1977). *Semantics* (2 vols.). Cambridge: Cambridge University Press.

McDougall, William. (1908/1961). *An introduction to social psychology*. London: Methuen.

Matsuki, K. (1995). Metaphors of anger in Japanese. In J. Taylor and R. E. MacLaury (Eds.), *Language and the cognitive construal of the world* (pp. 137–151). Berlin: Mouton de Gruyter.

Moffatt, Michael. (1989). *Coming of age in New Jersey: College and American culture*. New Brunswick, NJ: Rutgers University Press.

Munro, Pamela. (1991). ANGER IS HEAT: Some data for a crosslinguistic survey. Unpublished manuscript, Department of Linguistics, University of California at Los Angeles.

Newton-Smith, W. (1973). A conceptual investigation of love. In A. Montefiori (Ed.), *Philosophy and personal relations*. Montreal: McGill-Queen's University Press.

Oatley, Keith, & Johnson-Laird, Philip N. (1987). Towards a cognitive theory of emotions. *Cognition and Emotion, 1* (1) 29–50.

Ortony, Andrew, Clore, Gerald L., & Collins, Alan. (1988). *The cognitive structure of emotions*. Cambridge: Cambridge University Press.

Osgood, C. F. (1964). Semantic differential technique in the comparative study of cultures. *American Anthropologist, 66*, 171–200.

Padel, Ruth. (1992). *In and out of the mind: Greek images of the tragic self*. Princeton: Princeton University Press.

Palmer, Gary B. (1996). *Toward a theory of cultural linguistics*. Austin: University of Texas Press.

Palmer, Gary B., & Brown, Rick. (1998). The ideology of honour, respect, and emotion in Tagalog. In A. Athanasiadou and E. Tabakowska (Eds.), *Speaking of emotions: Conceptualisation and expression* (pp. 331–355). Berlin: Mouton de Gruyter.

Pape, Christina. (1995). *Die konzeptuelle Metaphorisierung von Emotionen: Untersucht am Beispiel von shame and embarrassment im Amerikanischen Englisch*. Unpublished master's thesis, University of Hamburg.

Parrott, W. G. (1995). The heart and the head: Everyday conceptions of being emotional. In J. A. Russell et al. (Eds.), *Everyday conceptions of emotion* (pp. 73–84). Dordrecht: Kluwer.

Peele, Stanton. (1975). *Love and addiction*. New York: Taplinger.

Plutchik, R. (1980). *Emotion: A psychoevolutionary synthesis*. New York: Harper and Row.

Quinn, Naomi. (1987). Convergent evidence for a cultural model of American marriage. In D. Holland and N. Quinn (Eds.), *Cultural models in language and thought* (pp. 173–192). New York: Cambridge University Press.

Quinn, Naomi. (1991). The cultural basis of metaphor. In J. W. Fernandez (Ed.), *Beyond metaphor: The theory of tropes in anthropology* (pp. 56–93). Stanford: Stanford University Press.

Radcliffe-Brown, A. R. (1922). *The Andaman islanders*. New York: The Free Press.

Radden, Günter. (1998). The conceptualisation of emotional causality by means of prepositional phrases. In A. Athanasiadou and E. Tabakowska (Eds.), *Speaking of emotions: Conceptualisation and expression* (pp. 273–294). Berlin: Mouton de Gruyter.

Radden, Günter, & Kövecses, Zoltán. (in press). Towards a theory of metonymy. In G. Radden and U-K. Panther (Eds.), *Metonymy in cognition and language*. Amsterdam: Benjamins.

Reddy, M. (1979). The conduit metaphor – a case of frame conflict in our language about language. In A. Ortony (Ed.), *Metaphor and thought* (1st ed., pp. 228–324). New York: Cambridge University Press.

Rimé, B., Philippot, P., & Cisalomo, D. (1990). Social schemata of peripheral changes in emotion. *Journal of Personality and Social Psychology, 59*, 38–49.

Rippere, Vicky. (1994). An empirical anthropological method for investigating common sense. In Jurg Siegfried (Ed.), *The status of common sense in psychology* (pp. 279–304). Norwood, NJ: Ablex.

Rosaldo, Michelle. (1980). *Knowledge and passion: Ilongot notions of self and social life.* Cambridge: Cambridge University Press.

Rosaldo, Michelle. (1984). Toward an anthropology of self and feeling. In Richard A. Shweder and Robert A. LeVine (Eds.), *Culture Theory* (pp. 137–157). Cambridge: Cambridge University Press.

Rosch, E. (1975). The nature of mental codes for color categories. *Journal of Experimental Psychology: Human Perception and Performance, 1*, 303–322.

Rosch, Eleanor. (1978). Principles of categorization. In E. Rosch and B. B. Lloyd (Eds.), *Cognition and categorization* (pp. 27–48). Hillsdale, NJ: Lawrence Erlbaum.

Rubin, Zick. (1970). Measurement of romantic love. *Journal of Personality and Social Psychology, 16*, 265–273.

Russell, J. A. (1991). Culture and the categorization of emotions. *Psychological Bulletin, 110*(3), 426–450.

Russell, James A., Fernández-Dols, José-Miguel, Manstead, Antony S. R., & Wellenkamp, J. C. (Eds.). (1995). *Everyday conceptions of emotion.* Dordrecht: Kluwer.

Sartre, Jean-Paul (1948). *The emotions: Outline of a theory.* New York: The Wisdom Library.

Schachter, S. (1971). *Emotion, obesity, and crime.* New York: Academic Press.

Schachter, S., & Singer, J. (1962). Cognitive, social, and physiological determinants of emotional states. *Psychological Review, 69*, 379–399.

Searle, J. R. (1990). Epilogue to the taxonomy of illocutionary acts. In Donal Carbaugh (Ed.), *Cultural communication and intercultural contact* (pp. 409–428). Hillsdale, NJ: Lawrence Erlbaum.

Shaver, P., Hazan, C., & Bradshaw, D. (1988). Love as attachment: The integration of three behavioral systems. In R. J. Sternberg and M. L. Barnes (Eds.), *The psychology of love.* New Haven, CT: Yale University Press.

Shaver, P., Schwartz, J., Kirson, D., & O'Connor, C. (1987). Emotion knowledge: Further exploration of a prototype approach. *Journal of Personality and Social Psychology, 52*, 1061–1086.

Shore, Bradd. (1996). *Culture in mind: Cognition, culture, and the problem of meaning.* New York: Oxford University Press.

Shweder, R. A. (1991). *Thinking through cultures: Expeditions in cultural psychology.* Cambridge, MA: Harvard University Press.

Siegfried, Jurg (Ed.) (1994). *The status of common sense in psychology.* Norwood, NJ: Ablex.

Smith, K. D. (1995). Social psychological perspectives on laypersons' theories of emotion. In J. A. Russell et al. (Eds.), *Everyday conceptions of emotion* (pp. 399–414). Dordrecht: Kluwer.

Smith, S. T., & Smith, K. D. (1995). Turkish emotion concepts: A prototype analysis. In J. A. Russell et al. (Eds.), *Everyday conceptions of emotion* (pp. 103–119). Dordrecht: Kluwer.

Smith, K. D., & Tkel-Sbal, D. (1995). Prototype analyses of emotions terms in Palau, Micronesia. In J. A. Russell et al. (Eds.), *Everyday conceptions of emotion* (pp. 85–102). Dordrecht: Kluwer.

Solomon, Robert. (1976). *The passions.* New York: Doubleday Anchor.

Solomon, Robert. (1981). *Love: Emotion, myth, and metaphor.* New York: Doubleday Anchor.

Solomon, Robert. (1984). Getting angry: The Jamesian theory of emotion in anthropology. In R. A. Shweder and R. A. LeVine (Eds.), *Culture theory* (pp. 238–254). Cambridge: Cambridge University Press.

Soyland, A. J. (1994). *Psychology as metaphor.* London: Sage.

Stearns, Peter N. (1994). *American cool: Constructing a twentieth-century emotional style.* New York: New York University Press.

Sternberg, R. J. (1986). A triangular theory of love. *Psychological Review, 93,* 119–135.

Storm, C., & Storm, T. (1987). A taxonomic study of the vocabulary of emotions. *Journal of Personality and Social Psychology, 53*(4), 805–816.

Sweetser, Eve. (1990). *From etymology to semantics.* Cambridge: Cambridge University Press.

Talmy, Leonard. (1988). Force dynamics in language and cognition. *Cognitive Science, 12,* 49–100.

Taylor, G. (1979). Love. In T. Honderich and M. Burnyeat (Eds.), *Philosophy as it is* (pp. 165–182). Harmondsworth: Penguin.

Taylor, John R., & Mbense, Thandi G. (1998). Red dogs and rotten mealies: How Zulus talk about anger. In Angeliki Athanasiadou and Elzbieta Tabakowska (Eds.), *Speaking of emotion: Conceptualisation and expression* (pp. 191–226). Berlin: Mouton de Gruyter.

Turner, Mark. (1987). *Death Is the Mother of Beauty. Mind, Metaphor, Criticism.* Chicago: The University of Chicago Press.

Turner, Mark. (1996). *The literary mind.* Oxford: Oxford University Press.

Walster, E. (1971). Passionate love. In B. I. Murstein (Ed.), *Theories of attraction and love.* New York: Springer-Verlag.

Wenger, M. A. (1950). Emotions as visceral action: An extension of Lange's theory. In M. L. Reymert (Ed.), *Feelings and emotions: The Mooseheart-Chicago symposium* (pp. 3–10). New York: McGraw-Hill.

Wierzbicka, Anna. (1972). *Semantic primitives.* Frankfurt: Atheneum Verlag.

Wierzbicka, Anna. (1986). Human emotions: Universal or culture-specific? *American Anthropologist, 88*(3), 584–594.

Wierzbicka, Anna. (1990). The semantics of emotions: *Fear* and its relatives in English. *Australian Journal of Linguistics, 10*(2), 359–375.

Wierzbicka, Anna. (1992a). Talking about emotions: Semantics, culture, and cognition. *Cognition and Emotion, 6*(3/4), 285–319.

Wierzbicka, Anna. (1992b). Defining emotion concepts. *Cognitive Science, 16,* 539–581.

Wierzbicka, Anna. (1995). Everyday conceptions of emotion: A semantic perspective. In J. Russell et al. (Eds.), *Everyday conceptions of emotion* (pp. 17–45). Kluwer: Dordrecht.

Young, P. T. (1943). *Emotion in man and animal.* New York: Wiley.

Yu, Ning. (1995). Metaphorical expressions of anger and happiness in English and Chinese. *Metaphor and Symbolic Activity, 10*(2), 59–92.

Author Index

Abu-Lughod, L., 189
Alston, W.P., 130
Arnold, M.B., 133
Averill, J.R., 13, 14, 18, 131, 136, 166

Barcelona, A., 25
Baxter, L.A., 6, 13, 26, 27, 87, 95, 96, 101, 102, 111
Berlin, B., 15
Besnier, N., 164
Bokor, Zs., 143, 170
Bradshaw, D., 126
Brown, R., 11, 189
Burnyeat, M.F., 138
Buss, D.M., 125, 126

Carstensen, L.L., 159
Churchland, P.S., 190–191
Cisalono, D., 11
Clore, G.L., 11
Collins, A., 11
Csábi, Sz., 29, 30

D'Andrade, R.G., 175
Darwin, C., 133
Davitz, J., 8
de Rivera, J., 9
Doi, 166
Duck, S., 6, 13, 87, 113

Ekman, P., 134, 159, 177
Emanatian, M., 162
Espenson, J., 56

Fauconnier, G., 85
Fehr, B., 3, 4, 11, 92

Fernández-Dols, J.-M.,19
Fónagy, I., 2
Friesen, W.V., 134, 159
Frijda, N.H., xiv, 4, 9, 15
Fromm, E., 51, 123
Fuller, M., 178

Geeraerts, D., 13, 136, 138, 147, 167–168
Gibbs, R.W., 6, 20, 22, 23, 116, 144, 173
Goldberg, A., 56
Grondelaers, S., 13, 136, 138, 147, 167–168
Guericke, D., 112

Harré, R., 15, 184, 185
Hatfield, E., 122, 126
Hazan, C., 126
Heider, K., 10, 11, 131, 159
Hochschild, A.R., 180
Holland, D., 6, 13, 32, 33, 114, 162

Irvine, J., 189
Izard, C.E., 134

Jäkel, O., 196–197
James, W., 131, 132
Johnson, M., 4, 15, 16, 17, 20, 24, 26, 44, 96, 101, 102, 105, 107, 109, 119, 159, 195, 198
Johnson-Laird, P.N., xiv

Kay, P., 15
Kendrick-Murdock, D.L., 33
King, B., 143, 144, 150, 157, 158, 166, 168, 172, 188
Kipnis, A., 6, 13, 32, 33

Kirson, D., 4
Kövecses, Z., 5, 6, 7, 11, 12, 13, 14, 18, 21, 22, 24, 25, 30, 35, 87, 115, 122, 136, 142, 148, 172, 173, 174, 178, 186
Kusumi, T., 152, 162

Lakoff, G., 4, 5, 11, 12, 13, 14, 15, 16, 17, 19, 20, 21, 23, 24, 26, 29, 39, 41, 44, 52, 53, 56, 68, 93, 94, 97, 101, 102, 103, 105, 107, 109, 115, 119, 142, 148, 159, 173, 194–195, 198, 199
Langacker, R., 20
LeDoux, J., xi–xii, 189–190, 192–193
Leeper, R.W., 132
Levenson, R.W., 159, 177
Leventhal, H., xiv
Levy, R.I., 143, 154, 188
Lutz, C.A., 13, 14, 15, 51, 147, 161, 168, 183, 185
Lyons, J., 7

Manstead, A.S.R., 19
Markan, S., 4
Matsuki, K., 143, 145, 152, 154, 168, 169, 187
Mbense, 165, 167, 169, 170, 171, 172, 187, 188
McDougall, W., 134
Moffatt, M., 175
Munro, P., 143, 154, 157, 159, 161

Newton-Smith, W., 126

Oatley, K., xiv
O'Connor, C., 4
Ortony, A., 11, 12
Osgood, C., 7, 9, 10

Padel, R., 138
Palmer, G.B., 11, 183, 189
Pape, C., 32
Parrott, W.G., 18, 129
Peele, S., 123
Philippot, P., 11
Plutchik, R., 132

Quinn, N., xiv, 13, 17, 86, 87, 95, 96, 101, 102, 111, 114, 115–122, 155

Radcliffe-Brown, A.R., 182–183
Radden, G., 5, 49, 75, 88, 89, 131
Reddy, M., 88, 89
Reischauer, 166
Rimé, B., 11
Rippere, V., 129
Rosaldo, M., 11, 189
Rosch, E., 3, 15
Rubin, Z., 125, 126
Russell, J.A., 3, 4, 11, 15, 19, 92, 164

Sartre, J.-P., 133
Sato, K., 4
Schachter, S., 7, 124, 132, 133
Scherer, K., xiv
Schwartz, J., 4
Searle, J.R., 2
Shaver, P., 3, 7, 11, 12, 92, 126
Shore, B., 116
Shweder, R.A., 9, 10
Siegfried, J., 19, 129
Singer, J., 7, 124
Smith, K.D., 4, 135
Smith, S.T., 4
Solomon, R., 8, 51, 122, 123, 133, 143, 147, 154, 157, 160
Soyland, A.J., 18
Stearns, P.N., 169, 174, 175, 176, 177, 177–178, 179, 180–181, 183
Sternberg, R.J., 123, 126
Storm, C., 92
Storm, T., 92
Sweetser, E., 20
Swidler, A., 178–179

Talmy, L., xv, 17, 62, 64, 67, 85
Taylor, G., 126
Taylor, J.R., 165, 167, 169, 170, 171, 172, 187, 188
Tkel-Sbal, 4
Turner, M., 20, 23, 85

Walster, 124, 126
Wellenkamp, J.C., 19
Wenger, M.A., 133
Wiers, R., 4
Wierzbicka, A., 7, 8, 11, 12, 15, 16, 47, 48, 189
Young, P.T., 131
Yu, N., 143, 150, 156, 168, 170, 172, 187

Subject Index

agonist, 62
anger in English, 13, 148–149, 173–174, 179
anger metaphors, 21–23
anger metonymies, 156–161
antagonist, 62
atama, 154
autonomic nervous system activity, 159–160

balance of strengths, 62
basic structure (of anger), 146, 155–156
bodily responses, xi
body in emotion, xii, 190
body-based constructionism, 183–186
brain and emotion, 192–193
brain states, xi
broader cultural context, its influence on conceptualization, 167–169, 179–181

cause of emotion, 64, 83–85
Chaga, 162
Chickasaw, 160–161
Chinese, 170, 171–172
cognitive linguistics, 20, 184
cognitive motivation, 159
conceptual metaphor, 4, 5; *see also* metaphor
conceptual metaphors, alternative, 177–179
conceptual metonymy, 4, 5, 177; *see also* metonymy
conceptual system, general, 193
conceptualized physiology, 159
conscious feelings, xi, xiii, 189–190, 191

"container" metaphors, their structure, 155–156
control, 197–198; as an aspect of emotion concepts, 43–44

desire/need, as an aspect of emotion concepts, 45
difficulty, as an aspect of emotion concepts, 45
discourse-pragmatic factors, 189–190
düh in Hungarian, 149–50, 168

embodiment, 159–160
emotion: as action, 51; as event, 51; as passion, 51; as state, 51; its cognitive model, 128; literal conception of, 12–13; nonliteral conception of, 12–13; multiple prototypes of, 13; *see also* meaning and emotion
emotion and morality, 194–196
emotion and rational thought, 196–197
emotion concepts, 127–129; and expert theories of emotion, 129–135; and expert theories, the nature of the relationship, 135–136; aspects of, 40–46; and Wierzbicka's semantic universals, 47–48
emotion language, 191–192; English and Hungarian, 140–142; expressive terms, 4; figurative expressions denoting aspects of emotion, 5; issues in, 14–19; its focus, 188; literal terms denoting emotions, 4
emotion metaphors: comparison with relationship metaphors, 109–113; their uniqueness, 16–17; *see also* metaphor

213

emotion response, 64, 65, 84
emotion schema, 64
emotion systems, versus a unitary emotion system, 192–193
emotion terms: basic, 2; descriptive, 2; expressive, 2; metaphorical, 4; metonymic, 4; prototypical, 3
emotional experience, content of, 186–187
emotional meaning, 186–189; *see also* meaning and emotion
emotions and events, the overlap between the two, 55–58
emotions and relationships, 193–194; the conceptual relationship between the two, 112–113
"essentialists," 182
event structure metaphor, 52–55, 193; and the subcategorization of emotion, 59
existence, as an aspect of emotion concepts, 41

faculties of the mind, 199
fear metaphors, 23–24
figurative language, *see* metaphor
folk psychology, versus scientific psychology, 190–191
folk theories of emotion, xiii, 58, 84; versus expert theories, 189; Western, 64
folk theories of love, and their relationship to expert theories, 126–127
force dynamics, 62; 192–193; shifting pattern of, 66
force schema, 62, 189
force system, as structuring the mind, 199
four humors, 167–168
friendship, 87; 174, 175, 177–178, 180; *see also* metaphor systems for friendship

generic space, 85

happiness metaphors, 24–25
hara, 152–154, 166, 167, 168
harm, as an aspect of emotion concepts, 46
honne, 168
Hungarian, 170

Ifaluk, 161
ikari in Japanese, 152–154, 166

intensity, as an aspect of emotion concepts, 41–42
intrinsic force tendency, 62

"lay views" vs. "scientific theories," 18–19; *see also* folk theories of emotion
linguistics and emotion, xi
love, 116–122, 174–175, 178–179, 180–181; the language of, 122–127; and scientific theories, 122–127
love metaphors, 26–29, 122–123
love metonymies, 123–125
lust metaphors and metonymies, 29–30, 31–32; in Chaga, 162

marriage, 115–122; dictionary definitions, 118–119; its expectational structure, 118–122
master metaphor: for emotions, 192; for relationships, 111; *see also* metaphor
meaning and emotion: the "core meaning" view, 7–8; the "dimensional" view, 8–9; the "embodied cultural prototype" view, 14; the "implicational" view, 9–10; the "label" view, 6; the "prototype" view, 10–13; the "social-constructionist" view, 13–14
metaphor, 188; and expert theories, 131–133; cognitivist theory of, 198; comparison of emotion and relationship metaphors, 109–113; elaborations of conceptual metaphors, 170–171; emotion-specific source domains, 48–49; generic-level, 64; the "master metaphor" for emotion, 61; range of conceptual metaphors, 169–170; specific-level, 64; the role of metaphor in cultural models, 115–122; the scope of, 35; in social constructionism and cognitive linguistics, 184; source domains that apply to all emotion concepts, 36; source domains that apply to most emotion concepts, 36–40; source domains that apply to one emotion, 40; *see also* event structure metaphor; master metaphor; *names of particular emotions*
metaphor and metonymy, the role of, 17–18
metaphor systems for friendship: the "communication" system, 88–92; the "complex systems" metaphor, 97–106;

the "emotion" system, 92–93; the "event" system, 108–109; the "positive-negative evaluation" system, 106–108; the "state" metaphor system, 93–97
metaphorical entailments, 148–154
metaphorical mappings, 155–156
methodological differences, between social constructionism and cognitive linguistics, 184
metonymies (of emotion) and expert theories, 133–134
metonymy, 188; elaborations of, 171–172; range of, 171; versus metaphor, 172, 176
Minangkabau, 159
mind, folk theory of, 199
morality, xiii, 199; *see also* emotion and morality
mune, 154

neurobiology and emotion, xi
niferash, 161
nonphysical unity, as an aspect of emotion concepts, 45–46
nu in Chinese, 150–152, 166, 167

passions, 59
passivity, as an aspect of emotion concepts, 42
physiology, 190; in anger, 159–160, 177
"positive-negative" evaluation, as an aspect of emotion concepts, 44
pride metaphors, 30–31
progress, as an aspect of emotion concepts, 46
prototype of anger: in Chinese, 144–145; in English, 143–144; in Hungarian, 144; in Japanese, 145
prototypes, 188; changing through time, 173–174; simultaneous multiple models, 174–176; universality of emotion prototypes, 15–16

prototypical cognitive models and expert theories, 129–131

qi, 150–152, 166, 167

rational thought, xiii, 199; *see also* emotion and rational thought
rationality, 180–181
related concepts: (of emotion) and expert theories, 134–135; (of love), 125–126
relationships, *see* emotions and relationships
"relativists," 182
resultant action, 68
resultant of force interaction, 62

sadness metaphors, 25–26
scenario structure (of emotions), 187
scientific theories of emotion, xiii; *see also* folk theories of emotion
shame metaphors, 32–33
social constructionism, 182–186
"social constructionists," 182
song, 13, 161
source domains (for emotions), *see* metaphor
subcategorizing emotions, 19
surprise metaphors, 33

Tahitian, 154
tatemae, 168

"universalists," 182

variation in the content of cultural models, 166–167
Victorian period, 174, 176, 177–178, 178–179, 180–181

Wolof, 154

Zulu, 165, 166, 168–169, 169–170, 170–171

Metaphor and Metonymy Index

Metaphors

ABSTRACT EFFORT IS PHYSICAL EFFORT, 98
ABSTRACT EXISTENCE IS PHYSICAL EXISTENCE, 98
ABSTRACT FUNCTION IS PHYSICAL FUNCTION, 99
ABSTRACT FUNCTIONING IS PHYSICAL FUNCTIONING, 99
ABSTRACT MAINTENANCE IS PHYSICAL MAINTENANCE, 98
ACTION IS MOTION, 83
ACTION IS SELF-PROPELLED MOTION, 52, 53, 56, 57, 77
AFFECTION IS WARMTH, 93
ANGER (DESIRE) IS HUNGER, 167
ANGER IS A BURDEN, 21
ANGER IS A BURNING SUBSTANCE (IN A PIPE), 170
ANGER IS A HOT FLUID (IN A CONTAINER), 4, 21, 22, 142–143, 148–150, 152–154, 170
ANGER IS A NATURAL FORCE, 21, 167, 171
ANGER IS A SOCIAL SUPERIOR, 21
ANGER IS A SUBSTANCE (FLUID/GAS) IN A CONTAINER, 146
ANGER IS AN OPPONENT, 21
ANGER IS A CAPTIVE ANIMAL, 21

ANGER IS EXCESS QI IN THE BODY, 151–152
ANGER IS FIRE, 21, 170
ANGER IS HARA, 153–154, 169
ANGER IS IN THE HEART, 169
ANGER IS INSANITY, 21
ANGER IS PHYSICAL ANNOYANCE, 49
ANGER IS THE MOVEMENT OF QI, 151–152
ANGER IS TRESPASSING, 49
ANGRY BEHAVIOR IS AGGRESSIVE ANIMAL BEHAVIOR, 21
ANGRY PERSON IS A FUNCTIONING MACHINE, AN, 21
ANGRY PERSON IS A PRESSURIZED CONTAINER, THE, 155–156, 160–161, 176
ATTEMPT AT CONTROL IS STRUGGLE WITH FORCE, 43
ATTEMPT AT EMOTIONAL CONTROL IS TRYING TO HOLD BACK A CAPTIVE ANIMAL, 43
ATTEMPT AT EMOTIONAL CONTROL IS TRYING TO KEEP A COMPLETE OBJECT TOGETHER, 43
ATTEMPT AT EMOTIONAL CONTROL IS TRYING TO OVERCOME AN OPPONENT, 43
ATTEMPT AT EMOTIONAL CONTROL

IS TRYING TO SUPPRESS FLUID IN A CONTAINER, 43

ATTRIBUTES ARE POSSESSED OBJECTS, 94

BAD THINGS ARE COLD, 44
BAD THINGS ARE DARK, 44
BAD THINGS ARE DOWN, 44
BAD THINGS ARE NONVALUABLE, 44
BEHAVIORAL RESPONSES ARE OTHER-PROPELLED MOTIONS, 59
BEING BAD IS BEING LOW, 194
BEING GOOD IS BEING UPRIGHT, 194
BEING HAPPY IS BEING OFF THE GROUND, 48
BODY IS A CONTAINER FOR THE EMOTIONS, THE, 146, 170

CAUSE OF ANGER IS PHYSICAL ANNOYANCE, THE, 40, 48
CAUSE OF ANGER IS TRESPASSING, THE, 21, 40, 48
CAUSED CHANGE OF STATE (EMOTION) IS MOTION CAUSED BY A FORCE, A, 59
CAUSED EVENTS ARE OTHER-PROPELLED MOTIONS, 58, 72
CAUSES ARE FORCES, 52, 57, 58, 61, 193
CAUSING HARM TO A PROUD PERSON IS CAUSING INJURY TO SOMEONE, 30
CAUSING HARM TO A PROUD PERSON IS CAUSING PHYSICAL DAMAGE TO A STRUCTURED OBJECT, 30
CHANGES ARE MOVEMENTS, 52
COMMUNICATION BETWEEN FRIENDS IS SHARING ONE'S INNERMOST (EXPERIENCE) OBJECTS, 91

COMMUNICATION IS SENDING, 89
COMPLEX SYSTEMS ARE COMPLEX PHYSICAL OBJECTS, 106, 112
COMPLEX SYSTEMS ARE LIVING ORGANISMS, 106
CONCEITED PERSON IS UP/HIGH, THE, 32
CONTROL OVER ACTION IS CONTROL OVER SELF-PROPELLED MOTION, 56
CONTROL OVER AN EMOTIONAL ACT IS CONTROL OVER MOTION, 59
CREATION IS MAKING, 98

DESIRABLE IS VALUABLE, 108
DESIRABLE THINGS ARE VALUABLE COMMODITIES, 106
DESIRE IS HUNGER, 45, 59, 78, 167, 170
DESIRES THAT CONTROL ACTION ARE EXTERNAL FORCES THAT CONTROL MOTION, 57
DEVELOPMENT IS GROWTH, 99
DIFFICULTIES ARE BURDENS, 45
DIFFICULTIES ARE IMPEDIMENTS TO MOTION, 52, 54, 56
DOING EVIL IS FALLING, 194
DYNAMIC RELATIONSIP BETWEEN TWO ENTITIES IS A PHYSICAL FORCE ACTING ON ANOTHER, 113

EFFECT OF AN INTENSE EMOTIONAL STATE IS INSANITY, THE, 74
EMOTION IS A BURDEN, 38, 64, 82–83
EMOTION IS A CAPTIVE ANIMAL, 37
EMOTION IS A FLUID IN A CONTAINER, 77
EMOTION IS A GAME, 39

EMOTION IS A GRAVITATIONAL FORCE, 83
EMOTION IS A HIDDEN OBJECT, 39
EMOTION IS A JOURNEY, 39
EMOTION IS A LIVING ORGANISM, 36
EMOTION IS A MAGICIAN, 72
EMOTION IS A MAGNETIC FORCE, 83
EMOTION IS A MECHANICAL FORCE, 83
EMOTION IS A MENTAL FORCE, 72–73
EMOTION IS A NATURAL FORCE, 37, 64, 71–72
EMOTION IS A NUTRIENT/FOOD, 39
EMOTION IS A PHYSICAL FORCE, 37, 83–85
EMOTION IS A PHYSIOLOGICAL FORCE, 77–80
EMOTION IS A SOCIAL FORCE/SOCIAL SUPERIOR, 37, 70–71
EMOTION IS A SUBSTANCE IN A CONTAINER, 65, 136
EMOTION IS A TRICKSTER, 72–73, 133, 136
EMOTION IS A UNITY, 39
EMOTION IS A WILD/CAPTIVE ANIMAL, 69–77, 133, 141
EMOTION IS AN ECONOMIC VALUE, 39
EMOTION IS AN ELECTRIC FORCE, 83, 132
EMOTION IS AN ILLNESS, 38
EMOTION IS AN INTERNAL SENSATION, 132–133
EMOTION IS AN OPPONENT, 37, 68–69
EMOTION IS FIRE/HEAT, 38, 64, 75–77
EMOTION IS FORCE, 61, 62, 64, 65, 111, 113, 192–199
EMOTION IS HUNGER, 39, 78
EMOTION IS INSANITY, 37, 59, 73–75, 133, 136
EMOTION IS INTERNAL PRESSURE, 64, 65–68
EMOTION IS LIGHT/DARK, 39
EMOTION IS MAGIC, 39
EMOTION IS PHYSICAL AGITATION, 80–82
EMOTION IS RAPTURE, 39, 74–75
EMOTION IS TEMPERATURE/HEAT, 93
EMOTION IS THIRST, 78
EMOTION IS UP/DOWN, 39
EMOTION IS VITALITY/LACK OF VITALITY, 39
EMOTION IS WAR, 39
EMOTION IS WARMTH/COLD, 39
EMOTIONAL BEHAVIOR IS ANIMAL AGGRESSION, 39
EMOTIONAL DESIRE IS HUNGER, 45
EMOTIONAL DIFFICULTIES ARE BURDENS, 45
EMOTIONAL DISTURBANCE IS PHYSICAL AGITATION, 81, 131–132
EMOTIONAL EFFECT IS PHYSICAL CONTACT, 83, 132, 136
EMOTIONAL EFFECT IS PHYSICAL MOVEMENT, 132
EMOTIONAL HARM IS PHYSICAL DAMAGE, 39, 46
EMOTIONAL PERSON IS A CONTAINER, THE, 37
EMOTIONAL PERSON IS A FUNCTIONING MACHINE, THE, 39
EMOTIONAL PERSON IS A PRESSURIZED CONTAINER, THE, 83
EMOTIONAL RELATIONSHIP IS A DISTANCE BETWEEN TWO ENTITIES, AN, 92
EMOTIONAL RESPONSES ARE OTHER-PROPELLED MOTIONS, 55, 58

EMOTIONAL SELF IS A DIVIDED SELF, THE, 38

EMOTIONAL STATES ARE BOUNDED REGIONS, 59

EMOTIONAL TENSION IS PRESSURE INSIDE THE CONTAINER, 141

EMOTIONS ARE NATURAL FORCES, 131–132

EMOTIONS ARE PHYSICAL FORCES, 58

EMOTIONS ARE SUBSTANCES INSIDE A PERSON/CONTAINER, 141

EVIL IS A FORCE, 194

EXISTENCE OF EMOTION IS BEING IN A BOUNDED SPACE, 36, 41

EXISTENCE OF EMOTION IS POSSESSING AN OBJECT, 36, 41

EXISTENCE OF EMOTION IS PRESENCE HERE, 36, 41

EXISTENCE OF EMOTION IS THE FUNCTIONING OF A MACHINE, THE, 41

EXPECTED PROGRESS IS A TRAVEL SCHEDULE, 52, 54

EXPERIENCES ARE OBJECTS, 88–89

EXTERNAL EVENTS ARE LARGE, MOVING OBJECTS, 52, 54, 58

FEAR IS A BURDEN, 23

FEAR IS A FLUID IN A CONTAINER, 23

FEAR IS A HIDDEN ENEMY, 40, 48, 49

FEAR IS A HIDDEN OBJECT, 23

FEAR IS A NATURAL FORCE, 23

FEAR IS A SOCIAL SUPERIOR, 23

FEAR IS A SUPERNATURAL BEING, 23, 40, 48, 49

FEAR IS A TORMENTOR, 23

FEAR IS AN ILLNESS, 23

FEAR IS AN OPPONENT, 23

FEAR IS INSANITY, 23

FRIENDS ARE CONTAINERS (THAT OPEN UP TO EACH OTHER), 91

FRIENDSHIP IS A JOURNEY, 108–109

FRIENDSHIP IS A LIVING ORGANISM (PLANT), 97, 104–106

FRIENDSHIP IS A MACHINE, 97, 101–103

FRIENDSHIP IS A POSSESSED OBJECT, 93–94

FRIENDSHIP IS A SPECIAL IMPLEMENT, 103–104

FRIENDSHIP IS A STRONG (PHYSICAL) BOND, 94–95

FRIENDSHIP IS A STRUCTURED OBJECT (BUILDING/IMPLEMENT), 97, 99–101

FRIENDSHIP IS A VALUABLE COMMODITY, 106–108

FRIENDSHIP IS AN ECONOMIC EXCHANGE, 95–97

FRIENDSHIP IS CLOSENESS, 92

FRIENDSHIP IS FIRE, 177

FRIENDSHIP IS SHARING ONE'S INNERMOST (EXPERIENCE) OBJECTS, 91

FRIENDSHIP IS WARMTH, 93, 177

GOOD THINGS ARE LIGHT, 44

GOOD THINGS ARE UP, 44

GOOD THINGS ARE VALUABLE, 44

GOOD THINGS ARE WARM, 44

HAPPINESS IS A CAPTIVE ANIMAL, 24, 141

HAPPINESS IS A FLUID IN A CONTAINER, 24, 170

HAPPINESS IS A NATURAL FORCE, 25

HAPPINESS IS A PLEASURABLE PHYSICAL SENSATION, 24, 40, 48, 49

HAPPINESS IS AN OPPONENT, 24

HAPPINESS IS BEING IN HEAVEN, 24, 40

HAPPINESS IS BEING OFF THE GROUND, 24, 40, 49, 170

HAPPINESS IS HEALTH, 24

HAPPINESS IS INSANITY, 25

HAPPINESS IS LIGHT, 170

HAPPINESS IS RAPTURE/HIGH, 24

HAPPINESS IS UP, 5, 170

HAPPINESS IS VITALITY, 24

HAPPY IS LIGHT, 24

HAPPY IS UP, 24

HAPPY IS WARM, 24

HAPPY PERSON IS AN ANIMAL THAT LIVES WELL, A, 24, 40, 48, 49

HARA IS A CONTAINER FOR ANGER, THE, 153–154

HUMAN RELATIONSHIPS ARE COMPLEX OBJECTS, 113

IDEAS ARE (VALUABLE) COMMODITIES, 107

IMPORTANT IS CENTRAL, 90

INCREASE IN INTENSITY IS GROWTH, 42

INCREASE IN THE INTENSITY OF EMOTION IS GROWTH, 41

INTENSITY IS AMOUNT/QUANTITY, 42

INTENSITY IS HEAT, 42

INTENSITY IS STRENGTH OF EFFECT, 42

INTENSITY OF EMOTION IS AN AMOUNT/QUANTITY (OF SUBSTANCE IN A CONTAINER), 41

INTENSITY OF EMOTION IS HEAT, 41

INTENSITY OF EMOTION IS STRENGTH OF EFFECT (OF FORCE), 41

INTERACTION IS AN ECONOMIC EXCHANGE, 96

INTERACTIVE RELATIONSHIPS ARE ECONOMIC EXCHANGES, 112

INTERNAL IS EXTERNAL, 83

INTIMACY IS CLOSENESS, 92

LACK OF CONTROL IS LACK OF CONTROL OVER FORCE, 44

LACK OF EMOTIONAL CONTROL IS A DIVIDED SELF, 43

LACK OF EMOTIONAL CONTROL IS A SUPERIOR, 43

LACK OF EMOTIONAL CONTROL IS INSANITY, 43

LACK OF EMOTIONAL CONTROL IS RAPTURE/HIGH, 43

LASTINGNESS IS STRENGTH, 99

LIFE IS A JOURNEY, 103–104, 108

LIFE IS A PLAY, 90

LONG-TERM, PURPOSEFUL ACTIVITIES ARE JOURNEYS, 52, 54

LOSS OF CONTROL IS LOSS OF CONTROL OVER FORCE, 43

LOSS OF EMOTIONAL CONTROL IS LOSS OF CONTROL OVER A STRONG FORCE, 43

LOVE IS A BOND, 26

LOVE IS A CAPTIVE ANIMAL, 26

LOVE IS A DISEASE, 26

LOVE IS A FLUID IN A CONTAINER, 26

LOVE IS A JOURNEY, 26

LOVE IS A NATURAL FORCE, 26, 123

LOVE IS A NUTRIENT, 26, 28

LOVE IS A PHYSICAL FORCE, 26, 123

LOVE IS A SOCIAL SUPERIOR, 26

LOVE IS A UNITY (OF COMPLEMENTARY PARTS), 26, 28, 119–222, 136, 178–179

LOVE IS AN ECONOMIC EXCHANGE (BASED ON MUTUALITY), 26, 28, 141, 178–179

LOVE IS AN OPPONENT, 26, 141

LOVE IS CLOSENESS, 26

LOVE IS FIRE, 5, 26, 140
LOVE IS INSANITY, 26, 123
LOVE IS MAGIC, 26, 123, 141
LOVE IS RAPTURE/A HIGH, 26, 123
LOVE IS SPORT/A GAME, 26
LOVE IS WAR, 26
LOVE IS A PHYSICAL FORCE (MAG-
NETIC), 141
LUST IS A GAME/PLAY, 29, 31
LUST IS A NATURAL FORCE, 29, 31
LUST IS A PHYSICAL FORCE, 29, 31
LUST IS A SOCIAL SUPERIOR, 29, 31
LUST IS A SUBSTANCE IN A CON-
TAINER, 31
LUST IS A TRICKSTER, 31
LUST IS A UNITY/BOND, 31
LUST IS A VICIOUS ANIMAL, 29
LUST IS AN OPPONENT, 31
LUST IS ANIMAL BEHAVIOR/WILD-
NESS, 31
LUST IS FIRE/HEAT, 31
LUST IS HEAT, 29
LUST IS HUNGER, 29
LUST IS HUNGER/EATING, 31
LUST IS INSANITY, 29, 31
LUST IS MAGIC, 31
LUST IS PAIN/A TORMENTOR, 31
LUST IS PRESSURE INSIDE A CON-
TAINER, 29
LUST IS RAPTURE, 31
LUST IS WAR, 29, 31
LUSTFUL PERSON IS A FUNCTION-
ING MACHINE, A, 29

MARRIAGE IS A PHYSICAL AND/OR
BIOLOGICAL UNITY OF TWO
PARTS, 120–122
MEANINGS ARE OBJECTS, 89
MEANS (OF CHANGE OF STATE/
ACTION) ARE PATHS (TO DESTI-
NATIONS), 52, 53
MENTAL ACTIVITY IS MANIPULA-
TION, 196–197

MIND IS A CONTAINER, THE, 89
MORALITY IS RESISTING A PHYSI-
CAL FORCE, 194–196
MORALITY IS STRENGTH, 194

NEGATIVE EMOTIONS ARE ILL-
NESSES, 44
NONPHYSICAL HARM IS PHYSICAL
DAMAGE, 46
NONPHYSICAL UNITY IS PHYSICAL
UNITY, 46, 119–120, 137

OBJECT OF LOVE IS A DEITY, THE,
27
OBJECT OF LOVE IS A POSSESSED
OBJECT, THE, 27
OBJECT OF LOVE IS A SMALL
CHILD, THE, 27
OBJECT OF LOVE IS A VALUABLE
OBJECT, THE, 27
OBJECT OF LOVE IS APPETIZING
FOOD, THE, 26
OBJECT OF LUST IS A POSSESSED
OBJECT, THE, 31

PASSIVE EXPERIENCES ARE THE
PHYSICAL EFFECTS OF FORCES,
42
PASSIVITY OF EMOTIONAL EXPERI-
ENCE IS THE PHYSICAL EFFECT
OF NATURAL/PHYSICAL FORCES,
THE, 42
PEOPLE ARE CONTAINERS (FOR THE
EMOTIONS), 65, 77, 92
PERSON IN CONTROL IS A CANONI-
CAL PERSON, A, 44
PERSON IS A CONTAINER, A, 90–
92
PERSON OUT OF CONTROL IS A DI-
VIDED SELF, A, 44
PRIDE IS A FLUID IN A CONTAINER,
30
PRIDE IS A SUPERIOR, 30

PRIDE IS AN ECONOMIC VALUE, 30
PROGRESS IS MOVEMENT TO A DES-
TINATION (IN A JOURNEY), 46
PURPOSES ARE DESTINATIONS, 52,
53

REAL SELF IS ONE'S INNERMOST
(EXPERIENCE) OBJECTS, THE, 91
RELATIONSHIPS ARE BUILDINGS,
112–113

SAD IS DARK, 25
SAD IS DOWN, 25
SADNESS IS A BURDEN, 25
SADNESS IS A CAPTIVE ANIMAL, 25
SADNESS IS A FLUID IN A CON-
TAINER, 25
SADNESS IS A LACK OF VITALITY,
25
SADNESS IS A LIVING ORGANISM,
25
SADNESS IS A PHYSICAL FORCE, 25
SADNESS IS A SOCIAL SUPERIOR, 26
SADNESS IS AN ILLNESS, 25
SADNESS IS AN OPPONENT, 26
SADNESS IS INSANITY, 25
SHAME IS A BURDEN, 32
SHAME IS A DECREASE IN SIZE, 32,
40, 48, 49
SHAME IS A FLUID IN A CON-
TAINER, 32
SHAME IS AN ILLNESS, 32
SHAME IS BLOCKING OUT THE
WORLD, 40, 48, 49
SHAME IS HAVING NO CLOTHES
ON, 40, 48, 49
SHAME IS HIDING AWAY FROM
THE WORLD, 32
SHAME IS PHYSICAL DAMAGE, 32
SHAMEFUL PERSON IS A DIVIDED
SELF, A, 32
SHAMEFUL PERSON IS A PERSON
HAVING NO CLOTHES ON, A, 32

SHAMEFUL PERSON IS A WORTH-
LESS OBJECT, A, 32
SHARING EXPERIENCES IS SHARING
OBJECTS, 89
STATES ARE LOCATIONS, 52
STATES OF AFFAIRS ARE COMMODI-
TIES, 107
SUBJECT OF FEAR IS A DIVIDED
SELF, THE, 23
SURPRISE IS A NATURAL FORCE, 33
SURPRISE IS A PHYSICAL FORCE, 33
SURPRISED PERSON IS A BURST
CONTAINER, A, 33

VANITY IS AN INDULGENT PERSON,
32

Metonymies

BLUSHING FOR LOVE, 124
BODY HEAT FOR ANGER, 156–157,
171, 172
BODY HEAT FOR EMOTION, 134
BODY HEAT FOR LUST, 32

CHANGE IN HEART RATE FOR EMO-
TION, 134
CHANGE IN RESPIRATION FOR
EMOTION, 134
CHANGE IN THE COLOR OF THE
FACE FOR EMOTION, 134
CRYING (TEARS) FOR ANGER, 171

DIZZINESS FOR LOVE, 124
DROP IN BODY TEMPERATURE FOR
FEAR, 5, 24

EFFECTS OF A STATE FOR THE
STATE, 134
EYEBROWS FOR HAPPINESS, 172

FACIAL EXPRESSIONS FOR EMO-
TION, 134

ILLNESS FOR ANGER, 171
INABILITY TO BREATHE FOR LOVE, 124
INABILITY TO SPEAK FOR ANGER, 171
INABILITY TO SPEAK FOR EMOTION, 75
INABILITY TO THINK FOR EMOTION, 75
INABILITY TO THINK FOR LOVE, 124
INCAPACITATING EFFECTS OF EMOTION FOR THE EMOTION, THE, 82
INCREASE IN BODY HEAT FOR LOVE, 123
INCREASE IN HEART RATE FOR LOVE, 124
INCREASE IN RATE OF HEARTBEAT FOR FEAR, 24
INSANE BEHAVIOR FOR ANGER, 177
INTERFERENCE WITH ACCURATE PERCEPTION FOR ANGER, 171
INTERFERENCE WITH ACCURATE PERCEPTION FOR LOVE, 124
INTERFERENCE WITH ACCURATE PERCEPTION FOR LUST, 32
INTERFERENCE WITH BREATHING FOR ANGER, 171
INTERNAL PRESSURE FOR ANGER, 157–158, 171, 171–172, 177
INTIMATE SEXUAL BEHAVIOR FOR LOVE, 124

JOYFUL (VISUAL) BEHAVIOR FOR LOVE, 124

LIGHT IN THE EYES FOR HAPPINESS, 172
LOVING VISUAL BEHAVIOR FOR LOVE, 124

MENTAL INCAPACITIES FOR THE EMOTIONS, 75

NAUSEA FOR ANGER, 171

PERSPIRATION FOR ANGER, 171
PHYSICAL AGITATION FOR ANGER, 5, 171, 177
PHYSICAL AGITATION FOR EMOTION, 82
PHYSICAL AGITATION FOR FEAR, 24
PHYSICAL AGITATION FOR LUST, 32
PHYSICAL CLOSENESS FOR LOVE, 124
PHYSICAL WEAKNESS FOR LOVE, 124
PHYSIOLOGICAL AND EXPRESSIVE RESPONSES OF AN EMOTION FOR THE EMOTION, THE, 134
PREOCCUPATION WITH ANOTHER FOR LOVE, 124

REDNESS IN THE FACE FOR ANGER, 142, 158, 177

SEX FOR LOVE, 124
SWEATY PALMS FOR LOVE, 124

WETNESS FOR ANGER, 188

Studies in Emotion and Social Interaction

First Series
Editors: Paul Ekman and Klaus R. Scherer

Handbook of Methods in Nonverbal Behavioral Research
Edited by Klaus R. Scherer and Paul Ekman
Structures of Social Action: Studies in Conversational Analysis
Edited by Max Atkinson and John Heritage
Interaction Structure and Strategy
Starkey Duncan, Jr., and Donald W. Fiske
Body Movement and Speech in Medical Interaction
Christian Heath
The Emotions
Nico Frijda
Conversations of Friends: Speculations on Affective Development
Edited by John M. Gottman and Jeffrey G. Parker
Judgment Studies: Design, Analysis, and Meta-analysis
Robert Rosenthal
The Individual, Communication, and Society: Essays in Memory of Gregory Bateson
Edited by Robert W. Rieber
Language and the Politics of Emotion
Edited by Catherine Lutz and Lila Abu-Lughod
Fundamentals of Nonverbal Behavior
Edited by Robert Feldman and Bernard Rimé
Gestures and Speech
Pierre J. M. Feyereisen and Jacques-Dominique de Lannoy
Landscapes of Emotion: Mapping Three Cultures of Emotion in Indonesia
Karl G. Heider
Contexts of Accommodation: Developments in Applied Sociolinguistics
Howard Giles, Justine Coupland, and Nikolas Coupland
Best Laid Schemes: The Psychology of Emotions
Keith Oatley
Interpersonal Expectations: Theory, Research, and Applications
Edited by Peter David Blanck
Emotional Contagion
Elaine Hatfield, John T. Cacioppo, and Richard L. Rapson
Exploring Affect: The Selected Writings of Silvan S. Tomkins
Edited by E. Virginia Demos